MW00785239

Cambridge International AS Level

Modern Europe
1750–1921

Nicholas Fellows
Mike Wells

HODDER
EDUCATION
AN HACHETTE UK COMPANY

Orders: please contact Bookpoint Ltd, 130 Park Drive, Milton Park, Abingdon, Oxon OX14 4SE. Telephone: +44 (0)1235 827827. Fax: +44 (0)1235 400401. Email education@bookpoint.co.uk Lines are open from 9 a.m. to 5 p.m., Monday to Saturday, with a 24-hour message answering service. You can also order through our website: www.hoddereducation.com

ISBN: 978 1 5104 4869 8

© Nicholas Fellows and Mike Wells 2019

First published in 2019 by

Hodder Education,
An Hachette UK Company
Carmelite House
50 Victoria Embankment
London EC4Y 0DZ

www.hoddereducation.com

Impression number   10 9 8 7 6 5 4 3 2 1

Year   2023 2022 2021 2020 2019

Cover photo © Classic Image/Alamy Stock Photo

Illustrations by Integra Software Services

Typeset in Palatino LT Std Light 10/13 by Integra Software Services Pvt. Ltd., Pondicherry, India

Printed by Bell & Bain Ltd, Glasgow

A catalogue record for this title is available from the British Library.

Contents

Introduction   iv
- **1** What you will study   iv
- **2** Structure of the syllabus   v
- **3** About this book   ix

CHAPTER 1   France, 1774–1814   I
- **1** What were the causes and immediate outcomes of the 1789 Revolution?   2
- **2** Why were French governments unstable from 1790 to 1795?   16
- **3** Why was Napoleon Bonaparte able to overthrow the Directory in 1799?   27
- **4** What were Napoleon Bonaparte's domestic aims and achievements to 1814?   38
- Study skills   50

CHAPTER 2   The Industrial Revolution in Britain, 1750–1850   56
- **1** What were the causes of the Industrial Revolution?   57
- **2** Why was there a rapid growth of industrialization after 1780?   66
- **3** Why, and with what consequences, did urbanization result from industrialization?   79
- **4** Why, and with what consequences, did industrialization result in popular protest and political change?   94
- Study skills   109

CHAPTER 3   Liberalism and nationalism in Germany, 1815–1871   117
- **1** What were the causes of the Revolutions in Germany in 1848–49?   118
- **2** What were the consequences of the 1848–49 Revolutions?   133
- **3** What were Bismarck's intentions for Prussia and Germany from 1862 to 1866?   143
- **4** Why was the unification of Germany achieved by 1871?   154
- Study skills   167

CHAPTER 4   The Russian Revolution, 1894–1921   174
- **1** What were the causes and outcomes of the 1905 Revolution up to 1914?   174
- **2** What were the causes and immediate outcomes of the February Revolution in 1917?   186
- **3** How and why did the Bolsheviks gain power in October 1917?   198
- **4** How were the Bolsheviks able to consolidate their power up to 1921?   207
- Study skills   220

Further reading   **224**

Glossary   **226**

Index   **231**

Introduction

This book has been written to support your study of the European Option: Modern Europe 1750–1921 for Cambridge International AS Level History (syllabus code 9489). The book has been endorsed by Cambridge Assessment International Education and is listed as an endorsed textbook for students studying the syllabus.

This introduction gives you an overview of:
- the content you will study for the European Option: Modern Europe 1750–1921
- the structure of the syllabus
- the different features of this book and how these will aid your learning.

What you will study

In the period from 1750 to 1921 Europe underwent a series of massive transformations. Its economy went from being agricultural to industrial, with Britain becoming the first industrial nation. This development led to rapid urbanization and the introduction of a new system of working, with the growth of the factory system. Politically, Europe also underwent a series of dramatic changes. In France the old order, the Ancien Régime, was overthrown as the country underwent a bloody revolution followed by years of warfare, firstly under a revolutionary government and then Napoleon Bonaparte. In Russia in the twentieth century, the old imperial government of the Tsar was overthrown and replaced by the world's first Communist government under Lenin and his Bolshevik party. During the nineteenth century the map of Europe and the balance of power was also transformed as the new state of Germany was created following an upsurge in liberal and nationalist feeling. These developments all destroyed the old order. How and why they happened are the focus of this book. The changes were often fast, accompanied by violence and protest as people struggled to adapt.

This book covers the following topics post-1750:
- Chapter 1 examines the causes of the French Revolution and how it developed so that Napoleon was able to emerge and establish his empire.
- The origins and development of the Industrial Revolution from 1750 to 1850 are considered in Chapter 2. It will also look at the response of the workers and governments to these developments.
- Chapter 3 traces the growth of liberalism and nationalism in Germany between the years 1815 and 1871. It will discuss the early attempts to unite a large number of states and the reasons why Prussia was able to emerge as the dominant force and how it united Germany.

- In Chapter 4 the discussion will focus on the collapse and overthrow of the imperial rule of the Tsar and its eventual replacement, following a second revolution in 1917 and civil war, by the Bolsheviks or communists.

 # Structure of the syllabus

The Cambridge International AS Level History will be assessed through two papers, a Document Paper and an Outline Study.
- Paper 1: For Paper 1 you need to answer one two-part document question on one of the options given. You will need to answer both parts of the option you choose. This counts for 40 per cent of the AS Level.
- Paper 2: For Paper 2 you need to answer two two-part questions from three on one of the options given. You must answer both parts of the question you choose. This counts for 60 per cent of the AS Level.

AS Level topics rotate between Papers 1 and 2 year-on-year – the prescribed topic for Paper 1 in the June and November series of any given year is not used for Paper 2.

Examination questions

For Paper 1 there will be two parts to each question. For part (a) you will be expected to consider two sources on one aspect of the material. For part (b) you will be expected to use all the sources and your knowledge of the period to address how far the sources support a given statement.

For Paper 2 you will select two questions from the option on Europe 1750–1921. There will be two parts to each question. Part (a) requires a causal explanation and part (b) requires you to consider and weigh up the relative importance of a range of factors. You will need to answer both parts of the question you choose.

Command words

When choosing the two essay questions, keep in mind that it is vital to answer the actual question that has been asked, not the one that you might have hoped for. A key to doing well is understanding the demands of the question. Cambridge International AS Level History use key terms and phrases known as command words. The command words are listed in the table on page vi, with a brief explanation of each.

Command word	What it means
Assess	Make an informed judgement
Compare	Identify/comment on similarities and/or differences
Contrast	Identify/comment on differences
Discuss	Write about issue(s) or topic(s) in depth in a structured way
Evaluate	Judge or calculate the quality, importance, amount or value of something
Explain	Set out purposes or reasons/make the relationships between things evident/provide why and/or how and support with relevant evidence

Questions may also use phrases such as:

- How far do/does X support?
- To what extent?
- Account for

Key concepts

The syllabus also focuses on developing your understanding of a number of key concepts and these are also reflected in the nature of the questions set in the examination. The key concepts for AS History are as follows:

Cause and consequence

The events, circumstances, actions and beliefs that have a direct causal connection to consequential events and developments, circumstances, actions or beliefs. Causes can be both human and non-human.

Change and continuity

The patterns, processes and interplay of change and continuity within a given time frame.

Similarity and difference

The patterns of similarity and difference that exist between people, lived experiences, events and situations in the past.

Significance

The importance attached to an event, individual or entity in the past, whether at the time or subsequent to it. Historical significance is a constructed label that is dependent upon the perspective (context, values, interests and concerns) of the person ascribing significance and is therefore changeable.

The icons above appear next to questions to show where key concepts are being tested and what they are.

Answering the questions

With Paper 1, the Document Paper, you have 1 hour and 15 minutes to answer the two parts to the question. On Paper 2, the Outline Study, you have 1 hour and 45 minutes to answer two two-part questions. It is important that you organize your time well. In other words do not spend 70 minutes on one question on Paper 2 and leave yourself just 35 minutes to do the second question. Before you begin each question, take a few minutes to draw up a brief plan of the major points you want to make and your argument. You can then tick them off as you make them. This is not a waste of time as it will help you produce a coherent and well-argued answer. Well-organized responses with well-supported arguments and a conclusion will score more highly than responses that lack coherence and jump from point to point.

The answers that you write for both papers will be read by trained examiners. The examiners will read your answers and check what you write against the mark scheme. The mark scheme offers guidance to the examiner, but is not comprehensive. You may write an answer that includes analysis and evidence that is not included in the mark scheme and that is fine. It is also worth remembering that the examiner who assesses your answers is looking to reward arguments that are well supported, not to deduct marks for errors or mistakes.

On Paper 1, Question (a) will be marked out of 15 and Question (b) out of 25. The total mark will be weighted at 40 per cent of your final grade. On Paper 2, Question (a) will be marked out of 10 and Question (b) out of 20. The total mark will be weighted at 60 per cent of your final grade.

Answering source questions

For the Comparison Question (a) you should be able to:
- make a developed comparison of the two sources
- show both similarities and differences in the evidence two sources give about a particular issue
- use contextual knowledge and source evaluation to explain the similarities and differences.

In order to attain the highest marks your answers for Question (b) should:
- evaluate the sources to reach a supported judgement as to how far the sources support the statement.

Answering essay questions

Both the short and long answer questions should:
- be well focused
- be well supported by precise and accurate evidence
- reach a relevant and supported conclusion or judgement
- demonstrate knowledge and understanding of historical processes
- demonstrate a clear understanding of connections between causes.

Your essay should include a significant opening paragraph or introduction that sets out your main points. Do not waste time copying out the question but do define any key terms that are in the question. The strongest essays will show awareness of different possible approaches to the question. You will need to write an in-depth analysis of your main points in several paragraphs, providing detailed and accurate information to support them. Each paragraph will focus on one of your main points and be directly related to the question. Finally, you should write a concluding paragraph. Help with developing these skills is offered throughout the book in the Study skills section at the end of each chapter.

What will the examination paper look like?

Cover

The cover of the examination paper states the date of the examination and the length of time you have to complete it. Instructions on the front are limited, but they do remind you that you should answer questions from only ONE section, Section A, the European Option. The cover will also tell you the total number of marks for the paper, 40 for Paper 1 and 60 for Paper 2, and will also tell you the number of marks for each question or part question.

Questions

Read through Section A, the European Option. With Paper 1 you will have no choice but to answer the Document Question from that section, but for Paper 2 you should choose which two out of three questions you can answer most fully.

With Paper 1 you might find it helpful to:
- spend 10 minutes reading the sources carefully
- identify the key terms and phrases in the question so that you remain focused on the actual question
- underline any quotations you will use to support your arguments.

If you spend about 10 minutes carefully reading the sources you will have about 1 hour left to answer the two questions. It is advisable to spend somewhere around 20–25 minutes answering (a) and 35–40 minutes answering (b).

With Paper 2 you might find it helpful to:
- circle the two questions you intend to answer
- identify the command terms and key words and phrases so that you remain focused on them.

Then spend time drawing up plans. If, for Paper 2, you allow 5 minutes to decide which questions to answer you will have 50 minutes for each question – 5 minutes to plan and 45 minutes to write answers to part (a) and (b). It is advisable to spend somewhere around 15–20 minutes answering (a) and 30–35 minutes on (b).

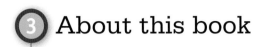

③ About this book

Coverage of the course content

This book addresses the key areas listed in the Cambridge International syllabus. The content follows closely the layout and sequence of the Cambridge syllabus with each chapter representing each topic. Chapters start with an introduction outlining key questions they address. Each key question is accompanied by content that you are expected to understand and deploy when addressing the key question. Throughout the chapters you will find the following features to aid your study of the course content.

Key terms

Key terms are the important terms you need to know to gain an understanding of the period. These are highlighted in the text the first time they appear in the book and are defined in the margin. They also appear in the glossary at the end of the book.

Key figures and profiles

Key figures highlight important individuals and can be found in the margin. Some chapters contain profiles that offer more information about the importance and impact of the individual. This information can be very useful in understanding certain events and providing supporting evidence to your arguments.

Sources

Throughout the book you will encounter both written and visual sources. Historical sources are important components in understanding more fully why specific decisions were taken and on what contemporary leaders based their actions. They also help to explain both causes and consequences of past developments. The sources are accompanied by questions to help you dig deeper into the history of Modern Europe, 1750–1921. To help with analysing the sources think about the message of the sources, their purpose, and their usefulness for a particular line of enquiry. The questions that accompany the source will help you with this.

Extension boxes

Sometimes it is useful to go beyond the syllabus to help further your understanding of the topic. The extension boxes will include a variety of additional information such as useful debates and historians' views.

Activities

Activities and tasks throughout the book will help you develop conceptual understanding and consolidate knowledge.

Summary diagrams

At the end of each section is a summary diagram which gives a visual summary of the content of the section. It is intended as an aid for revision. Try copying the diagram into your own set of notes and, using information from the chapter, provide precise examples to develop each point. This will help build your knowledge of the issues that relate to the key question.

Chapter summaries

At the end of each chapter is a short summary of the content of that chapter. This is intended to help you consolidate your knowledge and understanding of the content.

Refresher questions

Questions at the end of each chapter will serve as a useful tool to test your knowledge of what you have read. These are not exam-style questions, but will serve as prompts and show where you have gaps in your knowledge and understanding.

Study skills

At the end of each chapter you will find guidance on how to approach both writing a successful essay and also how to evaluate sources. These pages take you step by step through the exam requirements and show you the kinds of questions you might be asked. There is also analysis of and comment on sample answers. These are not answers by past candidates. We have written them to help you to see what a part of good answer might look like.

End of the book

The book concludes with the following sections.

Glossary

All key terms in the book are defined in the glossary.

Further reading

This contains a list of books that may help you with further independent research. At this level of study, it is important to read around the subject and not just solely rely on the content of this textbook. The further reading section will help you with this. You may wish to share the contents of this area with your school or local librarian.

Online teacher support

In an addition to this book there is an online teacher resource[*] for sale that will provide support for all three AS Level Paper 1 and Paper 2 options:
- The History of the USA, 1820–1941
- Modern Europe, 1750–1921
- International History, 1870–1945

The online material can be found here: **www.hoddereducation.com**

It includes:
- simple factual knowledge recall tests
- quizzes to test understanding of definitions and key terms to help improve historical understanding and language
- schemes of work
- worksheets to be used in the classroom or for study at home
- sample exam-style questions and answers
- links to websites and additional online resources.

[*] The online teacher support component is not endorsed by Cambridge Assessment International Education.

CHAPTER 1

France, 1774–1814

This chapter looks at why revolution broke out in France in 1789. It considers the nature and problems of the 'Ancien Régime' – the French monarchy which was eventually overthrown in 1792 after attempts to share power between the king and an elected assembly. It explains why there was so much political instability in the period 1790–95 and why the Revolution became more extreme. The rise to power of Napoleon Bonaparte in 1799 is considered, and also the changes that he brought to France as Consul and from 1804 as Emperor. You need to consider the following questions throughout this chapter:

★ What were the causes and immediate outcomes of the 1789 Revolution?

★ Why were French governments unstable from 1790 to 1795?

★ Why was Napoleon Bonaparte able to overthrow the Directory in 1799?

★ What were Napoleon's domestic aims and achievements to 1814?

KEY DATES

1774		Louis XVI comes to the throne
1787		Assembly of Notables to discuss financial problems
1789	May	Estates General meets
1789	20 June	Tennis Court Oath
1789	14 July	Storming of the Bastille
1789		October Days
1791		Flight to Varennes by Louis XVI
1792		War with Austria and Prussia
1793		Execution of Louis XVI
1793		Terror
1794		Coup of Thermidor

1795	Directory
1799	Coup of Brumaire. Bonaparte takes power
1802	Concordat with Papacy
1804	Civil Code
1804	Napoleon becomes Emperor
1805	War of Third Coalition
1808	Peninsular War
1812	Napoleon invades Russia
1814	Napoleon abdicates
1815	Hundred Days
1821	Napoleon dies on St Helena

What were the causes and immediate outcomes of the 1789 Revolution?

KEY TERM

Enlightenment This is the name given to the growth of scholarly and intellectual writing on many aspects of philosophy, science, the arts, economics, government, religion and politics in the eighteenth century. These writings were often critical of and questioned established religion, monarchical rule and social inequality, and were seen as a major cause of revolution.

The French Revolution had long-term and short-term causes. It was brought about by resentments in French society about inequality and privilege. These were reinforced by the writings of the **Enlightenment** and, more directly, by economic distress. In the short term it was brought about by the monarchy's failure to solve a growing financial crisis and Louis XVI's inability to manage the process of reform and rising political demands. The outcome of the events of 1789 were in the short term to bring about shared power by the king and an elected assembly but in the longer term to establish a republic and the abolition of monarchy which brought war and the rise of a military leader who declared himself Emperor in 1804.

Louis XVI

Born in 1754, he was the grandson of Louis XV. He came to the throne in 1774. Personally kind, he was not a dynamic or decisive figure. He was ridiculed for his inability to have children by his Austrian wife, Princess Marie Antoinette, until a minor operation made sexual relations possible for him. Though interested in many new ideas, particularly those connected to naval matters, he was unable to deal effectively with the growing problem of finance. He did not give support to a series of reforming ministers. His acceptance of advice to go to war against Britain in 1778 made the situation critical. He eventually agreed to summon the Estates General, the equivalent to a French parliament, which had not met since 1614, but then could not manage it. Shifting between support for change and a desire to use force to prevent it, he allowed events to get out of control. Forced to reside in the centre of Paris, not his palace at Versailles, by mob action in October 1789, his position became increasingly dangerous. He botched an attempt to flee in July 1791 and became a reluctant constitutional monarch. He unwisely supported a war policy in 1792 and was blamed for the French failures. He was overthrown as king in August 1792 and was executed in January 1793.

What were the problems of the Ancien Régime in 1774 and how were these affected by the policies of Louis XVI?

The term 'Ancien Régime' refers to the rule of the French monarchs before the Revolution of 1789. When Louis XVI came to the French throne in 1774 he inherited problems. Some of these were long term and were to do with how France was governed and the long-term inequalities of French society. Others, especially financial problems, were a result of costly wars fought in the reign of his grandfather Louis XV.

Long-term social problems

Louis XVI inherited a country that was deeply divided and unequal. France was made up of different classes, called Estates. Most of the French people were in the Third Estate. Of these some 80 per cent were peasants and the rest urban workers, tradesmen and a growing middle class. Above them were the First and Second Estates who had privileges that the mass of French people did not enjoy. The 0.5 per cent of churchmen who made up the First Estate owned 10 per cent of the land and were exempt from **direct taxes**. The official religion of France was Roman Catholicism and all French people had to pay a tax to the Church. Within the Church, members of the nobility held nearly all important and richer posts. The nobles, roughly 120,000 in number out of a population of some 28 million, were also exempt from direct taxes. Most of the leading officers in the armed forces, government ministers, provincial governors and important office holders such as the local administrators and diplomats were members of the aristocracy. Nobles also had the right as lords of the manor to hold courts and receive payments from their peasant tenants. These were known as **feudal dues** and were owed to them because of their noble status. This inequality and privilege caused discontent among the French middle classes who resented the lack of opportunity and the inequality in taxation. Many peasants resented the feudal payments, especially in times of hardship.

Long-term financial problems

Because of the tax privileges, the burden of taxation fell unequally. The French monarchy faced financial problems because it lacked a uniform and effective means of collecting taxes. There was a history of selling offices to raise money – not only positions in the legal system but also in the financial system. The crown relied on private individuals to collect taxes. Contracts were agreed to collect fixed sums in advance. Anything extra was profit for the collectors. Thus much money, which could have gone to the crown, went instead into the pockets of individuals. These intermediaries were known as 'tax farmers'. The French state could not collect enough taxes to meet expenses and had to rely on loans. In normal times there was a financial

KEY TERMS

Direct taxes Taxes levied on personal income or property.

Feudal dues Payments made to lords by peasants based on traditional privileges not contractual obligations.

ACTIVITY

Look at the long-term problems of France in 1774. Discuss with a partner or in a group which is the most serious of the problems and which is the least serious. Explain your view to the class.

shortfall, but two expensive wars fought by Louis XV – **the War of the Austrian Succession 1740–48** and the **Seven Years War 1756–63** – had increased the debts. In 1748 France had a debt of 1 billion livres and by 1763 this had risen to 1.8 billion. A lot of the taxes raised had to go on paying interest on a very large debt.

Long-term economic problems

There were also long-term economic problems. Most French people were peasant farmers and many of them made a bare living by **subsistence farming**. A run of bad harvests could mean severe hardships. France before 1774 was used to **bread riots** and hardship in many rural communities. Population growth had meant that urban population had grown. This was particularly true of Paris where there were very poor districts. The internal customs duties payable when supplies went from province to province added to the problems of food costs in bad years, and the customs posts were deeply unpopular.

Long-term political problems

The growing middle class, brought about by the development of trade and the growth of towns, saw considerable interest in ideas. Even before 1774 the French authorities faced a more literate public and the growth of criticism about the power of the clergy and nobles. Journals, books and newspapers increased in number. However, there was little formal outlet for discussion as France did not have a parliament as such, and the king was in theory absolute and could rule as he wished within the law. There was censorship and control over publications. The king could arbitrarily imprison his subjects and the only institutions that resembled a parliament, and indeed had the name '**parlements**', were in fact courts of law dominated by the nobles which merely registered royal edicts giving them the force of law. There was no equivalent to the British **parliament** which elected members and could vote on financial matters and initiate laws.

Short-term problems after 1774 and the impact of Louis XVI's policies

Louis XVI did little to solve these problems and, indeed, made them worse. His decision to go to war again against Britain in 1778 in support of the British colonies in North America that had rebelled against George III added to the debt quite considerably. Various attempts by reforming ministers to solve the financial problems were not sufficiently supported by the King to be successful.

The king and his queen, Marie Antoinette, did not set a good example by failing to curb their spending. However, the inherited debt and the high costs of war were more significant causes of financial problems.

There was little attempt to change France and to restrict privilege. Even tax reform proved to be impossible when the privileged orders resisted.

Louis persisted in relying on tax farming and merely asking the privileged classes to co-operate rather than enforcing major governmental change. The King was reluctant to make any political concessions. The decision to intervene in the American Revolution meant that many new ideas had come back to France about the right to resist **tyranny**, the right to be consulted about taxation and the right of all to 'life, liberty and the pursuit of happiness' as the American Declaration of Independence of 1776 said. Louis gave aid to rebels proclaiming these new ideas but was not prepared to make changes at home, which would have given his own subjects greater rights or liberty. For many, aristocratic privileges were a barrier to 'the pursuit of happiness' and Louis did little to reduce this.

As shown below, the King and his ministers were aware of the problems, but failed to solve them in a series of attempted reforms before 1799. These failures were crucial as they left the King with one choice: to appeal to the nation as a whole and summon the old French assembly – the Estates General – which had not met since 1614 to help him with the financial problems. In the end, this decision saw the beginning of the Revolution and the end of the Ancien Régime.

What were the pressures for change?

Changes in the social and intellectual life of France in the latter half of the eighteenth century led to greater demands for change and the governments of Louis XVI found themselves under pressure to respond to growing discontent among all classes.

Social pressures

The growth in the French middle class from about 700,000 in 1700 to 2.3 million by 1780 meant that this class was more numerous and likely to resent the privileges of the first two Estates. There was greater literacy and a growth in demand for books and journals, many of which were critical of the Ancien Régime. The businessmen and merchants resented restrictions on trade such as internal customs and lack of uniform weights and measures. There were large numbers of lawyers who wanted political change and also a society which gave more opportunities for people of talent to prosper regardless of how privileged their background was. Even among the clergy, the middle-ranking priests were resentful about the domination of the Church by aristocratic bishops and abbots. Within the cities there was also social discontent. Paris was the most populous with 620,000 people by 1789. The next largest city was Lyon with only 145,000. Thus, Paris was disproportionately large and influential. It had a large underclass of servants, casual labourers, peddlers, itinerant craftsmen and 25,000 prostitutes. Living in overcrowded and often unhealthy conditions, they resented restrictions imposed by employers and city authorities. Subject to hardship when bread prices rose, they often resorted to mob action. Like the more prosperous middle classes, they were reading more and had greater awareness of new ideas about the people having rights.

KEY TERM

Tyranny Oppressive rule.

ACTIVITY
Review the key terms covered so far and make sure that you understand them by writing a brief definition:
- Ancien Régime
- Parlement
- Feudal dues
- Estates General.

Economic discontent

A series of bad harvests during 1788–89 and a fall in trade and employment created a great deal of urban discontent. There were 80,000 unemployed people in Paris by 1789 and most larger towns and cities saw food riots in the spring and early summer. Food prices peaked in July 1789 and coincided with the outbreak of revolution. In the countryside peasants came under pressure from the 1760s as landowners tried to take over lands traditionally used by the villages as a whole. Landlords **enclosed** common land and forests that poorer farmers used for animal grazing and gathering wood, nuts and berries. By 1788 there were increasing instances of peasants refusing to pay dues and taxes and attacks on the manor houses (chateaux) of landlords. Though economic discontent produced violence and unrest by poorer people in both town and countryside, it was also an element in creating unrest among the middle classes. The increase in barriers to trade, especially between 1785 and 1787 when the tax farmers tightened collection and set up more customs posts, hit manufacturers and traders. State control of prices and the restrictions of the trade guilds which controlled production were resented by enterprising businessmen. The unfairness of the tax system made matters worse and seemed to show that there was a major need for change.

Political pressure

For many educated Frenchmen, the lack of political rights and a chance to participate in government was frustrating. The old parliament of France, the Estates General, had not met since 1614. The power of the monarchy had grown during the seventeenth century, especially under Louis XIV (1660–1715) who had promoted absolutism. His grand palace at Versailles was symbolic of the power of the central French state, imposing its will on the people in alliance with a privileged nobility and clergy. Alternative ideas of shared power and the participation of a wider political community had emerged in the eighteenth century. These reforming ideas were promoted by influential thinkers known as the *Philosophes*, and were part of a wider movement known as the Enlightenment.

Louis XIV and absolutism

Louis XIV, 1660–1715, established a more powerful monarchy after a period of political unrest in the mid-seventeenth century, which stressed the God-given authority of the monarch. This type of powerful monarchy was known as absolutism. Louis' power was expressed in his grand palace at Versailles and by his image in art and music as 'the Sun King'. Much of his reign was spent at war, which caused debts, and in practice there was unrest and division in France by 1715, so he left a problematic legacy to his successors Louis XV and Louis XVI of a monarchy that was absolute in theory but less so in practice.

In many European countries and in North America, there was a growth of interest in scientific knowledge and a discussion of all sorts of ideas. The interest in knowledge was reflected in the work of scholars like **Denis Diderot** who attempted to gather all knowledge into an encyclopedia. Greater knowledge led to treatises on change – there were works on agriculture, on industry, on finance, education, on the pursuit of happiness and on the nature of government. This expansion of intellectual activity was the work of an elite of thinkers and scholars. However, it had wider effects, particularly in matters of religion and politics.

There were doubts cast on traditional religious beliefs and the power of the Church to censor inquiries that threatened Christian beliefs. There was also the general questioning of traditions that affected belief in absolute monarchy. The most famous was the work of Jean Jacques Rousseau (a French-speaking Swiss writer, 1712–78) who questioned why, 'Man is born free, but is everywhere in chains' in his book *The Social Contract*, which suggested that men and women obey laws as part of an unwritten contract with those in power, not as a matter of blind obedience to God-given authority.

The new ideas affected not only the middle class but also some in the nobility. A major political writer was the Baron de Montesquieu (1689–1755) who argued that there should be a division between those who govern, those who discuss laws, and the judges to ensure a balance of power to protect the subjects from excessive state power. In Paris, Enlightenment ideas spread to the ordinary people, especially independent craftsmen and shopkeepers.

KEY FIGURE

Denis Diderot (1713–84) was an influential writer from the Champagne region of France who attempted to bring together knowledge into an encyclopedia begun in 1750 and completed in 1772. This quest for knowledge was highly influential and other Enlightenment writers followed suit; and as more was known and could be accessed, more could be questioned, so the effect was to promote more criticism of governments and institutions and to encourage more intellectual curiosity.

SOURCE B

An Enlightenment view of liberty. From Jean Jacques Rousseau, *The Social Contract* (1762)

The tyrant assures his subjects he will give them civil peace and tranquillity. Granted; but what do they gain, if the wars his ambition brings down upon them, his insatiable greed and the bad conduct of his ministers press on. What do they gain, if the very tranquillity they enjoy does not end the miseries? Tranquillity is found also in dungeons; but is that enough to make them desirable places to live in?

To renounce liberty is to renounce being a man.

How useful is Source B in explaining opposition to the Ancien Régime by 1789?

It would be wrong to think of the King as opposed to the Enlightenment. The queen, Marie Antoinette, was a great admirer of Rousseau. Louis was interested in various reforms. However, as he proved incapable of bringing about change to end the financial crisis and resorted to summoning the Estates General, he opened the way for discontents to be expressed and new political ideas to be discussed.

What was the reaction of Louis XVI to attempts to reform 1774–89?

The need to reform was pressing but Louis did not succeed in taking the initiative, despite being well-intentioned. Having appointed some able ministers, he failed to back them and let the situation get worse. He reluctantly agreed at last to a special assembly of notables to discuss the financial crisis in 1787 but this failed to get agreement and so he accepted the summoning of the Estates General and even allowed a nationwide consultation to put forward grievances. This was a huge gamble and might have worked had he himself led the movement for change but in fact it led to revolution and eventually his overthrow and execution.

Turgot and early attempts to reform

Faced with a deficit of 37 million livres, Louis XVI appointed an economic expert as his key minister – the Controller General of Finances. Given that the deficit was in modern terms at least £6000 million, some drastic action was needed and **Anne-Robert-Jacques Turgot** had plenty of ideas. He wanted to promote national wealth by freeing trade and reducing price controls; to end tax privileges and to improve communications to generate wealth. Appointed in 1774, he was dismissed in 1776 when the Queen and privileged aristocrats at court turned against him.

Necker and the *Compte Rendu*

His successor, a Swiss Protestant banker called **Jacques Necker**, was also inventive. He aimed to cut back on the sale of offices and reduce the share of the tax farmers in tax collected. To show transparency in government he published the national accounts in the *Compte Rendu* (report to the king) of 1781 – a bestseller as French people wanted to know the secrets of finance. This was a step too far for his enemies at court. He too was dismissed.

Calonne and the Assembly of Notables

His successor, the smooth and experienced aristocratic administrator Charles de Calonne, offered an ambitious three-pronged programme that would have economised spending, ended tax privileges in the payment of the key land tax, the taille, and increased prosperity by abolishing internal customs duties. He also proposed ending the unpopular **corvée**. When this did not meet with the approval of the parlement, Calonne turned to another striking proposal. In 1787, he called a special assembly of notables – of leading figures in the nation, aristocrats and royal princes. While not rejecting the reforms as such, the Assembly wanted to link them to greater political participation in government. The privileged classes were prepared to accept a reduction in their privileges but not without the calling of the Estates General. The failure to get agreement ensured that Calonne would go the way of his predecessors, and he was dismissed in April 1788.

KEY TERM 🔑

Corvée This was an obligation to work on the public roads or the king's highways. It was unpopular and as the nobles and clergy were exempt it caused a lot of resentment.

SOURCE C

A cartoon of 1788 shows the Assembly of Notables being called. The aristocratic delegates are shown as poultry being summoned to vote to be killed and eaten

> **What is the message of the cartoon in Source C?**

Brienne and the decision to call the Estates General

The attempts to reform continued. Calonne's successor, the aristocratic churchman Brienne, proposed to solve the financial problems by a new uniform land tax paid for by all. He also proposed other changes – reform of the customs barriers, provincial assemblies, civil rights for **Protestants** and the ending of torture. These progressive measures were rejected by the Assembly of Notables and also by the parlements, which refused to register them.

By 1788 the King had lost patience and he supported Brienne far more than he had supported the other reformers. When the parlements continued to refuse to register the changes, he exiled its members, announced plans to

KEY TERM 🔑

Protestants Followers of the religious reforms begun in the sixteenth century. There were wars between Catholics and Protestants in the sixteenth century. Protestants were granted toleration in 1598 but this was ended in 1685 when the Protestants, or Huguenots as they were called, were persecuted.

end parlements' rights to register edicts, or orders, and arrested leading members, including his own cousin who had expressed criticisms.

Would the King now rule as a real absolute monarch and force the privileged classes to accept change? This was one option open to him, but he did not follow it. Instead he announced another assembly – this time of the whole nation. On 8 August 1788 he declared that he would summon the Estates General.

- The leaders of the parlements had come to be seen as popular heroes resisting the power of the King, rather than selfish defenders of privilege.
- There had been demonstrations in their support, for example the 'Day of Tiles' in Grenoble.
- Louis and Brienne feared that if the King rejected both the Assembly of Notables and the parlements, and ruled as a real absolute monarch, then the state would not be able to borrow the money it needed to function.

The importance of this decision cannot be overstated.

- It led to widespread discussion of the grievances of the whole nation. Traditionally the calling of the Estates General was preceded by local meetings to draw up lists of grievances called *Cahiers de Doléances* (literally 'writing books of things which caused pain or distress').
- For the first time in the century there were elections for delegates to this grand meeting of the Estates.
- It led to considerable expectations of reform and change.
- Brienne was replaced by Necker who returned from Switzerland and was expected to take charge of a programme of change discussed and agreed by the whole nation.

ACTIVITY

Hold a balloon debate in which the key advisers in this chapter argue that they should stay in a hot air balloon which is sinking and has to lose a passenger! You will need to research 'your' adviser and argue that he was the best royal minister in the period 1774–1789.

'By February 1789 there was a revolutionary attitude in France.' To what extent does Source D support that statement?

SOURCE D

Some demands from the Third Estate in Carcassonne in Southern France in the Cahier drawn up in February 1789 at a special meeting

10 *Voting in the new assembly should be by head, not by estate.*

11 *No class, organization or individual citizen may lay claim to tax privileges.*

12 *The dues exacted from commoners holding lands should be abolished, and also regulations which exclude members of the Third Estate from certain positions, offices, and ranks which have hitherto been bestowed on nobles.*

13 *There should be no arbitrary orders for imprisonment … any tax exemptions. … All taxes should be assessed on the same system throughout the nation.*

14 *Freedom should be granted also to the press.*

The situation by 1789

The atmosphere created by this anticipation of change was heightened by high bread prices and unrest among the urban and rural population. The middle classes sensed an opportunity to introduce a new constitution and bring about fundamental change and an end to privilege. The level of political discussion was very high: debating societies talked about reform in the language of the Enlightenment – especially 'liberty'.

Only the most skilful monarch could have managed these expectations and avoided massive unrest. However, Louis was unable to grasp the widespread feeling for change. When the Estates General met it was announced that voting would be by Estate not by delegates. Necker had persuaded Louis to allow the Third Estate larger numbers of delegates, but the clergy and the aristocracy could outvote them. Also the first meeting of the long awaited Estates General was disappointing with Louis offering no programme and proceedings going in a slow and formal manner.

Louis had allowed every chance for serious reform to fail. By participating in yet another war – the **War of American independence** from 1778 to 1783 – the financial situation had been made worse. The King had failed to control his own nobles and to make them agree to reform. He had failed to back his own ministers. He had failed to see the consequences of suddenly allowing every district in France to meet to discuss grievances while having no plan to meet those grievances. In addition, he had not understood how to treat the Estates General or seen how important it was not to disappoint the high hopes for social, economic and political change.

What were the responses to Louis' actions during 1789 and how did the revolution develop?

The King's hesitations and initial refusals to allow the Estates General to vote by head and not by order – giving the first two Estates an automatic majority over the third, which represented the bulk of the nation – began a build-up of resentment against royal authority that grew when he was seen to oppose change. It was clear that Louis was reluctant to accept his new position as a constitutional monarch sharing his power with the representatives of the people. As change began to take place, the revolution grew more radical.

The King's response to the Estates General

When the Estates General met in 1789, it consisted of 278 nobles, 330 churchmen and 604 representatives of the Third Estate (i.e. the rest of the population). The King started badly by ordering each estate to its own meeting hall. This was in the eyes of the King not a national assembly but a meeting of three separate Estates, two of which could outvote the other. The old-fashioned class-ridden view of society was emphasized by the Third Estate being ordered to wear formal black clothes, in contrast to the colourful dress of the nobles. No plans for reform were announced in the opening ceremonies and valuable time was wasted in each Estate verifying the election results to ensure that the correct delegates were attending. The mismanagement drove the Third Estate to declare on 17 June that it was the assembly of the nation and not just an advisory body called by the King. When it appeared that they were locked out of their meeting room, they met in a tennis court (in modern terms, more like a large squash court, see Source E below) on 20 June and declared they were a 'national assembly' and swore an oath not to disperse until France had a constitution.

The Tennis Court Oath

This was a key moment of the revolution and confirmed the change in the Estates General. Originally called by the King to advise him on terms that he decided, it had become a very different body by 17 June. It had declared that it was the representative body of the nation – even though this was far from the truth as the bulk of the French people were peasants and the bulk of the representatives from the Third Estate were middle-class urban dwellers and professionals. The oath taken on 20 June moved this idea forward by binding the members to form a new constitution that would formally end the absolute power of the king and give the people the right to elect representatives. This would mean that the government would be responsible to the nation and not just the king. This was truly revolutionary. The occasion was seen as so important and historic that the great artist Jacques-Louis David was commissioned to paint it in 1790 (see Source E). However, before he could finish many of the original members had fallen victim to revolutionary violence so his sketch is a somewhat poignant commentary on the view that those who start revolutions rarely finish them.

SOURCE E

The Tennis Court Oath painting by Jacques-Louis David

> **Look at Source E. How does the artist seek to portray the great importance and drama of this event?**

The King was not to be moved. On 23 June he held a meeting of the Estates and told them to go away and consider and discuss proposals for reform separately. The Third Estate refused to obey the king. When 47 nobles joined them, Louis gave way and agreed that there should be one body and the three Estates should join.

Thus, by June 1789, Louis was facing a situation that he had never intended. There was a new national assembly committed to a new constitution, which would involve regular elections. Claims had been made openly for the nation to be involved in government and decision-making.

The storming of the Bastille

The revolution had begun, quite bloodlessly, before the event that France now celebrates as its beginning – the storming of the Bastille on 14 July. The King helped to bring this about by appearing to be preparing for the use of military force to restore his authority by summoning troops to the capital. He provoked a crisis by dismissing the reforming minister Necker on 11 July.

However, Paris had become a hotbed of political agitation; unemployment and high bread prices had created discontent. The authorities had virtually lost control of the capital. Impromptu public meetings and the speeches of radical political agitators had created a mood of excitement. The King's actions did not help, but the conditions for an outburst were already there.

Crowds attacked customs posts, then, fearing military action to suppress the assembly, they searched for arms. First they took weapons from the Invalides military hospital and then moved to the fortress of the Bastille. This had largely fallen out of use and was used to house a few prisoners, but its sheer bulk was a symbol of royal authority. The troops stationed there fired on the crowds. Other disobedient troops joined the attackers and there was bloodshed, culminating in the mob killing the prison's governor, the Marquis de Launay.

SOURCE F

A Parisian newspaper reports the storming of the Bastille, July 1789

The conquerors, glorious and covered in honour, carry their arms and the spoils of the conquered, the flags of victory, the victory laurels offered them from every side, all this created a frightening and splendid spectacle. The people, anxious to avenge themselves, allowed neither De Launay nor the other officers to reach the place of trial; they seized them from the hands of their conquerors, and trampled them underfoot one after the other. De Launay was struck by a thousand blows, his head was cut off and hoisted on the end of a pike with blood streaming down all sides … This glorious day must amaze our enemies, and finally usher in for us the triumph of justice and liberty. In the evening, there were celebrations.

> **How useful is Source F as evidence about the atmosphere in Paris in July 1789?**

The British ambassador reported to the government in London on 30 July 1789 on the events of 14 July.

The fate of the Governor M.de Launay, is generally lamented, for he was an Officer of great merit and always treated the prisoners committed to his charge with humanity: it may be observed that the mildness of the present reign in France is strongly characterised by the small number of persons who were discovered in confinement in the Bastille: yet these considerations were not sufficient to check the fury of the populace, animated by the success of the attack and heated with the spirit of vengeance.

> **How does the tone and the content of Sources F and G differ? Which do you think is the more reliable source?**

KEY TERM

National Guard An armed force of citizens formed to keep order in July 1789.

To maintain order the Paris propertied classes (the electors of delegates to the Estates General) created a new city council and a **National Guard** – signs that the King's authority was being ignored. The King accepted this on 17 July.

The Great Fear, the August Decrees and the Declaration of the Rights of Man

The King had paid the price for failing to be decisive in leading a movement for reform or decisively using the ample military forces at his disposal to end the revolution. Events now went forward at a pace that left him out of control.

There was a marked increase in peasant unrest in the wake of rumours that the nobles were going to stop reform and attack them. This 'Great Fear' resulted in the burning of many chateaux and the destruction of records of taxes and dues. In the towns, too, there was the overthrow of traditional authority. The Assembly in Paris was caught up in the national mood for radical change. It voted for the abolition of feudal dues on 4 August 1789, and on 26 August passed the Declaration of the Rights of Man and of the Citizen – a bold statement that Frenchmen were citizens not subjects, with rights not merely the duty to obey the monarch.

ACTIVITY
Reread the section on 1789 and find arguments and facts to support each of the following statements:
- 'The loss of royal authority by July 1789 was mainly the fault of the king himself.'
- 'The loss of royal authority was because of a situation that was too difficult for the king to control and he should not be held responsible.'

Then decide which you think is more convincing and why.

Extracts from the Declaration of the Rights of Man, 26 August 1789

1 *Men are born and remain free and equal in rights.*

2 *The aim of all political association is the preservation of the natural and imprescriptible rights of man. These rights are liberty, property, security, and resistance to oppression.*

3 *The principle of all sovereignty resides essentially in the nation. No body nor individual may exercise any authority which does not proceed directly from the nation.*

4 *Liberty consists in the freedom to do everything which injures no one else.*

5 *Law can only prohibit such actions as are hurtful to society.*

6 *Law is the expression of the general will.*

> **What can you learn from Sources F and H about the development of the Revolution during the summer of 1789?**

The King could do little except observe these major changes in French society and government. They were the unintended consequence of the decision to summon the Estates General and the failure to gauge the situation.

The 'March of the Women' and the October Days

By October, Louis was having second thoughts. He did not embrace change. He resented his loss of status as representative of the nation and made some half-hearted moves to restoring what he thought was the natural order of monarchy. He summoned troops from the Flanders Regiment, who were known to be loyal to him personally, to his palace at Versailles. At a reception for some of the officers, the revolutionary red, white and blue cockade (emblem) was trampled underfoot.

With food prices high and with a great deal of hardship fuelling radical agitation in the poorer districts, another burst of popular fury erupted. This 'March of the Women' was led by the fishwives of the Paris markets protesting about the price of bread. A great demonstration was held and a march on Versailles took place. The National Guard and its indecisive commander, the **Marquis de la Fayette**, followed the crowds to Versailles where there was bloodshed, as royal guards were killed and the palace invaded on 5 October 1789.

Up to this point both the King and his ministers and the national assembly had been meeting at Versailles. The events of 5 October forced both King and assembly to move to the centre of Paris. Louis went in a humiliating procession, jeered by crowds, to take refuge in the Tuileries Palace, where he was at the mercy of the mob far more.

The Assembly now moved to establishing a new reformed France and to drawing up a new constitution. Its name now – the **Constituent Assembly** – showed that it was working as an independent body, not as part of a royal government.

The role of the King in the development of the Revolution in 1789

The King was in many ways the author of his own misfortunes and his fatal inconsistency ended chances of a royal-based reform programme and also an effective suppression of revolution. However, the economic situation was not within his control and neither was the growth of the population of Paris and the radical ideas of the Enlightenment. He also inherited financial problems and an inefficient financial and administrative system. There were disturbances in other countries in the late eighteenth century and the use of force was not always effective, as was shown in the successful rebellion of the American colonies against Britain. Thus, while Louis' responses to the developments of 1789 can be seen as intensifying the Revolution, they cannot completely explain the loss of royal control by the end of 1789.

KEY FIGURE

Marie-Joseph Gilbert du Motier, Marquis de la Fayette (1757–1834) was a high-ranking noble from the Loire who was a professional soldier. Moved by the idea of liberty, he volunteered to help the American colonists in their war against Britain in 1777. He became a hero in America. In 1789 he was made commander of the new National Guard and helped to write the Declaration of the Rights of Man. He was not able to control the march on Versailles in October 1789 and was increasingly concerned about the radicalism of the revolution. He fled abroad in 1792.

KEY TERM

Constituent Assembly An elected body whose task is to draw up a new constitution, or a set of rules under which a country is to be run.

ACTIVITY

Reread the chapter and explain why each of the following was important in the development of the Revolution in 1789:

- The Storming of the Bastille
- The Tennis Court Oath
- The Declaration of the Rights of Man
- The October Days

Now rank these events in order of importance: 1=least important, 5=most important and explain your reasons.

a Long- and short-term causes of the Revolution

LONG

↓

1 Finance

↓

2 Tensions in society

↓

3 The Enlightenment

SHORT

↓

1 Foreign policy

↓

2 Finance

↓

3 Failure of reform

↓

4 Political crisis 1787–88

↓

5 Economic crisis

b How did the Revolution develop?

Drawing up Cahiers

↓

Estates General

↓

Crown reaction

↓

Storming of the Bastille

↓

Provincial Revolt

↓

Great Fear

↓

August Decrees

↓

Declaration of the Rights of Man

↓

Nationalization of Church land

↓

October Days

SUMMARY DIAGRAM

What were the causes and immediate outcomes of the 1789 Revolution?

 # 2 Why were French governments unstable from 1790 to 1795?

The achievements of the National Assembly which became the Constituent Assembly were remarkable, but it became increasingly difficult to ensure that France was stable after 1790. The opening up of political debate had led to all sorts of different ideas – some very radical – while at the same time there was conservative concern about the pace of change, so France became very divided. The situation was made worse by war from 1792. The new constitution took until 1791 to be formed and by then many had lost faith in the King and there were also powerful republican groups. With the overthrow of the King power passed to the radical revolutionaries but their reign of terror was too extreme for many and they were overthrown in 1794 and a more conservative government called the Directory ruled until 1799. Threatened by both royalists and radicals they relied more and more on military power.

The views and aims of revolutionary and counter-revolutionary groups

The events of 1789 had moved France very quickly from an absolute monarchy to a **constitutional monarchy**. There had also been an unprecedented amount of political discussion and interest in political developments. This had led to a wide range of views being expressed and the formation of new political clubs which pressed for change. The opponents of the Revolution – or the counter-revolutionary groups – also emerged. Thus, France became very divided, and political arguments went beyond mere discussion and became violent, leading to instability in government, extremism and loss of life.

Revolutionary groups

The discussions about the Cahiers and the relaxation of censorship and government control led to an expansion of political activity and the expression of a range of radical political ideas. The most influential groups that demanded radical change were members of political clubs called the Cordeliers and the Jacobins. Middle-class radicals founded the Cordeliers Club in 1790 as the Society of the Friends of the Rights of Man and of the Citizen. Its members encouraged working-class membership. The leading speakers **Georges-Jacques Danton** and **Camille Desmoulins** wanted to extend the Revolution to ensure that it represented the ordinary people and they also wished to end the monarchy. The Jacobins originated in a meeting of deputies from Brittany to the Estates General. A discussion club in a former convent of St Jacques, it was initially moderate, but it split in July 1791. Those who believed in a constitutional monarchy left to form a club called the Feuillants. This left the Jacobin club as a gathering of more radical members who, like its leading speaker Maximilien Robespierre, looked for power for the people, an end to the monarchy, a sweeping away of the old elites and a new Republic of virtue that would see a rebirth of France. He and many radicals saw the people as natural and pure, as opposed to the corrupt court and nobility. These ideas were expressed in a newspaper called 'The Friend of the People' organized by Jean-Paul Marat.

KEY TERM

Constitutional monarchy
A state where the hereditary ruler shares power to a greater or lesser extent with an elected assembly.

KEY FIGURES

Georges-Jacques Danton (1759–94) was a radical lawyer who took a leading part in the overthrow of the monarchy in 1792 and was Minister of Justice in 1792. A powerful orator, he disagreed with Robespierre about the severity of the Terror, urging more moderation and was tried and executed as a traitor to the Revolution in 1794.

Camille Desmoulins (1760–94) was a radical lawyer who did much to incite the crowds in Paris in July 1789 prior to the storming of the Bastille. He wrote prolifically and published revolutionary newspapers but he disagreed with Robespierre, his former friend, and paid for that with his life in 1794 when he was guillotined.

Maximilien Robespierre

Born in Arras in 1758, Robespierre was the son of a lawyer. He trained in law in Paris and specialized in defending poorer people. Robespierre was elected to the Estates General in 1789. He developed radical ideas and was a member of the Jacobin club. Though opposed to war in 1792, he was a passionate believer in the Revolution and the end of the monarchy. He took the major role in the overthrow of the Girondins and was a leading member of the Committee of Public Safety, supporting extreme measures of terror against perceived opponents. Highly influential with the Paris crowds, he became powerful and aimed to implement controversial changes such as the Cult of the Supreme Being in place of traditional religion. He lost support among the people and the Convention and was arrested, condemned and executed in July 1794.

Less radical, but still anxious for change, was another leading group, the Girondins. Called after the Gironde region where many of its members came from, this group supported revolution but were prepared to accept a constitutional monarchy. They were initially the allies and supporters of a journalist and intellectual, Jacques-Pierre Brissot, and included the influential political leaders Jean Roland and his wife.

Clubs and parties in the French Revolution

There were no political parties in the modern sense and the titles below refer either to the places where like-minded people met to discuss political events, like the former Convent of St Jacques (hence Jacobins), or to names given to them.

Name	Nature	Some leading figures	Key aims
Cordeliers	Radical revolution	Danton, Desmoulins	Ending the monarchy; more power to the people
Jacobins	Initially moderate but became more radical	Robespierre, St Just, Couthon, Marat	Ending the monarchy; opposing enemies of the Revolution; encouraging a dedication to revolution as a rebirth of French life; more democracy
Feuillants	Moderate	Barnave, Lameth, Duport	A constitutional monarchy with limited voting for the people
Girondins	Revolutionaries but willing to accept constitutional monarchy	Jacques-Pierre Brissot, Jean Roland, Mme Roland	Supported war in 1792
Enragés	Extreme anti-monarchists and republicans	Hébert, Roux	Social revolution; ending of aristocracy; power to the people

Even more extreme revolutionary ideas emerged in Paris such as the Hébertists. These were sometimes known as the Enragés (the angry ones) and called for a popular democracy, the destruction of the old privileged classes and the role of the king, and policies to share wealth among the poor.

What had begun as a moderate and bloodless revolution that called for a constitutional monarchy that would consult its subjects about key elements such as taxation had turned by 1792 into a much more extreme movement as the political clubs and groups struggled for power and did not hesitate to gain the support of the Paris people. The monarchy was overthrown in a violent coup in August 1792, and the King was tried and executed in January 1793, showing the increased influence of the more extreme groups.

This development of radicalism had been feared by royalists since 1789. Many nobles and the King's brothers had left France and established themselves over the border in the lands of the German Archbishop of Trier. These émigrés, as they were known, urged other European monarchs to intervene to restore the power of Louis. They promoted resistance to the Revolution in France.

Many Frenchmen did not agree with the changes. There was particular resentment among many Catholics at the religious policies that ended the special position of the Catholic Church, took over its lands and made priests officials of the state (The **Civil Constitution of the Clergy**). Opposition to the new ideas and to the control being exerted by the revolutionary assemblies in Paris gave rise to counter-revolutionary movements which split France and led to civil war. These were strong in Brittany where local forces known as **Chouans** opposed the Revolution in favour of a restoration of the power of the Church and the King. In la Vendée in the west there was resistance and revolutionary armies fought bitter struggles against opposition. This often involved mass executions such as those at Nantes in 1793 and in Lyon where special forces were sent from Paris to overthrow the royalist government that had been set up in the city.

However, violence was not just a result of royalist ideas being pitted against revolutionary ideas. The more extreme Jacobins denounced and had executed the Girondin leaders and also their rival radicals. The leader of this terror was Robespierre and he brought about the downfall and death of his one-time friends Danton and Desmoulins. Brissot and the Rolands were tried and executed. But political murder was not all on one side. A Girondin, Charlotte Corday, murdered Marat in his bath and was herself tried and executed. Robespierre and his supporters were overthrown by force in July 1794.

The Revolution brought new ideas about religion, with Robespierre supporting a Cult of the Supreme Being to replace Christianity. This was a broadly religious movement with special ceremonies in praise of key civic

ACTIVITY

Make sure you understand these key terms by writing a short definition of each one:

- Counter Revolution
- Emigre
- Jacobin
- Girondin
- Civil Constitution of the Clergy.

KEY TERMS

Civil Constitution of the Clergy The name given to the new official position of the church in the Revolution which placed it under state control.

Chouans The name given to those who fought against the Revolution in Western France, especially in Brittany and Maine from 1793. They were a mainly peasant force.

virtues. The Jacobin St Just had ideas about revolutionising education, distributing wealth among the people and having true democracy and when war broke out from 1792 (see below) the revolutionaries had the idea of a total war with a citizen army being supported by the entire population. There were calls not only for democracy for men but even for political equality for women – though this was frowned on by the male-dominated revolutionary groups. Nevertheless, a few thinkers like the Marquis de Condorcet supported the feminist ideas of Olympe de Gouges and **Théroigne de Méricourt**. However, these won little general sympathy and were seen as part of the political extremism brought about by revolution.

Why were there so many changes of government 1790–95?

The Estates General renamed itself the National Assembly on 17 June 1790 and on 9 July became the National Constituent Assembly. While the King continued to appoint ministers, the Assembly passed legislation, which transformed and modernized France, and finally produced a written Constitution in September 1791. A new elected assembly called the **Legislative Assembly** lasted from September 1791 to 1792. France was still a monarchy but the King was suspended in August 1792 and France became a republic in September with a new National Convention. Rule passed to committees of this convention. Revolutionary violence increased from September 1792 until an extensive Terror was established during 1793–94 with political groups attacking their enemies and sending them to execution while suppressing all resistance to the Revolution with great violence. The Terror ended in 1795 when France had yet another constitution under a government of Directors who ruled France until a military coup in 1799 brought Napoleon Bonaparte to power. Thus, the period from 1790 to 1795 was one of considerable change and political instability.

The Constituent Assembly reorganized local government, ended nobility and passed important measures freeing trade and ending guild restriction. It confirmed the end of feudalism and began a process of bringing in uniform laws. But its main function was to give France a constitution. When it had introduced a new constitution its members who had been active since the calling of the Estates General in 1789 passed a law that former deputies were not eligible to sit in the new Legislative Assembly. Thus, valuable experience was lost.

The attempt to make the new constitutional monarchy work was weakened by the King attempting unsuccessfully to flee France in July 1791, which made him seem a traitor to his own people and increased calls for a republic. The rising influence of the more extreme revolutionary groups like the

Jacobins and the growth of counter-revolution in France led to instability. This was also caused by disputes over religion with the King opposing the Civil Constitution of the Clergy and then the outbreak of war in 1792 and early defeats of France's forces made for instability. Popular disturbances in Paris brought the monarchy to an end in August 1792.

The new Republic faced the strains of war both against foreign nations and also its own people in the provinces. It had bitter political in-fighting between different groups and came to rely heavily on terror. The emergence of highly radical leaders dominated by abstract ideas made the Republic vulnerable. When it seemed that Robespierre might extend the Terror, he was overthrown by former allies. But even with the end of the most extreme factions, there was limited stability with both royalists and radicals in danger of taking over. In 1795 there was yet another attempt to institute a new constitution with the formation of the Directory. Though this lasted until 1799, it was not led by inspiring leaders and was dangerously dependent on military successes by ambitious generals.

Thus, after 1790 the Revolution did not settle to a moderate constitutional monarchy as many hoped but could not sustain a more radical form of government either. It has been rightly claimed that the Revolution did not throw up an outstanding leader who could unite the nation.

Economic problems 1790–95

The bad harvests and high prices, together with longer-term economic problems in many areas of the countryside, had contributed to the events of 1789. The constitutional monarchy that had emerged was helped by better harvests in 1790. However, in 1791 once again harvests were bad. There were food riots in Paris in January and February 1792 and the rate of unemployment rose. This was partly because of the effects of the Revolution. The departure of many aristocrats and richer elements in French society meant that the demand for luxury goods fell. Those involved in many trades that supplied items such as lace, silk clothes, expensive shoes and all sorts of consumer goods found that their incomes fell and many workshops closed. The outbreak of a slave revolt in the French West Indian colony of St Dominique disrupted imports of some key items such as coffee and sugar and disrupted the profitable West Indies trade.

Inflation and paper money

Economic conditions were made worse by the issuing of paper money by the government. The new notes were called assignats and they were, in effect, transferrable **IOU**s based on the wealth that the state had gained from taking over Church lands. However, their value was unstable and this resulted in **inflation**. French people were reluctant to use this paper money so causing a shortage of currency, which inhibited trade.

ACTIVITY
Discussion point
Consider the following statement: 'The Constitution of 1791 was doomed to fail.' Below are some points to help with your thinking.

- Think about what was necessary for it to succeed.
- Think about whether there was too much extremism and too little trust in the king.
- Think about whether anything in history is 'doomed to fail'.

KEY TERMS

IOU A way of writing 'I owe you' – a promise to repay a loan.

Inflation Rising prices.

Worsening problems

These economic problems were accompanied by problems that accompanied the decision to go to war in 1792 against Austria and subsequently Prussia and Britain. The war brought the threat of foreign invasion and stirred up fears and resentments, which were in part fuelled by food shortages and high prices at a time when trade was highly disrupted first by revolution and then by war.

The hardships of the people of Paris were expressed in resentment against the old ruling classes. The **sans-culottes** demanded harsher measures against enemies and suspects who they saw as priests who would not swear an oath of loyalty to the new constitutional Church, to aristocrats, to traders and merchants who hoarded food and deprived the poor, and to the King and the royal family.

Louis resolutely refused to accept laws in the Legislative Assembly against so-called non-juror priests and also to accept that the property of the aristocratic émigrés should be confiscated.

As with the revolutionary journées, or 'days', of 1789, economic hardship was a major contributor to a fresh outbreak of popular unrest in Paris that led to the end of the monarchy on 10 August when crowds supported by radical politicians, and provincial troops who had come to defend Paris, attacked the royal guards at the Tuileries and brought an end to the monarchy.

The economic problems continued into 1793. The value of the paper money assignats fell by 50 per cent and grain supplies were at dangerously low levels. The new Convention tried to impose controls in response to popular demands for actions against hoarders. However, price controls merely meant less grain was brought to market and illegal trading or the black market flourished, raising prices even more and creating more social discontent. The more extreme elements in the Convention called for death for hoarders and new taxes on the rich.

KEY TERM

Sans-culottes Richer men wore breeches and stockings on their legs but the poorer men wore trousers – so they were literally 'without breeches'. The sans-culottes were politically active and often not the very poorest of the people of Paris but small shopkeepers and artisans who resented the rich and were influenced by the radical ideas of clubs like the Jacobins. They took a key role in many of the political disturbances of the Revolution in Paris.

SOURCE I

Jacques Roux, a radical member of the Paris local government (Commune) petitions the Convention, in June 1793. He refers to currency speculation involving the paper money (assignats)

Have you outlawed speculation? No. Have you decreed the death penalty for hoarding? No. Have you controlled trade (to ensure plentiful and cheap food)? No. Have you banned the exchange of assignats for specie? Have you visited the poorer floors of the houses of Paris? You would have been moved to tears by the tears and signs of an immense population without food and clothing.

How useful is Source I as evidence for the grievances of the people of Paris in 1793?

The political situation worsened – the moderate revolutionary Girondin government faced considerable demonstrations from the Paris crowds and radical elements of the National Guard which overthrew it in June 1793, leading to a more radical Jacobin government and to the political violence known as the Terror (see pages 19–21).

The civil war that had broken out in the countryside by 1793 disrupted food supplies even more. The needs of war against European enemies absorbed resources and raised prices. In September 1793 the Jacobin government passed the Law of the General Maximum. This controlled prices but also wages. The Jacobin leaders believed in the Revolution passionately but that meant fighting a war. They did not put the interests of the urban workers before the need for stable prices. They prevented higher wages and took action against strikes by tradesmen such as plasterers, bakers, butchers and printers. In March 1794 there was renewed attempt by the government to control wages.

The discontent in Paris that had once resulted in the creation of a new constitutional monarchy and then helped to destroy the monarchy and to support a radical regime and a revolutionary Terror was now turning against the Jacobins and their leader Robespierre. The sans-culottes made no attempt to save Robespierre from being overthrown by his enemies in the Coup of Thermidor on 17 July 1794. Initially a period of cheaper food had led to popular support for the radical revolutionaries, but fear of wage reductions led to a loss of this support. After Robespierre's fall, price controls were first reduced and then ended. For the first time since 1791 there were serious rises in bread prices and real wages fell back to 1789 levels.

> **ACTIVITY**
> Draw a spider diagram to show the problems facing France in 1793. On your diagram, label the most serious problem as 1, the next most serious problem as 2, and so on.

SOURCE J

Government Report 1795

The worker's wage is far too low to meet his daily needs: the unfortunate pensioners and small investors have to sell their last sticks of furniture; the shop keepers and small businessmen find their capital and income eaten up; the civil servants also suffer economic privation.

> **Compare and contrast Sources I and J as evidence for hardship in France 1793–95.**

Arms production was reduced, causing hardship, and supplies of food from the countryside were reduced because peasants refused to accept discredited paper money. The gap between poor and rich seemed once again to be considerable and on 1 April 1795 there were bread riots and an attempt to take over the Convention. It was met with determined resistance and repression. Hunger and distress led to a wider revolt on 20 May known as the Revolt of Prairial. The sans-culottes surrounded and entered the Convention, demanding lower prices and action against the rich. But when they dispersed the authorities used troops to surround the main working-class districts.

Economic distress continued but it could no longer fuel effective crowd action. The Revolution had given rise to high hopes for economic change, which it was not able to deliver.

Foreign threats and the impact of war on France

The initial events of the Revolution did not lead Louis XVI's fellow monarchs in Europe to rush to his defence. He had exploited the problems of Britain in the American War of Independence and had intervened in the Netherlands in 1788 to take advantage of a revolt against Austrian rule in neighbouring Belgium. When his brothers and other nobles left France, they established themselves in Coblenz, over the border in modern-day Germany. At this time, Germany was over 1000 independent mini countries under the nominal control of the Holy Roman Empire. The émigrés were sheltered by sympathetic German archbishops but did not get the support they needed for an invasion of France by the largest German powers, Austria and Prussia. The European powers were not entirely displeased to see France weakened by revolution.

However, as the Revolution became more radical, especially after Louis tried unsuccessfully to flee and it was clear he was a virtual prisoner in his own country in July 1791, there was more concern. In August 1791 the King of Prussia, Frederick William, and the Emperor of Austria issued the Declaration of Pillnitz, threatening intervention in support of Louis. The Austrian Emperor Leopold was the brother of Marie Antoinette and was becoming concerned for her safety.

SOURCE K

From the Declaration of Pillnitz, August 1791

> *His Majesty the Emperor and His Majesty the King of Prussia … declare together that they regard the actual situation of His Majesty the King of France as a matter of communal interest for all sovereigns of Europe. They hope that that interest will be recognized by the powers whose assistance is called in … to strengthen, in utmost liberty, the foundations of a monarchical government of the French. In that case, aforementioned Majesties are determined to act promptly and unanimously, with the forces necessary for realizing the proposed and communal goal. In expectation, they will give the suitable orders to their troops so that they will be ready to commence activity.*

How far does the evidence in Source K show that the Revolution was faced by united and dangerous enemies?

Thus the threat from foreign powers and the dangers of the émigrés led some in France to demand war. This was pushed by the Girondins, the more moderate revolutionary group led by Jacques-Pierre Brissot. They hoped to unify the nation behind a pre-emptive war to defend the Revolution and also to spread revolutionary ideas. It was opposed by Robespierre who argued that it could actually lead to counter-revolution if it failed. The King supported the war against his own fellow monarchs hoping that it would bring about a restoration of royal power.

The war changed the whole nature of the Revolution. France declared war on Austria in April 1792 and against Prussia in June. Great revolutionary enthusiasm was not enough to prevent French forces being driven back as they attempted to invade the Austrian Netherlands. France now faced invasion and worse. In July the Prussian commander issued the Brunswick Manifesto threatening to destroy Paris if the King were harmed. This created a panic in Paris that was made worse when Prussian forces took the fortress of Verdun.

The threat of a counter-revolution supported by Austrian and Prussian forces led to a wave of suspicion. Treachery was blamed for the military failures and a state of emergency was declared. Provincial troops were summoned to Paris to defend the Revolution. The Paris crowds invaded the Tuileries Palace on 20 June and forced the King to wear the **red cap of liberty**. However, in the heightened atmosphere of war this was not going to be enough. Louis had incurred suspicion for vetoing measures against émigrés and had opposed calling up extra troops. On 10 August mobs attacked the Tuileries Palace, massacred the royal guards, forced the imprisonment of the King and a suspension of the monarchy.

The immediate threat of invasion was ended by a revolutionary victory at the Battle of Valmy, but the monarchy was doomed by then and a Republic was declared. The fevered atmosphere of war brought a massacre of suspects in the Paris prisons. The wave of violence continued relentlessly. The King was tried and executed in January 1793. Civil war erupted in the south and west. French threats to the Netherlands together with revulsion at the death of the King brought about war with Britain. Revolutionary France was now isolated in Europe and faced a coalition of major European nations which was capable of aiding the opposition within France itself.

The Battle of Valmy, 20 September 1792

Prussian forces invaded France and were met by a French force led by Dumouriez and Kellermann. A rapid Prussian advance might have been decisive but the Prussians decided to attack a French force, blocking their retreat to Germany. An artillery duel made the Prussians stop their attack and a further clash at Jemappes in November ended the Prussian invasion. Though fought by members of the former royal French army, not revolutionary hordes, the battle was decisive in saving the Revolution.

The feeling of betrayal was increased when the victor of Valmy, French generals Lafayette and Dumouriez, deserted to Austria. The Girondin ministers who had been so anxious for war now faced a popular uprising supported by their political enemies. The war led to a second French Revolution that toppled the moderates and brought the more extreme elements into power from 31 May to 2 June 1793.

The National Convention and its Committees – Public Safety and General Safety – was dominated by Robespierre who enjoyed the support of the Paris sans-culottes and offered a policy of total war. All national resources were taken for war. There was conscription, new arms workshops were set up; suspected opponents were arrested and controls put on prices and wages. Political representatives were sent to dismiss and often execute defeatist or inadequate generals.

SOURCE L

Decree of the Convention, August 1793, instituting national conscription

From this moment until that in which the enemy shall have been driven from the soil of the Republic, all Frenchmen are in permanent requisition for the service of the armies. The young men shall go to battle; the married men shall forge arms and transport provisions; the women shall make tents and clothing and shall serve in the hospitals; the children shall turn old linen into lint; the aged shall betake themselves to the public places in order to arouse the courage of the warriors and preach the hatred of kings and the unity of the Republic.

It is, accordingly, authorized to form all the establishments, factories, workshops, and mills which shall be deemed necessary for the carrying on of these works, as well as to put in requisition, within the entire extent of the Republic, the artists and working men who can contribute to their success.

> **How useful is Source L for showing the impact of war on the people of France? Answer by explaining ways in which you think it is useful and then consider any limitations you think this evidence has.**

KEY FIGURE

Lazare Carnot (1753–1823) was a mathematician and military leader who organized the French revolutionary army after 1793. He did much to introduce the idea of total war.

Utmost violence was used against internal opponents, with mass killings in the provinces and public execution by guillotine in Paris. Marie Antoinette was a victim in October but those killed were often accused of undermining the war effort rather than just being nobles executed in a class war.

The idea of a citizen army and a ruthless political terror were the direct consequences of war, though they had their roots in some of the revolutionary ideas discussed since 1789. However, without the threat of war it is unlikely that revolutionaries like Robespierre would have gained power. The author of the war effort was **Lazare Carnot** and his organization anticipated the total war of the twentieth century. By 1794 the threat of invasion had lessened and there was greater control of rebellious areas of France itself – at an estimated cost of some 200,000 lives.

The war offered opportunities for talented younger officers to emerge and the large forces raised by the revolutionary regime were effective in reducing the threat and in French conquests. By July 1794, the foreign threat was no longer strong enough to justify a possible extension of terror and the economic controls were being resented. In July Robespierre fell and though the war was continued by his successors, it did not dominate the course of the revolution to such an extent.

> **ACTIVITY**
> Make notes on pages 24–26 on the importance of the Revolutionary War. Pick out key points about the impact of the war and use sub-headings and bullet points as much as possible.

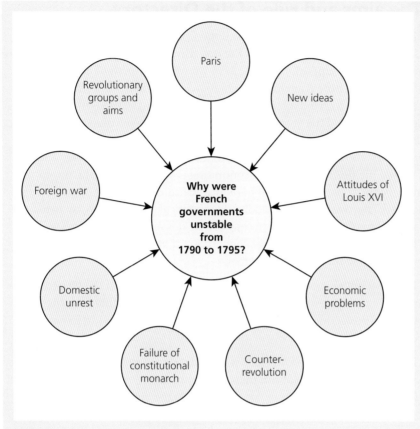

 # Why was Napoleon Bonaparte able to overthrow the Directory in 1799?

The most notable military victories of the Revolution were won by a young Corsican commander trained in France called Napoleon Bonaparte. Making his name by taking a leading part in driving Britain out of the southern French port of Toulon in 1793 he went on to gain powerful friends in the Directory and was appointed to command the army of Italy in 1796. He achieved spectacular successes and went on to a very well-publicized campaign in Egypt, which while failing in the long term produced some short-term victories that caught the public imagination and led to him being used by plotters to overthrow the Directors in 1799.

The aims and rule of the Directory

The members of the Convention and the Committees of Public Safety and General Security who organized the overthrow and execution of Robespierre and his leading supporters in July 1794 were known as the Thermidorians, after the date of the coup in the revolutionary calendar – Thermidor (July). Their aim was to avoid a bout of terror that might have brought them to their deaths and to end the supremacy of Robespierre. They wanted to distance the government from the radical ideas of Robespierre on religion and avoid what they saw as the absurdities of his Cult of the Supreme Being. They doubted the need or wisdom of continuing the Terror, given the improved military situation, and wanted to reduce the control of the state on economic activity. They were mainly middle-class political figures who distrusted the radical Paris Commune, which they saw as dominated by the sans-culottes. They also distrusted the radical constitution that the Jacobins had drawn up but which had never been implemented.

The defeat of the popular risings of April and May opened the way to a new and less extreme revolutionary regime that was more in line with the ideas of 1791 in protecting property and preventing the state having too much power.

The Constitution of the Directory was not instituted until 1795. The Directory was a ruling committee of five men. They constituted the executive branch of government and were chosen for five years by the upper chamber of the legislature, which was the Council of the Elders (Conseil des Anciens). This consisted of 250 members all of whom had to be over the age of 40. They chose the Directors from a list submitted by the second chamber, the Council of Five Hundred, who had to be at least 30 years old. Both houses were elected by all men over 21 who paid direct taxes. There were 5.5 million of these taxpayers out of a population of about 30 million. They voted for a special group called electors who in turn chose the members of the two councils. These were men who were even wealthier and there were high property qualifications, which meant that only 30,000 men were eligible. There were annual elections for these elite electors but they chose only a third of the two houses each year to ensure continuity. The Directors served for five years with one retiring each year on the basis of drawing lots.

This elaborate arrangement aimed to ensure certain outcomes.
- The Directors would not be as powerful as a monarch or as powerful as the Convention's previous committees. No future Robespierre could emerge.
- The voting would be in the hands of wealthier elements who would not threaten stability or vote for measures to benefit the masses at the expense of taxpayers.
- The restriction in age would ensure that more mature men would dominate and not younger and more radical men.

KEY TERM 🔑

White Terror This was politically inspired violence used by the enemies of the Revolution (the so-called 'Whites') against its supporters.

The Directory was brought in at a time when the Thermadorians had reduced the power of the sans-culottes and the political clubs. The threat of invasion was much less than in 1792–93 and internal unrest, while not suppressed, had been lessened. However, problems remained.

- The fall of Robespierre had encouraged considerable violence by royalists in the provinces – the so-called **White Terror** – and there was a danger that there might be a restoration of the monarchy.
- The power of the radicals had been diminished but there was still a danger from the sans-culottes.
- There were ongoing economic problems that might cause instability and the financial position was not secure.
- France faced the hostility of many European powers and Britain in particular was a persistent foe whose strong finances and powerful navy threatened France.
- There was still a need to maintain large military forces and the regime was dependent on military victory.
- There was always the danger of a military coup.

The reputation of the Directory and opposition to it

The Directory did not throw up a single inspirational figure and its reputation has been of a weak and unsuccessful government that fell victim to intrigues and the emergence of a strong military leader. Napoleon Bonaparte ended the regime and introduced a stronger and more purposeful government. The elements that have been seen as weak are as follows:

- The constitution did not allow for firm government and the Directory faced a series of attempts to overthrow it, both from royalists and from the radicals – the so-called **neo-Jacobins**.
- The regime was corrupt and financially inefficient.
- There was overreliance on censorship and repression in the absence of genuine support.
- The regime depended on military success and the plunder from military campaigns.
- The regime was weakened by internal intrigues that finally brought the Directory to an end in 1799.

However, defenders of the Directory point out that the challenges to it were met more firmly than was the case with previous revolutionary regimes. In October 1795 the Directory faced a challenge from 25,000 royalist demonstrators in Paris protesting against measures to ensure that the new councils would be dominated by those loyal to the Republic. On 13 Vendemiaire in the **revolutionary calendar** (5 October) the Directory used a young commander, Napoleon Bonaparte, to protect them with artillery and his 'whiff of grapeshot' – deadly cannon used at point blank range – dispersed the demonstrations.

KEY TERMS

Neo-Jacobins The main impetus of radical revolution had been slowed by the fall of Robespierre and the suppression of the more extreme groups. However, the ideas of the Jacobins had not died and there was a radical opposition to the Directors that saw the regime as betraying the core principles of the Revolution. These groups were not a united party and have been known as the neo- (or near) Jacobins. They were later suppressed severely after a failed attempt on Napoleon's life.

Revolutionary calendar In order to break from the past, the Revolution in October 1793 renamed the months and started numbering the years from the start of the Revolution. The months were named after their characteristics – so November, for example, became Brumaire – the foggy month. Year 1 was 1793–94.

ACTIVITY

Find points to support each of these interpretations:

1 The Directory's poor reputation is justified and it achieved little.

2 The Directory was more successful than is often claimed and does not deserve its poor reputation.

Then consider which you think is more convincing and why.

Napoleon Bonaparte

Napoleon Bonaparte was born in Corsica in 1769. His
family were minor aristocrats and his father was a
lawyer. Napoleon was sent to France to study as a
result of the family's collaboration with the French who
had recently taken over the island. He trained as a
professional soldier and became a lieutenant of artillery
– the least fashionable and aristocratic part of the army.
Serious and withdrawn, he read widely and was deeply
interested in the French Revolution. He returned to
Corsica to try to lead the revolution there but was
driven out by local feuds and the Bonapartes moved to
France. His friendship with some leading Jacobins led to
him being able to take a leading part in the battle to
expel British forces from the port of Toulon. This gave
him a good reputation and marrying the mistress of one
of the Directors, **Paul Barras**, made him known in
political circles. He commanded a force that dispersed a
mob trying to overthrow the Directory in 1795 and his loyalty was rewarded by a
command of the army of Italy. This was the breakthrough as by rapid movement
and skilled tactics he defeated the enemy forces of Piedmont and Austria and
imposed a peace treaty in 1797 giving France control of Northern Italy.

In 1798 he led a daring expedition to Egypt to cut off British Mediterranean trade
routes to the East. Successful on land, his ships were destroyed by the British
admiral Nelson. Leaving his army he returned to France where he was taken up by
opponents of the Directory and took part in a coup in November 1799 to establish
a new constitution. Once within reach of power, he took his opportunity to
dominate the new government as First Consul and became **Consul for Life** in
1802. He oversaw a batch of highly important internal reforms as Consul including a
major reform of French law. He declared himself Emperor in 1804. However, his
main concern was war. He led a brilliant campaign in central Europe 1805–07
defeating Austria, Prussia and Russia and dominating Europe. To defeat Britain he
tried to strangle British trade by forbidding British exports but this backfired and led
him into wars in Spain and Portugal and also in Russia in 1812. French forces could
not hold on to Spain and Portugal when British troops supported local forces. The
invasion of Russia was on a very large scale but was unsuccessful and saw a
humiliating and costly retreat. Still believing in victory he fought a campaign in
Germany in 1813 against Prussia and Austria but could not prevent the invasion of
France in 1814.

Losing the loyalty of key figures in his government and faced with unfavourable odds
against much larger allied forces and having lost control of the seas to Britain, he
abdicated in April 1814 and was exiled to the small island of Elba in a miniature and
humiliating parody of Empire. He returned to France in 1815 for a brief restoration
of his imperial rule but was defeated by British, Dutch and Prussian forces at
Waterloo and exiled finally to the remote Atlantic island of St Helena where he died
of cancer in 1821.

In March a threat from the radical left, a conspiracy by François Noel (Gracchus) Babeuf, a radical democrat, was discovered and Babeuf was arrested and executed in 1797.

Threatened by royalist victories in the elections of September 1797 that might have seen a royalist takeover, the Directors took decisive action and in the so-called Coup of Fructidor arrested two right-wing Directors and 27 deputies. Though the constitution in theory weakened the executive, in practice the Directors overcame threats and were not afraid to take decisive measures. Mass conscription was continued and the Law of Hostages of 1799 gave the government considerable powers of arrest, imprisonment and confiscation of property of those aiming to overturn the regime in any area that was designated 'disturbed'.

ACTIVITY

Research the events of Vendemiare in 1795 and assess how accurate the portrayal in Source M is.

What does Source M suggest about the methods used by the Directory to maintain order?

SOURCE M

The defeat of the royalist uprising of Vendemiaire, 1795

Individually, some of the Directors, particularly Paul Barras, had a reputation for corruption but the Directory did see financial reform. The Minister of Finance from 1796 to 1797, Dominique-Vincent Ramel de Nogaret, introduced impressive reform measures that improved the collection of the main land tax by drawing up new registers of property and establishing regular tax offices in each department. His measures helped to end the assignat inflation and by a bold measure of renouncing part of the debt (the so-called bankruptcy of two thirds) he made repayments of the remaining amounts more realistic.

It was true that this was not a regime that could appeal to the public for support or offer much in the way of inspired leadership. There was a reliance on force and on intrigue. In 1799 in the Coup of Prairial (June) the more conservative directors plotted against the neo-Jacobin directors. It was to extend this that the conservatives, led by Sieyès and Pierre Ducos, aimed at a purge of the two councils with the assistance of a compliant general. By a deal with Bonaparte, **Emmanuel-Joseph Sieyès** and his conspirators brought about the end of the Directory in November 1799 (see below). However, given the strains of war and the internal divisions, it could be argued that the Directory did well to maintain itself in power for so long and to keep parliamentary government going.

The Directory did depend on military success. It inherited the war of the First Coalition, which was ended by spectacular military victories by General Bonaparte in Italy leading to the Treaty of Campo Formio in 1797, which gave France lands in Northern Italy. The Directors also received much needed revenue from plunder. Bonaparte was a leader of considerable military ability, but he had been appointed as a young man by the Directors who should get some credit. However, in 1798 another European coalition was formed against them. With Bonaparte away on a campaign in Egypt in 1798, there was less success, heavy cost and less plunder to fund the government.

By 1799 there was talk of a '*margouillis national*', which means a national mess in French. There was a range of problems:
- The problems of inflation had been replaced by the problems of falling prices and economic downturn.
- Military successes were less frequent and there was less money coming into France from plunder of conquered territories.
- There was growing opposition, especially the increasing threat from a revival of Jacobinism and popular unrest. However, there were also opponents who were royalists and supported an end to the Revolution.
- The Directory was divided and some of its members were plotting a military coup to strengthen the government and put down opposition.

The Directory had ceased to attract much support. When the coup of November 1799 resulted in the formation of a consulate dominated by Bonaparte, there was little attempt by any significant forces to oppose this. For all its achievements, the Directory could not guarantee stability or maintain internal unity.

KEY FIGURE

Emmanuel-Joseph Sieyès (1748–1836) was a clergyman and political thinker. His pamphlet 'What Is the Third Estate?' was a key document of the French Revolution and encouraged middle-class support for change. He masterminded a coup to put Napoleon in power in 1799 but had little influence after that.

The military reputation and political ambitions of Napoleon Bonaparte up to 1799

Napoleon Bonaparte was able to rise because of the opportunities open to a young soldier of talent as a result of the Revolution. He first achieved major success in his part in driving the English out of the port of Toulon in 1793. He manoeuvred cannon onto high ground in order to attack his enemies and showed personal bravery and initiative.

The Italian campaign created the image of a new kind of general fighting a new kind of war. Here was a people's commander, speaking directly to his men, being in the thick of the fighting, sharing the hardships of his troops and being prepared to lead from the front. In his dispatches he promoted his own abilities and created an image of a true revolutionary general. He worked hard to boost morale, addressing his forces in an inspirational manner, taking the trouble to know them and winning their loyalty. He revitalized a tired and dispirited army and led them against a divided enemy with old-fashioned tactics. The essence of the Italian campaign was speed and concentrating forces against the weak points of his enemy. He rapidly defeated the forces of the Italian state of Piedmont and then faced the stronger forces of the Austrian Emperor. Rapid and decisive campaigning led to Austrian withdrawal and a peace signed in 1797 at Campo Formio. Bonaparte negotiated this treaty personally and it led to French control of Northern Italy. The spectacle of Italian forces in the historic city of Venice was thrilling for the French public, loot flowed into France, and Napoleon became a state-builder, setting up a new government in Milan.

Bonaparte was not the only successful general during the Directory, but he was the only one to give so much attention to establishing an image by publishing bulletins designed to show his genius. This suggests that he had political ambitions.

SOURCE N

Bonaparte's speech to his troops, March 1796

Soldiers, you are naked, ill fed! The Government owes you much; it can give you nothing. Your patience, the courage you display in the midst of these rocks, are admirable; but they procure you no glory, no fame is reflected upon you. I seek to lead you into the most fertile plains in the world. Rich provinces, great cities will be in your power. There you will find honour, glory, and riches. Soldiers of Italy, would you be lacking in courage or constancy?

> **How useful is Source N in explaining Bonaparte's success in Italy 1796–97?**

The Egyptian Expedition, 1798

His next campaign was deliberately designed to grab the imagination and admiration of France and was one of the boldest moves in the war. He took his forces to Egypt, then part of the Ottoman Empire, in order to cut the trade links between Britain and India, one of its richest imperial possessions. The aim was for France to dominate the Eastern Mediterranean, but Bonaparte also took with him scholars to make the expedition part of an enlightened project to gain knowledge of the ancient civilizations of the Middle East.

The modern light artillery and the carefully planned military tactics that he had developed would be effective against the limited resources of the forces of the rulers of Egypt, the Mamluks, and would be sure to enhance the general's reputation. But Bonaparte had not counted on British naval power. The British navy led by Horatio Nelson attacked the French fleet at anchor in the Nile at Aboukir Bay, cutting the French forces off from the homeland. On land Bonaparte achieved his spectacular victories near the Pyramids and went on to dominate Egypt and invade Syria. However, the campaign was marked by plague and by massacres of prisoners. It also petered out when France was unable to take the key coastal town of Acre. To the French public, however, Bonaparte was the heroic conqueror of Egypt and when he slipped past the British ships and got back to France, he was greeted as a hero.

Was this reputation deserved?

Bonaparte claimed to have found a weak and ineffective army, which he revitalized by his personal energy and leadership. Though the army had had limited success it did consist of 41,000 men, many of whom had battle experience. Napoleon's reputation was based on a smaller French force winning victories against larger odds. It is true that he was outnumbered. The Piedmontese had 25,000 men and the Austrians had 38,000 in Italy. However, the two enemies did not establish a joint command so Bonaparte was able to use his forces against weaker Piedmontese forces and then go on to tackle Austria.

Bonaparte was lucky in the initial battles. An attack on the Piedmontese at Ceva 16–17 April 1796 did not achieve much, but the government of Piedmont decided not to pursue the campaign and its forces fell back on Turin. The campaign against Austria did include some spectacular incidents – an attack led by Bonaparte on the bridge at Lodi over the river Adda made him famous but was not militarily significant as the Austrians were already retreating. The decisive battle at Rivoli in January 1797 was not against aged and incompetent Austrian generals and though the French were successful it was not as a result of brilliant tactics but sheer determination. Bonaparte did maintain a war of movement against Austria but he also tried to take the fortified city of Mantua for eight months. The city did fall in February 1797.

On the other hand, Bonaparte was flexible and did see that he must ensure that Piedmontese forces were defeated before they joined with Austria. When attacked he did improvise very effectively, as at the final great battle at Rivoli. Whatever the importance of incidents such as the struggle for the bridge at Lodi 10 May 1796, his personal involvement in positioning artillery and encouraging his forces to attack led him to gain a high reputation among his men. This was a major element in bringing victory.

Even though the campaigns of 1798 were against an enemy with limited artillery and knowledge of modern tactics, they were very effective. Bonaparte used the latest ideas of deploying his forces in what was known as the 'ordre mixte', alternating lines and columns and using lighter artillery to maximum effect. His personal reputation was boosted by acts of individual bravery, especially visiting plague victims at Jaffa, helping to move them and not fearing to touch them.

SOURCE O

Bonaparte's senior military surgeon gives an account of his actions towards plague victims, 1798

His presence among plague victims brought great consolations; he made the doctors treat several patients in front of him. They were piercing the swellings to relieve pain. He touched those who were most distressed to prove to them that they had an ordinary illness. He helped lift, or rather carry, the hideous corpse of a soldier whose tattered uniform was befouled by the bursting of abscessed wounds.

> **How far does Source O support the view that Bonaparte was a great leader?**

Military historians continue to debate his reputation. However, the victorious outcome in Italy and the successes on the battlefield in Egypt spoke for themselves to a French public deprived of heroic leadership. Bonaparte had the political skill to make the most of what he had achieved and to construct his own legend. Even after his fall in 1815 in lonely exile on St Helena he rewrote history, adding heroic speeches to his troops in 1796 that he had not actually made at the time.

Napoleon's political ambitions

Bonaparte did not see himself merely as a commander. He had taken an active part in politics in Corsica after the Revolution, so much so that his enemies made it necessary for him to return to France and take his family with him. He had taken a keen interest in revolutionary writings and politics, had associated himself with the Jacobins and had the support of Robespierre's brother. He escaped possible execution after their fall, but showed an interest in state-building both during the Italian campaigns where he set up a revolutionary state in Milan and also in Egypt where he took a keen interest in establishing a model state.

Bonaparte prepared the ground for taking power by carefully calculated bulletins and the promotion of a heroic image. He was also more than ready to co-operate with the politicians of the Directory who wanted to have the services of a politically minded general to back a coup to strengthen the executive and to purge political enemies. He later claimed that he had planned to take power all along. His wide reading and interest in reforms suggest that he was confident in a sense of mission to maintain the gains of the Revolution. At the same time he wanted to give back to France unity and internal discipline, which would allow it to become a great European power again. More critical views have seen him as an ambitious general eager to promote himself and his family and to extend the authority he enjoyed as a military commander to France as a whole.

The coup of 1799

It is often debated whether the coup of 1799, which brought the Directory to an end and began the rule of Bonaparte, was a result of the weaknesses of the existing regime or his own strengths and popular appeal.

It is true that the coup did not overthrow a flourishing or particularly popular government. There had been attempts to overthrow the Directors from conservatives and from neo-Jacobins. The regime relied heavily on force to maintain itself and there was the ongoing threat from European powers that had formed the **Second Coalition** against France in 1798.

However, a study of the history of previous republics that had ended with the emergence of a strong dictatorial figure led many to fear that a military-backed coup would destroy the gains of the Revolution. There was no certainty that, despite his high reputation, Bonaparte would be acceptable as the leader of a coup. Also, the leaders of the coup did not aim to establish a military dictatorship but rather to remove the threat of a return to Jacobinism and to strengthen the executive power.

The chief plotters were Emmanuel Sieyès and Pierre Ducos who enlisted the support their fellow Director Paul Barras. They had support in both councils but not enough to act without the threat of military action that was to be provided by Bonaparte. A crisis was engineered when the Directors resigned – the two Jacobins being forced to leave office by the others. The meetings of the two councils were moved from central Paris to the outskirts at St Cloud to prevent any popular demonstrations. There, Bonaparte and loyal troops were gathered.

What was expected to be a short and successful takeover turned out to be a botched and farcical event.

The Council of Five Hundred (see page 28) put up more resistance than expected to the establishment of a new government. When they protested Bonaparte entered the Chamber but was met by furious opposition and shouts of 'Outside the law.' This was dangerous. If the troops had failed to support him, then Bonaparte could have been arrested as a plotter. At a crucial time he wavered, but the day was saved by his brother Lucien who claimed that Bonaparte's life was being threatened. The troops rushed into the meeting room and the deputies rushed out.

KEY TERM

Second Coalition The First Coalition or alliance of different European states against France had broken down in 1797. Britain was ready to finance another group of nations and in 1798 Britain, Austria, Russia, Portugal, Naples, some German states and the Ottoman Empire (Turkey) signed alliances to co-operate in a coalition against France. The coalition was weakened by Bonaparte's victory over Austria in 1800.

ACTIVITY

Write a profile of Bonaparte from the point of view of a writer in 1799 explaining his character and achievements, and assessing his future prospects.

SOURCE P

Bonaparte gave a different version in a proclamation on 10 November 1799

The councils being assembled at St Cloud. Several members of the council of five hundred, armed with daggers and fire-arms, circulated around them nothing but menaces of death. I then repaired to the council of five hundred without arms, and my head uncovered, such as I had been received and applauded by the elders. Twenty assassins threw themselves upon me, and sought my breast. The grenadiers of the legislative body, whom I had left at the door of the hall, came up and placed themselves between me and my assassins. At this time the cry of 'Outlaw!' was raised against the defender of the law. They pressed around the president [Napoleon's brother Lucien Bonaparte], threatened him to his face. I gave orders to rescue him from their power, and six grenadiers of the legislative body brought him out of the hall. Immediately after the grenadiers of the legislative body entered into the hall, and caused it to be evacuated.

> **How useful is Source P as evidence for the events of 10 November 1799? Answer by using the provenance of the source and your own knowledge.**

Sieyès was ready with a new constitution increasing the power of the government. The Directors were replaced by three Consuls initially ruling for ten years. The name derived from the rulers of the Republic of Ancient Rome. However, this was not a dictatorship as there was an elected legislature. In this most complex arrangement the lower house had two bodies. The first was the Tribunate of 100 members aged 25 and above. The second was the Legislature consisting of 300 members over 30. The upper house was the Senate consisting of 60 members over 40 years old. The actual government was dominated by Napoleon as First Consul – the other two fell into obscurity. He appointed the Senate who in turn appointed the members of the Tribunate and Legislature. The democratic element, such as it was, came from the male population (some 6 million) choosing a Communal List (600,000) who in turn chose a Department List (60,000) who chose the National List (6000) from whom the Senate chose the Tribunate and the Legislature. The First Consul and his Council of State proposed any new laws. These were approved by the Senate. They were discussed by the Tribunate and voted on by the Legislature.

Bonaparte justified the changes in a speech in November 1799 by stressing the decline between 1797 and 1799.

SOURCE Q

A speed by Bonaparte in 1799

I left you peace, I find war. I left you conquests, I find enemies at our borders. I left you the millions (of francs) from Italy. I find misery and extortionate laws! Where are the brave hundred thousand soldiers, my companions of glory now?

> **How useful is Source Q in explaining whether Bonaparte was able to take power in 1799 because of the weakness of the Directory? What knowledge would you use to test the accuracy of his comments?**

The coup had succeeded in strengthening the government, which could not be removed for ten years and was sure of any of its measures being passed. In 1802 Bonaparte was made Consul for Life, ending any chance of a change of government. In 1804 he declared himself Emperor (see pages 41–43).

The coup had removed the instability, as with the support of the army and with little power remaining with the assemblies there was little chance of any attempted coups such as had threatened the Directors being successful.

The new regime retained some democratic elements. The new constitution was referred to all males to vote on in a plebiscite or referendum. Also initially all adult males voted for the first of the lists of people who would eventually make up the Legislature. However, this was very far from the most democratic of the constitutions of the French Revolution and it was the one that gave elected assemblies the least power.

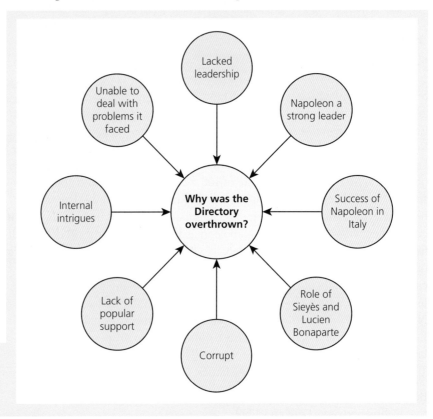

SUMMARY DIAGRAM

Why was Napoleon Bonaparte able to overthrow the Directory in 1799?

What were Napoleon Bonaparte's domestic aims and achievements to 1814?

Though much of Bonaparte's energies went into military campaigns, there was a period from 1800 to 1804 where he gave his attention to domestic changes and this produced some of the most important achievements of his career. After 1804 his conquests in Europe preoccupied him but the reforms spread into Europe and he continued to take an interest in domestic policy.

Napoleon Bonaparte's initiatives as First Consul

Bonaparte's immediate domestic aims were to maintain his authority and to enable him to defeat his internal opponents and ensure that the French state could support the defence of France and its conquests since 1793 against foreign powers. However, during the Consulate he initiated important changes in France which showed that he was not merely pursuing power for its own sake. In order to sustain the new balance between 'liberty' and 'order' of 1799 he extended his power in 1802 to become Consul for Life. This was presented to the people for approval in the tradition of the Revolution but in fact the results were rigged and only token opposition was shown.

Local government

Local government was controlled by the change in the way that France's 83 departments were ruled. Prefects were appointed with wide responsibilities to allow Bonaparte to maintain control of the different regions. His power extended to major towns as he also appointed mayors and nominated members of town councils.

This seemed to go against the ideal of democracy and the rights of the people of the Revolution, but it did carry on some of its ideas. There was uniform administration for all French citizens, even if it was directed from a central authority. Appointments were made on merit and not through privilege. Members of the French middle class were given posts in local government on merit, and sound and efficient government was promoted.

Legal reform

The revolutionary idea of efficient and uniform administration in place of the old privilege and huge regional and local differences that had existed before 1789 was also reflected in important legal reforms. There had been widespread discussions of introducing one uniform legal code for the whole of France. This had led to lengthy discussions, but the military mind of Bonaparte was applied to the problem and he encouraged the production of a Civil Code in 1804 and later commercial and criminal codes by 1807. Thus laws were made uniform throughout France.

Education

Another key revolutionary idea had been equality and opportunities open to talented people regardless of class. One requirement for this was that there should be an educational system open to all. This was beyond the scope of what was possible, but Bonaparte showed a keen interest in educational change to produce the administrators and officers that France needed. In 1802 the Consul initiated 45 state academies or lycées which provided scholarships for 6400 boys. Beneficiaries were mainly the sons of officers and officials. The aim was to offer technical education of a high standard. After 1805 there were more state secondary schools established. The 300 new schools were tightly organized with a common national curriculum and strict regulations as to timetable and the content of lessons. In neither secondary education nor higher education was there much stress on free enquiry, rather the development of skills useful to the nation and the promotion of a sense of national unity and obedience.

The Concordat

Religious change was an important element of the Consulate. Religious disputes had divided France since 1790 and many priests had rejected the state Church established by the Revolution and had refused to swear an oath of loyalty. Religion had motivated much of the opposition to the Revolution in the provinces and it was vital for national unity that Catholics were reconciled to the state. Napoleon began negotiations with Pope Pius VII in 1800 and an agreement was reached in 1801 and published in 1802 called the Concordat. Catholicism was recognized as the religion of the majority of French people. The Church was, thus, given a special position but it remained state controlled with its clergy being paid by the state and leading appointments being made by the First Consul. A new structure with 10 archbishops, 60 bishops and 3000 parishes was established. As the Church had suffered a lot from anticlerical actions during the Revolution it was reassuring for it to be given something of its old status back; but Napoleon retained a lot of control. Key appointments were made by him and the state retained its control over registering births, deaths and marriages which it had taken in 1790. After the Concordat, French Catholics did not feel however, that supporting the state was somehow to be disloyal to the Catholic Church.

Public finance

The period of peace between 1801 and 1804 allowed Napoleon to initiate other important measures as Consul. There were improvements in tax collection that built on the work of the Directory. Registers showing liability for the main direct tax on land were improved and the collection of both indirect and direct taxes was made more rigorous and less corrupt.

An important financial measure was the creation of a Bank of France in 1800. Britain and the Low Countries (the Netherlands and Belgium) had established national banks in the seventeenth century. This allowed secure issuing of paper money and made lending to the state more secure. In order to bring greater financial stability to help trade and to make borrowing easier the Consul introduced a new currency – the *franc de germinal* – based on gold and silver coins whose content of precious metal was closely controlled. This finally ended the danger of inflated paper currency.

The significance of domestic reforms

The energy that Bonaparte put into establishing a new and more stable, if less democratic, state and into putting into practice changes that the revolutionary regimes had discussed but had not managed to implement makes the Consulate one of the most dynamic periods for domestic change in the nineteenth century.

The nature and impact of domestic policy generally will be discussed below but the initiatives of the Consulate have led some to consider Napoleon as the heir to both the Enlightenment (see pages 6–8) and the Revolution. For others, the initiatives were deeply flawed because of the authoritarian nature of the regime and the underlying motive for change has been seen less as the national good but more the cementing of a military dictatorship.

In December 1804 the whole nature of the regime was changed by the decision of the Consul for Life to go a step further towards personal power and declare himself Emperor.

The inauguration of the Empire

The Consulate was a monarchy in all but name. Bonaparte enjoyed more power than Louis XVI had done as constitutional monarch after the changes from 1789. He had put into practice reforms, which had proved impossible for Louis and his ministers from 1774. He had given France greater internal stability than the Ancien Régime, virtually ending the riots and disturbances that had often accompanied bad harvests even under strong kings.

However, this stability depended heavily on the energy and personality of the Consul and not on a system. In the event of Bonaparte's assassination or death in battle, then France could easily be plunged once again into instability and civil war.

There were two elements that may have led to the Empire of 1804. The first was undoubtedly Bonaparte's ambition and desire to promote his family. He had a strong belief in his destiny to rule and a great desire that his family and his descendants should be rewarded. His position was a strange one. There were few republics in the Europe of his day. Hereditary monarchy was the norm even when the monarchs as in Britain shared power with elected assemblies or aristocratic elites. The US was a Republic but even in that more democratic country, a strong elected ruler had been established by the constitution of 1787. But there the president could change without a violent civil war. In France that would not be likely. Once Napoleon fell, then it was likely that the Consular system would fall with him. However, if he became a hereditary monarch then the nation could get used to the idea of his son inheriting the crown and the underlying system could continue with the support of a new aristocracy led by the Bonaparte family.

The other impetus for an Empire came not so much from Bonaparte, but from the notables. The Council of State and the Tribunate and Senate were in favour of a monarchy. There had been plots against the Consul, particularly those masterminded by the Breton opposition leader Georges Cadoudal. The fear of royalist plots was great enough for Bonaparte to order the kidnap and execution of the exiled Bourbon prince – the Duc d'Enghien – from Germany in 1804, one of his most controversial and shocking acts. The army leaders too were in support and Bonaparte had received a great many petitions to take the next step and make himself hereditary ruler.

ACTIVITY

Make a table. In the first column list the major reforms of the Consulate:

- Legal reforms
- Education
- The Concordat
- Financial reforms.

In the second column explain briefly what each achieved.

In the third column 'mark' each reform out of 6 – with 6 being the 'top mark'. In the fourth column explain your 'mark'.

Look at your 'top mark reform' – perhaps it is legal reform. Now plan an essay about that reform, for example:

'Assess the view that The Code Napoleon was the most important of the reforms of the Consulate.'

Despite Josephine's objections and some fears that he would be seen as overambitious and might end up in a similar position to Louis XVI, he took the decision to establish the Empire in May 1804. Backed by a plebiscite he held a grand ceremony in Notre Dame with the Pope present in December. The Empire was proclaimed at the same time as the Civil Code and Napoleon made it clear that his new imperial status was based on the people and the senate.

SOURCE R

Napoleon on His Imperial Throne by Jean-August-Dominique Ingres, painted in 1806

> **Look at Source R. What image is the artist trying to project?**

The Empire saw a change in style. A new aristocracy appeared with special robes and symbols. His brothers were given grand titles. Heavy symbolism appeared. Napoleon linked himself to royal traditions before the Bourbons. He took as his personal symbol the bee. This had been a favoured symbol of the ancient Merovingian kings of France, especially Childeric (436–481). Charlemagne (747–814) was also featured in paintings and tributes. Court ceremonials became grander.

Emperors are at a higher level than mere kings, so members of his family could be elevated to kingship. Louis his brother became King of Holland. Joseph was first of all King of Naples and then King of Spain. Jerome became King of Westphalia in Germany. Even one of Napoleon's generals, Murat, became King of Naples. The Empire was supported by rewards that went beyond Napoleon's family. The Legion of Honour was extended to 25,000 people who received grants of land as well as the prestige and the Napoleonic elites – officers, administrators, wealthy supporters – were given posts and honours. The elites were known as 'the masses of granite' on which the Empire was built. The Empire also saw impressive public buildings and public works. But Napoleon himself was careful to retain the image of the simple soldier. On campaigns that took him out of France for a long period – 1805–07, 1809 and 1812–13 – he dressed very plainly and shared a lot of the hardships of his men.

SOURCE S

Napoleon reflects on his situation as Emperor (1809)

My empire will be destroyed if I cease being fearsome – if my son is not a great military commander – if he is not able to do what I do – then he will fall off the throne. Among established kings, a war's only purpose is to take a province or capture a city. But with me, it's always a question of my existence of a monarch.

To secure his dynasty he divorced Josephine and married the Austrian princess **Marie-Louise of Parma** in 1810. She produced a male heir – the Duke of Reichstadt. However, the chances of establishing a dynasty were in practice remote. Napoleon the Emperor faced relentless opposition from Britain and undertook years of campaigning against the other European monarchs. In the end, the survival of the Empire was based on his ability to defeat his enemies on the battlefield rather than any real legitimacy.

The nature and impact of Napoleon's reforms (legal, education, social and financial)

The legal reforms

The Civil Code of 1804 and its extension in 1807 set out a uniform law system for all of France. It established the clear principle that law was the creation of the state and it was nothing to do with local custom, or religion

KEY FIGURE 🔑

Marie-Louise of Parma (1791–1847) was an Austrian archduchess, the daughter of the future emperor Francis II. Brought up to hate Napoleon, she was married to him in 1810 after his defeat of Austria in 1809. Though he said 'I have married a womb' and hastened to use her to give birth to a son and heir in 1811, she developed affection for him. She was regent in 1813 and 1814 while he campaigned. She never saw Napoleon after January 1814. She went on to rule the Italian cities of Parma and Piacenza with her lover Count Neipperg. Her tomb in Vienna has Parma violets placed on it daily.

How far does Source S support the view that Napoleon was an insecure emperor? Does your own knowledge suggest that he was right to wage war?

ACTIVITY

Which of these comments on why Napoleon became Emperor seems more accurate?

- 'An act which showed his vanity and ambition.'
- 'The Act of a responsible statesman.'

Explain your view by reference to the chapter.

or the traditional rights and privileges of nobles. The Code had some major effects on French life.

- Property could be bequeathed more freely and did not all have to pass to the eldest son.
- The ending of feudal rights that the Revolution had brought about was confirmed in law.
- Privileges such as those of the Church were ended.
- The property rights of those who had gained land from the Church or from the nobility during the Revolution were confirmed.

These elements together with the very fact that there was one national, uniform law code could be seen as beneficial for many property owners and met a lot of the demands expressed in the cahiers of 1789. However, there were elements that were a lot less liberal.

- The Code permitted the reintroduction of slavery in French overseas colonies to protect the rights of the owners of slaves who had lost their human property during the Revolution.
- Husbands' and fathers' authority over women and children was reinforced. Married women could not own property in their own right. Wives who survived their husbands did not automatically inherit their property. Husbands were favoured in disputes about custody rights of children; divorce requirements were stricter for women than men. Women could only gain divorce if husbands had been unfaithful and if the other woman was actually brought into the family home, but any infidelity on a woman's part was grounds for divorce.
- Fathers' rights to control their children were reinforced and employers' rights over their workers were also recognized.

Thus male authority was strengthened in society – over wives, children, workers and slaves. The main support for the regime came from property owners as they were the main beneficiaries of the reforms.

Education

Educational reform at secondary level was for boys. There was little provision for either primary education or for girls' education, which continued to be met by private teaching or by the Church. The aim was to provide an elite of well-trained civil servants and officers. There was little offered in the way of intellectual speculation. In higher education there was more development in the Empire. The so-called 'University' was decreed in 1806 and established in 1808. Here the aim was for one institution to bring 26 academies together in a centralized system of higher state education. Mostly the plans concerned scientific and technological developments, but the idea was never developed because of the demands of war after 1805. A feature of educational reform was regimentation and overall control and utilitarian rather than speculative content and teaching. The scale of the lycées and secondary schools remained too limited for the reforms to have a widespread impact, but an important model was established for future French education.

Social changes

The effects of the changes aimed to have a major effect on French society. The religious changes ensured that toleration was an official policy even though the Catholic Church was recognized as the main religious body. The divisions in society caused by opposition to religious change were reduced and the hostility towards 'godless revolutionary government' from provincial areas lessened.

The greater access to positions in the state met a lot of the middle-class grievances of the pre-revolutionary period and increased the status and wealth of the French middle classes. Property owning was made more secure by legal changes that recognized the ownership of previous noble and ecclesiastical land. However, the gap between richer and poorer elements increased. The urban lower middle class lost any political influence, and workmen were more controlled by the use of livrets – a record of behaviour kept by employers that made it hard for those workers who did not conform to get future employment.

The heavy spending on war and the extensive programmes of buildings and public works provided employment, but the main beneficiaries of the Napoleonic regimes were the notables – the richer middle classes who had brought about the Revolution. The old nobles, though encouraged to support the regime, remained suspicious and many stayed in exile. The poorer peasants and the sans-culottes gained little from the regime and generally did not participate in the upward social mobility of a growing middle class.

Financial and economic

The Consulate had provided a stable currency and a new national bank. The inflation of the revolutionary period was contained. The Empire consciously promoted industry. The Revolution had moved France into free trade, ending customs barriers. The fall of Robespierre ended restrictions on wages and prices. Manufacturers and employers gained from the end of guild restrictions and the restrictions on workers' organizations. Napoleon gave them tariff protection by putting import duties on foreign goods. His conquests gave them access to wider European markets. Control of other European countries gave France a chance to restrict foreign production that came into competition with French industries. A new commercial law code and uniform weights and measures helped business. Roads and canal building helped trade and business communications.

However, the downside was the loss of capital available to be invested into industry. This money was instead devoted to Napoleon's extensive and prolonged wars, which restricted cash and resources available for other economic projects. Also, the war disrupted valuable trade with Britain as Napoleon attempted to cut off British products from being sold in Europe by his Continental System in 1806. As Britain was the major manufacturing country in the world, this hit French consumers and merchants. It also meant that valuable British colonial raw materials were not as easily available. The activities of the British navy also hit French merchants and overseas traders. Britain relished seizing valuable French cargos and also captured valuable French overseas colonies.

Napoleon's use of propaganda and other means of control

There were beneficiaries from Napoleon's rule and many were excited by the resurgence of France as a great European power and by the expansion of France into Europe. However, for others, Napoleon's regime betrayed the Revolution and was simply a military dictatorship. To counter opposition, the regime depended on a lot of images and propaganda. Much of this was inherited from the Revolution whose leaders were adept at using all sorts of propaganda messages to gain support. However, Napoleon also relied heavily on repression and the use of police, informers and threats. There has been some historical discussion about whether Napoleonic France was a 'police state' – that is whether it relied on a high level of surveillance, censorship and punishment of dissent to stay in power. Some have seen Napoleon as a forerunner of twentieth-century dictatorships such as communist Russia, fascist Italy or Nazi Germany. Parallels have been drawn with the glorification of the national leader as almost a superhuman being and the widespread system of spying and information gathering together with wide police powers and the repression of opponents.

The control of the media was important for Napoleon and he is quoted as saying 'Four hostile newspapers are more to be feared than a thousand bayonets.' The explosion of newspapers and journals had been a major feature of the Revolution, but the Napoleonic regime reduced newspapers considerably. Sixty newspapers were closed in 1800 alone, and the remaining ones were subject to strict censorship. The government produced its own version of events in an official paper called 'Le Moniteur'. Both as Consul and Emperor, Napoleon took a close personal interest in ensuring that there was control of the arts and literature. Publishers had to gain official approval before printing plays, novels and pamphlets. A developed system of official censorship was in place by 1810 affecting all printed material, with punishments for those not submitting to the official code of practice.

Censorship was part of a much tighter police system. A former supporter of the Terror, **Joseph Fouché** was an efficient minister of police and daily reports were sent to Napoleon on matters of security. The jurisdiction of the police was wide and included monitoring opinion, ensuring that food prices were not too high to avoid discontent, policing economic measures, chasing deserters and maintaining a system of spying and surveillance.

A distinction was made between these quasi-political activities and the normal maintenance of law and order and suppressing crime, which was in the hands of the gendarmerie, which was run on military lines. The state had effective control over the judicial system as the regime selected judges and could remove them from office. In the departments (administrative regions of France) the prefects had considerable powers of surveillance and suppression of both opposition and crime. Under the control of the Ministry of the Interior, the prefects and their deputies oversaw a wide range of local activities and the central government had effective agents in local areas.

Key debate: Was Napoleonic France a police state?

A police state is a state whose main characteristic is repression by a police or security force empowered to override the rights of the individual in order to protect the state.

Historians such as Michael Broers and Michael Sibalis have suggested that there was a police state.

- There were special tribunals for crimes against the state.
- From 1810 there were state prisons for political offences.
- There were roundups of suspects.
- The police forces were increased significantly; for example, the Corps of Gendarmes went from 10,000 to 15,000 in the first year of the Consulate.

However, local studies suggest that enforcement of decrees was not on a level of a twentieth-century policed state. In Rouen, for example, there were few detentions and prefects were often too overwhelmed by their other responsibilities to hunt down suspected critics.

On the positive side, the regime provided spectacular victories especially in the years 1805–07 when Austria, Prussia and Russia were defeated. Control of the press helped to ensure that news reporting was favourable. There were visible signs of national glory such as the Arc de Triomphe. Napoleon was portrayed in a heroic way in paintings and in tangible artifacts such as medallions. There was a distinct cult built up round him that helped to sustain popular support, even when his wars began to go far less well after 1812.

ACTIVITY

1 Explain the meaning of the term 'police state'.
2 From the chapter and your own reading list the evidence that Napoleonic France was a 'police state'.
3 What evidence might show that this is not an appropriate description?
4 Write the first paragraph of the following essay question: Was Napoleonic France a 'police state?

SOURCE T

An English visitor to Napoleon's France. Anne Plumptre, *Narrative of Three Years Residence in France 1802–1805*, published in 1810

I was as perfectly free as I am in England, I went whithersoever I was desirous of going, and was uniformly received with the same politeness and hospitality as while peace still subsisted between the two countries. I never witnessed harsh measures of the government but towards the turbulent and factious; I saw everywhere the works of public utility going forward; industry, commerce, and the arts encouraged; and I could not consider the people as unhappy, or the government as odious … I have found speech everywhere as free in France as in England: I have heard persons deliver their sentiments on Bonaparte and his government, whether favourable or unfavourable, without the least reserve; and that not in private companies only and where some one among the company might be a spy of the police for any thing that the others knew to the contrary – yet this idea was no restraint upon them.

> **How useful is Source T as evidence for the amount of freedom in Napoleonic France? You should consider both the provenance of the evidence and your own knowledge in making your decision.**

SOURCE U

A famous critic of Napoleon's tyranny, Germaine de Staël, whom Napoleon exiled, writes critically of the Empire after its fall. *Considerations on the Principal Events of the French Revolution*, LF ed., Germaine de Staël, 1817 (source: https://oll.libertyfund.org)

It is generally after long civil troubles that tyranny is established, because it offers the hope of shelter to all the exhausted and fearful people. This was true of Bonaparte. His scheme for arriving at the domination of France rested upon three principal elements – to satisfy men's interests at the expense of their freedom, to dominate public opinion by lies, and to give the nation war instead of liberty.

> **What different messages about Napoleonic France are given in Sources T and U?**

SUMMARY DIAGRAM

What were Napoleon Bonaparte's domestic aims and achievements to 1814?

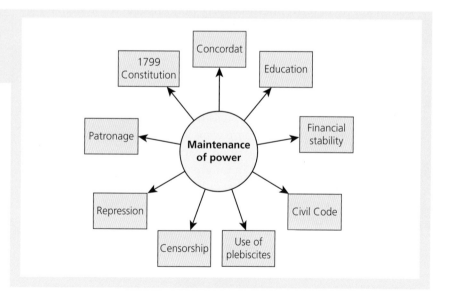

Chapter summary

The revolution that broke out in France in 1789 was a result of long-term flaws in the French monarchy and French society. The nobility and higher clergy were exempt from most taxes and enjoyed a privileged position when it came to gaining positions of power and responsibility. The bulk of the population were tenant farmers who had to put up with a range of feudal payments to noble landlords and who had none of the tax privileges enjoyed by the privileged classes. The middle classes, growing in wealth and confidence, saw their progress blocked by privileged aristocrats and resented the unequal taxation. Inspired by the ideas of the Enlightenment, they saw little chance of the political reforms they were reading about. The monarchy suffered from severe financial problems brought on by war which brought it to the verge of bankruptcy. From 1787 there were bad harvests and high prices. There were demands for a body which represented France to be called to bring about reforms.

Louis agreed to summon a meeting of the Estates General. Hopes for change were dashed by wrangles over voting procedures. The Third Estate declared that it was a National Assembly. Louis took no decisive action but seemed to threaten to use force. In the panic, crowds seeking arms stormed the Bastille fortress in Paris, In the summer of 1789, unrest spread through the French countryside and, in a wave of enthusiasm for change, the Assembly promised to end. In October hungry crowds forced the royal family and the Assembly to move from Versailles to Paris and the process of drawing up a new constitution was begun. Rapid changes were made ending aristocratic titles, reorganizing local government and bringing the church under civil control.

In the midst of this, new political ideas and discussions developed as political clubs and groups formed. Some of these were radical enough to demand an end to the monarchy. This came in 1792 after the new constitution of 1791 failed to work and the King rashly encouraged war against Austria and Prussia. In September a Republic was declared. The King was executed in January 1793.

Both internal civil war and external war led to a period of revolutionary terror in 1793–94 until there was a reaction against extremism and a more moderate constitution. The regime depended on military success and the rising general Bonaparte became a famous figure. In 1799, discontented politicians plotted a coup and enlisted Bonaparte in the plot. Bonaparte ruled France as consul, then consul for life, then emperor in 1804. As consul, Bonaparte oversaw some very important changes to France in law, education, government, finance and religion. The decision to proclaim himself Emperor was to give his regime more stability and sense of permanence. However, it really relied on military successes and prestige. The wars were fought with enormous success from 1805–07. By then, Napoleon dominated Europe. However, failures in Spain and then a disastrous expedition to Russia in 1812 saw the regime start to unravel. Though Napoleon raised very large armies to replace the half a million men lost in Russia, he could not achieve victory on a large scale again. He was forced to abdicate in 1814. He returned in 1815 but was defeated by the British and Prussians at Waterloo.

Refresher questions

1 What were the financial problems facing the French monarchy by 1789?

2 What economic hardships faced the people of France in 1788?

3 What was the Tennis Court Oath?

4 How did Louis XIV mishandle the Estates general in 1789?

5 What happened in the Terror?

6 Why did the Directory fall?

7 What shows Bonaparte's military abilities before 1799?

8 How did the reforms of the Consulate change France?

9 Why did Napoleon decide to become emperor?

10 What is a police state? What might show that Napoleonic France was a police state?

 Study skills

Paper 1 guidance: Source questions

Understanding and interpreting sources

In your examination for Paper 1 you will be presented with four sources and a question made up of two parts. You will have to answer both parts of the question. The first question will ask you to read two sources and compare and contrast them – see where they agree and disagree or assess how useful they are as evidence. For the second question you will need to read all four sources and consider how they support a particular view.

In the examination, you need to show key skills in approaching evidence.

- You have to interpret evidence. You need to link it to the issue in the question and decide what the evidence is saying about the issue. In the example below the issue is:

  How far was the French Revolution brought about by the financial problems of Louis XVI?

- You will need to consider how useful the evidence is. This involves thinking carefully about who wrote it, why it was written and how typical it might be.

- This really involves knowledge of the whole situation in 1789, but it is also important to look at the type of evidence you are dealing with. The use of knowledge is a skill that will be developed in the next two chapters. Here it is important to ask 'How is this source linked to the issue in the question?' and 'Was the person who produced this source in a position to know, and is there a reason why he or she might hold that view?'

However, you can only move on to these questions once you are sure you understand the relevance of the sources to the question.

The activity below will help you to establish the basic relevance of the four sources. You do not need to create a table in an examination but the activity will help you with the vital first step – the skill of interpreting the sources.

 Activity

Look at Sources A–D. Make a copy of the table below. You will see that one part has been done for you. Now fill in the rest for Sources B to D.

Source	What is this source saying about the key issue?	What evidence from the source shows this?
A	Indicates serious financial problems and bad conditions. Does not say problems will cause a revolution but says they are serious and would be made worse by war. Real threat to the Crown because of the financial situation	'poor condition of the people' – danger of bankruptcy; dangerously weaken the crown
B		
C		
D		

On the basis of what they say about the importance of finance, group the sources. Which ones are most obviously saying that finance is the key and which ones suggest that it is not just finance, but other issues?

SOURCE A

The finance minister outlines his views to Louis XVI (Turgot, memorandum, August 1774)

There must be no increase in taxation because of the poor condition of the people.

There must be no more loans because each loan reduced royal revenue because of the interest payments.

There is only one way and it is to make our expenses lower than our debts, low enough for us to save money to pay off old debts. Without this, the first cannon shot (if we were to go to war) would force the state into bankruptcy and dangerously weaken the crown.

SOURCE B

A courtier and later royalist recalls the 1786 reform proposals of the Minister of Finance, Calonne (The Marquis de Bouillé, *Memoirs*, 1821)

The most striking of the country's troubles was the chaos in the finances, the result of years of extravagance made worse by the expense of the American War of Independence, which had cost the state over 1200 million livres.

Calonne had a bold and wide-ranging plan, which the King promised to support. This would have changed the whole system of financial administration. The worst problems were the unfair distribution of taxation; the cost of collecting taxes and the abuse of privilege by the richest section of taxpayers.

SOURCE C

A noble member of the Assembly of Notables states his objection to Calonne's reform plans, 1787

The King does not have the authority to bring in a new tax payable by all. Only the Estates General could give the necessary consent for such a tax.

A permanent tax should not be payable by everyone. Farmers have the resources of the crafts, labour and trade, which noblemen and clergymen do not have. It would not be fair that while the nobleman fights and the priest celebrates divine services, they should not have the privilege of not paying a permanent tax.

SOURCE D

An English traveller in France records the views expressed by guests at a dinner party he attended in 1787 (From Arthur Young, *Travels in France*, 1792)

There was a great confusion in the finances, with a deficit that was difficult to provide for without calling an Estates General.

There were no talented ministers to provide any solution to the financial crisis.

There was a king on the throne without the resources of mind that could govern in such a moment.

The court was depraved and thought only of pleasure.

A great unrest existed among all ranks of men, eager for change.

A strong current of liberty had increased since the American Revolution.

Comparing and contrasting two sources

In the examination you may be asked to compare and contrast two sources. It is important not to just describe what one says and follow it by describing what the other says.

- There should be a point by point comparison (where the sources agree) and contrast (where the sources disagree).
- The comparisons should be illustrated by brief quotations from both texts.
- There should be some explanation of the differences by looking at who was writing and why.

To help practise the skill of comparing and contrasting sources and planning an answer it might be helpful to draw up a table like the one below:

Points on which the sources agree	
Parts of each source which show this	
Reasons as to why the sources might agree (provenance)	

Points on which the sources disagree	
Parts of each source which show this	
Reasons as to why the sources might disagree (provenance)	

ACTIVITY

Practise this skill by filling in the table for the two Sources T and U on page 48.

Paper 2 guidance: Essay questions

Understanding the wording of the question and planning an answer

In Paper 2 of your examination you will have to answer two types of essay question for two topics. The first question is a short answer essay which will ask you to explain an issue or event, the second is a long essay. Most of the advice applies to answering the long essays but there is also guidance on how to tackle the 'explain' or short essay questions.

Understanding the wording of the question

It is very important that you read the wording of the question you are answering very carefully. You must focus on the key words and phrases in the question; these may be dates, the names of leading figures or phrases such as 'How successful …?' Unless you directly address the demands of the question you will not score highly.

The first thing to do is to identify the command words; these will give you the instructions about what you have to do.

In Question (a) you will be asked to **explain** an event or why something happened.

In Question (b) you may be asked:
- to make a judgement about the causes or consequences of an event
- to consider to what extent or how far a particular factor was the most important in bringing about an event
- to make a judgement about a particular government or ruler.

Here are two examples.

1 'The most important reason for the French Revolution (to 1789) was the spread of the ideas of the Enlightenment.' How far do you agree?

   You could also be given a statement such as this one. Although this question requires you to consider reasons, you must consider the spread of the Enlightenment and write a good paragraph on it, even if you argue that it was not the most important reason. However, even if you think it was the most important, you must still explain why other factors were less important.

2 How far was Louis XVI responsible for his own downfall?

In this essay you would need to analyse what personal failings led to his downfall. However, in order to reach the highest levels you would need to judge the relative importance of this factor in order to reach a balanced conclusion, not simply produce a list of mistakes of the King.

Planning an answer

Once you have understood the demands of the question, the next step is planning your answer. The plan should outline your line of argument. This means that you will need to think about what you are going to argue before you start writing. This should help you to maintain a consistent line of argument throughout your answer. It also means that your plan will be a list of reasons about the issue or issues in the question which will ensure an analytical response. Simply having a list of dates would encourage you to write a narrative or descriptive answer and this would result in an unsuccessful essay.

Consider the first example on page 53: 'The most important reason for the French Revolution (to 1789) was the spread of the ideas of the Enlightenment.' How far do you agree?

Your plan should be structured around issues such as the following:
● Why was the Enlightenment important?
● What other reasons are there?
● Why are these reasons important?
● Are they more or less important than the Enlightenment?
● What is your overall view having looked at the key factor and the other causes?

A plan for this essay might take the following form:

1 The Enlightenment: what key ideas influenced the Revolution, e.g. Rousseau and the Social Contract; Voltaire and scepticism about religion? Montesquieu and the idea of a balance of power? Make the view that it was the most important factor clear by linking these ideas to events, e.g. the Declaration of the Rights of Man; the calls for a National Assembly to reflect the sovereignty of the nation; the Tennis Court Oath.

2 Other factors: privilege and financial problems that led to the calling of the Estates General. Possible links to enlightened ideas.

3 The desire of the middle classes for greater opportunity; Sieyès. More informed and politically aware urban population again linked to spread of ideas.

4 Economic grievances: bad harvests, urban unemployment, peasant discontent – less linked to ideas.

5 Political mistakes of King and government in handling 1789 crisis: perhaps this disappointed those who were led by the study of new ideas to expect change.

6 Conclusion: weighs up the relative importance of Enlightenment ideas and brings together interim conclusions in previous paragraphs. Perhaps arguing that though few might have read the Enlightenment philosophers the key ideas were very powerful among the educated middle class of the Third Estates in the Estates General and other grievances were linked to them **or** argue that the ideas had been common for years before the Revolution but it took short-term factors like bad harvests and a financial and political crisis which led the King to call the Estates General to bring a revolution that included some of the ideas.

Planning answers to these questions will help you put together a structured answer and avoid the common mistake of listing reasons with each paragraph essentially saying 'Another reason for the French Revolution was …'

Planning an answer will help you focus on the actual question and not simply write about the topic. In the second question you might write all you know about the King but not explain why he was or was not responsible for his downfall. Under the pressure of time in the examination room, it is easy to forget the importance of planning and just to start writing; but this will usually result in an essay that does not have a clear line of argument, or changes its line of argument halfway through, making it less convincing and so scoring fewer marks.

QUESTION PRACTICE

The focus of this section has been on planning. Use the information in this chapter to plan answers to the following questions:

1 How far was Louis XVI to blame for the loss of royal authority by October 1789?

2 To what extent was the Terror the result of the threat of external war?

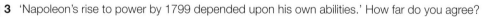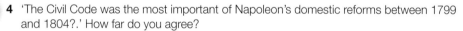

3 'Napoleon's rise to power by 1799 depended upon his own abilities.' How far do you agree?

4 'The Civil Code was the most important of Napoleon's domestic reforms between 1799 and 1804?.' How far do you agree?

EXPLAIN QUESTIONS

1 Explain why it was so hard for Louis XVI to solve his financial problems.

2 Explain why the constitutional monarchy failed.

3 Explain why Robespierre fell from power in 1794.

4 Explain why Napoleon became First Consul in 1799.

CHAPTER 2

The Industrial Revolution in Britain, 1750–1850

This chapter looks at the industrialization of Britain in the period from 1750 to 1850. This period was particularly significant in the development of the nation. It transformed an economy from one dependent upon land to the first industrial economy in the world. The chapter will investigate the causes of this transformation and examine the social and political consequences of these developments. This chapter examines these developments through the following questions:

★ What were the causes of the Industrial Revolution?

★ Why was there a rapid growth of industrialization after 1780?

★ Why, and with what consequences, did urbanization result from industrialization?

★ Why, and with what consequences, did industrialization result in popular protest and political change?

KEY DATES

1761	Opening of Bridgewater canal	1811–12	Luddite activity
1764	James Hargreaves' Spinning Jenny	1830	Stephenson builds railway line between Manchester and Liverpool
1769	Richard Arkwright's Water Frame		
	James Watt patents a steam engine	1830–01	Swing Riots
1771	First cotton spinning mill, Cromford, Derbyshire	1832	Great Reform Act
1781	Development of rotary motion allowing steam power to be applied to machines	1833	First Factory Act
		1839	People's Charter drawn up
1785	Edmund Cartwright's Power Loom	1846	Repeal of the Corn Laws
1791–94	Canal mania	1848	First Public Health Act

What were the causes of the Industrial Revolution?

There were many reasons for the Industrial Revolution, with historians putting different emphasis on factors rather than arguing that it was due to one particular issue. Unlike political revolutions, such as the French Revolution, it is impossible to date either the start or end of the Industrial Revolution although it would be difficult to deny that Britain in 1850 was a vastly different country from that of 1750, with changes taking place in agriculture, the process and organization of manufacturing, patterns of trade and transport, as well as impacting on all aspects of life. This section will consider the causes of those changes.

The agricultural revolution

Before the eighteenth century, agricultural change had been slow and production was mostly for **subsistence** rather than the market. In part this was due to poor communications that meant produce could not be taken further than local markets. Even when there were improvements, these were usually confined to local areas and depended on individuals with new ideas spreading only slowly. There was also little incentive for the tenant farmers to increase efficiency or production, as the benefits from improving land would usually go to the landlord. Although the tenant farmers had access to **common land** to graze their animals, such a system allowed the inter-breeding of animals which did little to enhance their quality (Source A).

> **ACTIVITY**
>
> Read pages 57–60 and construct a flow diagram to show how agricultural developments aided industrial developments.

> **KEY TERMS**
>
> **Subsistence** The growing of enough food to feed just your family.
>
> **Common land** Village land where everyone who was not a landowner could graze animals and use it as a source of wood and food.

SOURCE A

William Marshall, *The Rural Economy of Yorkshire*, 2 vols, 1788

Upon the waste commons of the West Riding the kind of sheep bred are more miserable than can be imagined. They generally belong to poor people and are in small lots so that they can never be improved. This will apply to the whole of the sheep on the common that are not stinted; the numbers put on beggar and starve the lot.

> **How useful is Source A in explaining the problems of increasing agricultural productivity?**

> **ACTIVITY**
>
> Find arguments and evidence in the section on the agricultural revolution to support each of the followings statements:
>
> • 'The increase in agricultural productivity was the result of the influence of individuals.'
>
> • 'The increase in agricultural productivity was due to the increased land under production.'
>
> • 'The increase in agricultural productivity was due to new farming techniques.'
>
> Then decide which you think is more convincing as an explanation and why.

Table 2.1 Population growth 1701–1831

Year	Population in millions
1701	5.3
1771	6.9
1801	9.2
1831	13.9

However, a growth in population as seen in Table 2.1 on page 58 resulted in an increased demand for food, but also other goods. It would supply a larger labour force that could work in towns as there was no consequent rise in employment opportunities in the countryside. There is a considerable debate among historians as to whether this rise was due to a falling death rate or a rising birth rate.

Population growth

Historians still debate the causes of population growth in the eighteenth and nineteenth centuries. Some argue that the major cause was a fall in the death rate and point to the ending of outbreaks of plague, the prevention of disease, improved nutrition and food supply – in part due to the agricultural changes – and a reduction in infant mortality. Others argue that it was due to a rise in the birth rate as the average age of marriage dropped, due in part to a rise in real wages; other factors historians have considered include new economic opportunities, changing patterns of employment and the generous outdoor relief payments to the poor.

The increase in food production that characterized the early eighteenth century onwards has been described as an 'agricultural revolution'. There were a number of elements to the agricultural changes and modernization that was witnessed in the period. One of the most notable features of the period after 1750 was the **enclosure** of land. Parliament passed over 4000 Acts of Enclosure in the century after 1750 as owners of land petitioned Parliament to pass Acts as they realized it would allow them to increase their profits by adopting more efficient methods. This led to a further 20 per cent of land being enclosed and it completed a process begun in the Middle Ages. However, this often involved villagers losing their right to graze animals on common land, while it provided landowners with the opportunity to breed selectively (see Source B).

KEY TERM

Enclosure The enclosing of land by hedges or fences in order to divide up large open fields.

ACTIVITY

Make a list of the causes of the Agricultural revolution and explain how each brought about the revolution. Which do you think was the most important cause? Explain your choice.

SOURCE B

A. Young, *The Farmer's Tours through the East of England*, 1771, vol. 1, pages 110–113

Mr Bakewell of Dishley, one of the most considerable farmers in this country, has in so many instances improved on the husbandry of his neighbours, that he merits particular notice in this journal. His breed of cattle is famous throughout the kingdom; and he lately sent many to Ireland. He has in this part of his business many ideas which I believe are particularly new; or hath hitherto been totally neglected. This principle is to gain the best, whether sheep or cow, that will weigh most in the most valuable joints. The general order in which Mr Bakewell keeps his cattle is pleasing; all are fat as bears; and this is a circumstance which he insists is owing to the excellence of the breed.

The period also witnessed an increase in the amount of land under cultivation. The growing population and increased demand meant that it was now worthwhile for landowners to use more marginal land for production. As a result, the area of land under cultivation rose from 10 million acres in 1750 to 15 million by 1850, much of which was given over to grain crops. Enclosure also allowed farmers to use more modern techniques (see Source C).

SOURCE C

A. Young, *Annals of Agriculture*, vol. V, 1786, pages 120–4

Charles Lord Viscount Townshend resigned the seals in May 1730; and, as he died in 1738, it is probable that this eight years was that of his improvements round Raynham. There is reason to believe that [he] actually introduced turnips in Norfolk; but the idea that he was the first who marled there is erroneous. But to be the father of the present great foundation of Norfolk husbandry, which had quadrupled the value of all the dry lands in the county, is an honour that merits the amplest eulogy. He certainly practised the turnip culture to such an extent, and with great success, that he was copied by all his neighbours.

> **Compare Sources B and C in their views about the improvements in agriculture.**

The development of crop rotation practices, which saw a change from the traditional two-year cultivation and one-year fallow used under the old **open field system** to the four-course rotation, did much, as Young explains in Source C, to improve the soil and boost crop yields, but also support a larger livestock population. This meant that fewer animals had to be slaughtered in the winter, and the body weight of animals increased, boosting meat production.

Although the period witnessed a number of changes through individuals such as Bakewell and Townshend (described above) and the introduction of mechanization with developments such as Jethro Tull's seed drill, one of the most important factors in the improvements was the spread of knowledge.

> **KEY TERM** 🔑
>
> **Open field system** The division of large open fields into strips where each villager was allocated a number of strips across the fields.

> **ACTIVITY** 🌀
>
> Explain why the spread of knowledge was important in developing the agricultural revolution.

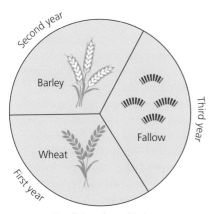

**Traditional method
A three-year rotation**

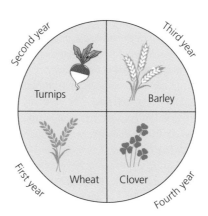

Norfolk four-course rotation

Figure 2.1 Diagram illustrating the two systems of crop rotation

Much of the credit for that should be given to writers such as **Arthur Young**, **William Marshall** and **Thomas Coke**, whose works meant farmers were made aware of practices such as crop rotation, drainage, **marling** and hoeing, all of which helped to increase production.

Agricultural developments were therefore an essential pre-requisite for industrial development for a number of reasons:

- A growing urban population could be fed.
- The home market consumed all the food produced but the supply ensured there were no shortages and therefore a stable society.
- Agricultural workers provided a market for some of the goods that would be produced in the towns.
- Landowners made considerable profits which were often invested in industrial enterprises, such as canal building.

Agriculture was both a supplier to the new industries providing, for example, wool for the textile industry, and also a customer as agricultural labourers bought the new products.

The development of capitalism: investment, trade and commerce

The industrial changes that took place in the period from 1750 to 1850 would not have been possible without **capitalism**. This was essential if money was to be invested in the new machines and technology. At the start of the period this was less of a problem as industrial enterprises, such as small-scale textile factories, were relatively cheap to establish as the early machinery was relatively cheap. Despite this, it still required sufficient funds to provide the buildings, the machines and purchase the raw materials (see Source D).

SOURCE D

David Whitehead of Rawtenstall, *Autobiography*, c.1830

In 1817 my brothers and I agreed that the firm should be called Thomas Whitehead and Brothers. Brother Peter attended to his warping and at nights assisted me in planning. We had not been brought up mechanics but had good ideas of mechanism and we soon made a great improvement in our machinery. We had got a large stock of weft on hand which did not sell well. I bought some warps and began to manufacture. I got a few weavers in the neighbourhood of Balladenbrook. I got my mother who lived at New church to weave for us, and a few weavers more at New church. Balladenbrook was a small place and had no shop to sell food. The workpeople complained of having so far to go to buy other grocery. Warbourton, who had the mill of whom we took the room, had a woollen engine and carded woollen for country people. His business was not doing so well for him. He said if we had no objections he would deliver the mill up to us. We went with him to Mr Hargreaves of whom he rented the mill, but did not agree with Mr Hargreaves about the mill at this time. We found that with all the money we could collect together we had little enough. We got mother to go and see if she could prevail of old Mr. Thomas Hoyle of Manchester to lend us a hundred pounds. My grandfather Lionel Blakey was one of the Friends (Quakers), as was also Thomas Hoyle. They were relations and fellow playboys.

> **What can we learn from the writer of Source D about the problems in establishing industrial enterprises?**

Despite the problems facing the Whiteheads, there is clear evidence that more money became available during the period with historians suggesting that the proportion of **Gross Domestic Product** invested rose from about 6 per cent in 1760 to more than 11 per cent by the 1820s. This money came from a variety of sources. In the last section it was mentioned that profits from agriculture were used, but there were also profits from overseas trade, which also played a significant role in stimulating manufacturing, as can be seen below.

Capital could be raised in a variety of ways. At the start of the period loans were often arranged locally with lawyers drawing up contracts between lenders and borrowers. Relatives and friends were also often a useful source of finance, whereas borrowing from banks was unusual. This was because banks were often unwilling to undertake long-term lending, preferring short-term loans, and it would not be until the nineteenth century that they would play a greater role in industrial development. However, loans from relatives and friends were often given at a rate of about 5 per cent which was particularly attractive given the vast profits that a successful enterprise could make. Once the firm was established, then the profits often provided the source of investment, known as 'plough-back'. However, as the scale of industrial enterprises increased, for example with the construction of canals, then a different form of investment was required.

In order to meet the demands of larger enterprises that individuals or small groups could not meet, and to deal with the fears that if an enterprise failed then all investments would be lost, joint stock companies were established. These companies were owned by shareholders and were liable only for the debts according to the amount they had invested. This protected investors as they had limited liability for any losses, thus reducing the risk. This meant that they would not have to pay back debtors if the company collapsed.

Trade and commerce

The availability of funds allowed economic developments to take place, but this was given further stimulus by overseas trade and commerce. Overseas trade made available some of the raw materials, such as cotton, that played a vital role in the development of industry, but it also meant that there was a market for the finished product. Developments in trade also had a beneficial impact on transport developments, particularly with ports and the growth in the merchant fleet. Overseas trade, also required the development of a financial system that could provide credit and insurance. Developments in this area not only benefited overseas trade, but also the domestic market and helped to turn London into the world's financial capital. However, although foreign trade was important, domestic trade was even more important (see Source E).

KEY TERMS

Capitalism The system by which private owners and companies increase their wealth by trade and invest for profit.

Gross Domestic Product The annual total value of goods produced and services provided in a country.

ACTIVITY

Explain the reasons why the nature of investment in industry changed during the period.

SOURCE E

D. Macpherson, *Annals of Commerce*, 1805

The home trade is with good reason believed to be a vast deal greater in value than the whole of the foreign trade, the people of Great Britain being the best customers to the manufacturers and trades of Great Britain.

The period certainly saw growing demands at home for consumer goods and this becomes clearer as many of the marketing methods with which we are familiar are seen to have their origins in the eighteenth and nineteenth centuries. There is certainly evidence of circulars, advertisements and even special offers being available. Growing consumption at home was a feature of the period with the possession and use of domestic goods enhancing one's status and displaying social rank, with attempts to imitate the spending habits of one's social betters. The *British Magazine* commented in 1763:

The present rage of imitating the manners of high life hath spread so far among the gentlefolks of lower life, that in a few years we shall probably have no common folk at all.

How far cheaper food, brought about by the changes in agriculture, led to a consumer boom is a matter of debate, but there were many reasons why people wanted to own goods and this provided a further stimulus for industrial development.

Early mechanization: steam engines and spinning machines

Steam power and the mechanization of industry were closely linked, with many of the developments in machinery dependent upon steam power. However, although steam engines would play a central role in the process of industrialization, it must not be forgotten that water power was just as important. In fact, until 1820 more cotton yarn was produced using water power than steam. However, the use of steam power was crucial in the rapid industrialization, as it allowed larger and more powerful machines to be deployed. Initially steam power had been used simply to drain mines by pumping water from them. However, the partnership of **James Watt** and **Matthew Boulton** in the late eighteenth century transformed manufacturing. Watt developed a steam engine that needed much less fuel to power it and together with Boulton produced a more efficient engine in 1781 that was cheaper to run. Perhaps most importantly, a modification to the engine allowed rotary motion rather than a simple up and down motion and this meant that steam power could now drive machines (see pages 67–68). The spread of steam engines became much quicker after 1800 when Watt's patent expired and other inventors were able to develop and improve the machine.

Steam power allowed larger machines to be developed and therefore the growth of the modern factory to house them. It also increased productivity dramatically, and had a massive impact on the jobs that were done mechanically, transforming the roles of many workers. However, it was not just in factories that the development of the steam engine had an impact, but also in agriculture. In the nineteenth century steam ploughs and threshing machines were developed which made farming more mechanized and efficient, but also reduced the number of labourers needed, often forcing them to leave the land and look for jobs in the fast-growing industrial towns.

Steam would also have a huge impact on transport in the later period of industrialization (see pages 67–69). It would allow railways to be built and therefore make it easier and quicker to carry large amounts of goods, both raw materials and finished products, around the country at a far faster rate than was possible either by road or water. Steam engines also had an impact on overseas trade as steam ships were developed, which by the end of the period would also ensure that sailing ships powered by the wind were replaced.

The development of machinery probably saw its greatest advances in the textile industry. This was particularly seen in the manufacture of cotton goods rather than in woollen manufacture, which was much more conservative and resisted change. It was the cotton industry of South Lancashire that was the first area to embrace the new developments and these are summarized in the table below.

ACTIVITY

1   Construct a spider diagram to show the impact of steam power. In what ways did the use of steam power change during the period?

2   Hold a balloon debate in which the key inventors in the textile industry argue that they should stay in a hot air balloon which is sinking and has to lose a passenger. You will need to research your inventor and argue that he was the most significant inventor.

Table 2.2 Developments in the textile industry, 1730–90

Date	Invention	
1733	John Kay's Flying Shuttle	This speeded up the weaving process by moving the shuttle across the loom automatically and ended the need for the weaver to thread it by hand. It was not in widespread use until the 1750s as handloom weavers resisted it, even attacking Kay's home in 1753. They feared that the faster process would mean fewer jobs. It was used on domestic handlooms and therefore did not create a demand for textile factories.
1764	James Hargreaves' Spinning Jenny	As a result of the Flying Shuttle there was a demand for a more yarn to meet the weaving process. The spinning wheel could not meet this demand and the Jenny was the first attempt to increase production, initially allowing a spinner to produce eight threads. However, the thread was not strong and could be used only for the weft. Despite this, it was used in the cotton industry and improvements allowed up to 100 threads to be produced. Similar to the Shuttle it could be used in homes as it was hand-powered. By 1780 there were some 20,000 in use in Lancashire.
1769	Richard Arkwright's Water Frame	The Water Frame allowed a stronger thread to be made than that from the Jenny and allowed a cloth made entirely from cotton to be produced. The size of the frame meant that it was less suited to domestic production. It led Arkwright to open the first factory at Cromford in Derbyshire. The success of Cromford meant that the process spread and by the 1780s steam engines were being applied to the spinning process in Lancashire. This had an impact on factory location as they no longer needed to be close to a supply of water, instead a supply of coal became an important issue.
1779	Samuel Crompton's Spinning Mule	The Mule incorporated the best features of the Jenny and Water Frame. It combined the fine quality of the thread produced by the Jenny with the strength of the thread from the Frame. This allowed a wide range of cloth to be produced. Crompton failed to apply for a patent for his machine, which allowed others to copy and develop it. By the early nineteenth century there were Mules producing up to 300 threads and in 1825 a machine was developed that could spin 2000 threads.
1785	Edmund Cartwright's Power Loom	The increased output from spinners meant that there needed to be developments in weaving. The increased demand for weaving was initially satisfied by an increase in the number of handloom weavers. Demand for their work meant that they enjoyed a period of boom that would last until the 1830s. It was only then that power-driven weaving took over despite the development of a power loom by Cartwright in 1785.

An engraving of a spinning mule

It was therefore in spinning that the first developments in mechanization took place. In part this was due to the resistance of the handloom weavers who were determined to preserve their high wages, resorting to violence at times (see page 96). However, applying steam power to weaving was also more difficult, while the number of handloom weavers meant there was less urgency to create a factory-based weaving industry. This development took off only in the period after 1820.

The textile industry and the technological developments played a crucial role in the industrialization of Britain, and the changes made clear the crucial link between the industry and the steam engine. Friedrich Engels also made the link clear in his book *The Condition of the Working Class in England* (1844) when he observed 'These inventions gave rise to an industrial revolution which altered the whole of civil society; one, the historical importance of which is only now beginning to be recognized.'

Early developments in transport: canals and roads

Transport in the pre-industrial age depended upon roads and horses and rivers or the sea. The condition of the roads was particularly poor as their maintenance depended upon the local community who saw little to be gained from improving them for the benefit of outsiders. Initial attempts by the government to bring about improvements through encouraging the local population saw little success. Rivers were useful as a means of transport as barges could carry much heavier loads than horses and the journey was much smoother with less likelihood of goods being damaged. However, journeys were slow and the water depth often varied according to the season. Some trade was carried by sea, probably the most famous being coal

ACTIVITY

Which was more important in the development of the industrial revolution:

- the steam engine
- spinning machines?

Explain your choice

brought from the coalfields of the North East to London, but many areas were a long way from the coast. All of this limited internal trade and would need to be improved if economic growth were to take place (see Source G).

SOURCE G

Adam Smith, *An Inquiry Into the Nature and Causes of the Wealth of Nations*, 1776

A broad-wheeled wagon, attended by two men, and drawn by eight horses, in about six weeks; time carries and brings back between London and Edinburgh near four ton weight of goods. In about the same time a ship navigated by six or eight men, and sailing between the ports of London and Leith, frequently carries and brings back two hundred ton weight of goods. Six or eight men, therefore, by the help of water-carriage, can carry and bring back in the same time the same quantity of goods between London and Edinburgh, as fifty broad-wheeled wagons, attended by a hundred men and drawn by four hundred horses. Were there no other communication between those two places, therefore, but by land-carriage, as no goods could be transported from the one to the other, except such whose price was very considerable in proportion to their weight.

In the eighteenth century, Britain began to build private or turnpike roads that people had to pay to use. These were better constructed and maintained. But the horses and carts that used them to carry goods could not move the large loads that could be carried on rivers. The improvements in the roads did allow faster travel and enabled people to travel between some of the major towns and cities at a much faster rate, but they did not provide the answer for the movement of heavy raw materials or finished goods.

Although the major rivers of Britain had always played a role in the movement of goods, there were difficulties in using them as a transport network. They were widened to take increasing traffic in the early eighteenth century, but in many instances they did not link up the necessary places, and their meandering meant that travel was slow. However, between 1760 and 1840 this network was completely transformed with the construction of 4000 miles (*c.* 6500km) of canals. Their routes could be planned in the interests of trade, linking industrial centres and encouraging the development of settlements along their routes. The system allowed the major coalfields and agricultural regions to be linked to ports (see Source H).

ACTIVITY

Create a table with 3 columns. In the first column state the method of transport, in the second column note down the problems in using the methods and in the third column decide how successfully the problems were overcome.

SOURCE H

Adam Smith, *An Inquiry Into the Nature and Causes of the Wealth of Nations*, 1776

Good roads, canals and navigable rivers, by diminishing the expense of carriage, put the remote parts of the country more nearly upon a level with those in the neighbourhood of the town. They are upon that account the greatest of all improvements. They encourage the cultivation of the remote, which must always be the most extensive circle of the country. They are advantageous to the town, by breaking down the monopoly of the country in its neighbourhood. They are advantageous even to that part of the country. Though they introduce some rival commodities into the old market, they open many new markets to its produce.

How far do Sources G and H agree in their views about how transport improvements helped economic growth?

It was the construction of the Bridgewater Canal in 1761 between Manchester and the coalfields on the estate of the Duke of Bridgewater at Worsley that is usually seen as the start of the 'canal age'. Its construction halved the price of coal in Manchester and made the economic opportunities of the construction of canals clear to both the investors and users. This was reflected in two periods of intense development, the first in the early 1770s and then in the 1790s, a period known as 'canal mania'.

Canals were particularly important in the transport of coal as one barge could carry 50 tons and was therefore much cheaper than the traditional way of using pack horses. The lower transport cost was of great benefit to both industrial and domestic consumers and encouraged the use of steam power. Profits for mine-owners increased as demand soared, while canal companies also made considerable profits, much of which were often reinvested in further industrial developments. The reduction in the cost and the availability of coal also had a massive impact on the iron industry (see pages 73–74). However, it was not just industry that gained, but also agriculture as access to wider markets improved. Canals also meant that goods could be carried more cheaply and easily to ports and exported overseas. This would be particularly important for the Lancashire cotton industry with canal links to Liverpool enabling not only exports of the finished goods but also imports of the raw materials at a cheaper rate than carriage by pack horse. However, there were losers. In the textile industry it had been the handloom weavers who had suffered from new development; in transport it was those who made a living by pack horses, carts and carriages.

ACTIVITY

Construct a spider diagram to show the main reasons for industrial development. Briefly explain how each factor helped. Which do you think was the most important factor? Explain your answer.

SUMMARY DIAGRAM

What were the causes of the Industrial Revolution?

How much development was there in the period to 1800?

Limited development	Development
Limited transport development until 1790s Few factories – still cottage industry Limited use of steam power	Agricultural improvements Increased demand for goods Textile industry sees technological changes Increased investment

② Why was there a rapid growth of industrialization after 1780?

The period after 1780 saw an even more rapid growth in the economy than the period from 1750 to 1780. This was due to a number of reasons. Steam engines became more efficient and were applied to large-scale machinery which encouraged the growth of the factory system. These developments and developments in transport led to an increased demand for both coal and iron, which ensured that technological developments were not confined to the textile industry. Meanwhile the building of a large number of canals, known as 'canal mania' at the end of the eighteenth century, and the development of rail network towards the end of the period meant that markets were opened up allowing internal trade to develop. At the same time, Britain, as the first industrialized nation, was able to sell goods around the world and develop an overseas market which was a further stimulus to investment and growth.

Development of the factory system: steam power and machines

Although the steam engine was developed in the period before 1780 and Watt had produced an improved model by 1769, it was the expiry of his patent in 1800 that allowed others to improve on his design. These new engines had a far greater fuel efficiency and were accompanied by the development of high pressure engines that were both lighter and cheaper than Watt's model. These developments led to a significant change in the manufacturing process and the location of factories as the **domestic system**, which was already in decline because of the water mill, was replaced by the factory system (see Source I).

KEY TERM 🔑

Domestic system The making of goods within the home whereby clothiers would purchase the raw materials, bring them to workers in their cottages and collect the finished product.

SOURCE I

Report of the Inspectors of Factories for the half year ending 30 April 1860

In the early days of textile manufactures, the locality of the factory depended upon the existence of a stream having sufficient fall to turn a water-wheel; and although the establishment of the water-mills was the commencement of the breaking-up of the domestic system of manufacture, yet the mills necessarily situated upon the streams, and frequently at considerable distances the one from the other, formed part of a rural, rather than an urban system; and it was not until the introduction of steam-power as a substitute for the stream that factories were congregated in towns, and localities where the coal and water required for the production of steam were found in sufficient quantities. The steam-engine is the parent of manufacturing towns.

According to Source I, why did the location of factories change in the period from 1750 to 1850?

As a result Cromford, which depended upon water power, remained a village while new towns with their factories developed in Lancashire and Yorkshire (see Table 2.3).

Table 2.3 Population in 000s of factory textile towns

Town	Population pre-1801 (000s)	Population 1801 (000s)	Population 1851 (000s)
Blackburn	6	12	47
Bolton	12	18	61
Bradford	4	13	104
Halifax	7	12	34
Leeds	24	53	172
Oldham	5	12	53

ACTIVITY

What can we learn from Tables 2.3, 2.4 and 2.5 about industrial development in the period from 1750 to 1800?

The importance of steam power, particularly in the nineteenth century in the development of the cotton industry, becomes even clearer when Tables 2.4 and 2.5 below are considered.

Table 2.4 The location and sources of power 1838–50

County	Changes in the number of mills	% decline in water power	% increase in steam power
Cheshire	−21	35	16
Derbyshire	−21	21	65
Lancashire	+49	5	57
Yorkshire	+54	11	143
Totals	+61	16	56

Table 2.5 Power looms and handloom weavers (in 000s) in the cotton industry 1795–1860

Date	Power looms	Handlooms
1795		75
1813	2.4	212
1820	14	240
1829	55	225
1833	100	213
1835	109	188
1845	225	60
1850	250	43
1861	400	7

The cottage industry method of production was no longer viable. As demand for goods had increased, employment had reached the limits of available labour and this meant that those with the necessary skills received very high wages. As a result, the high wages became the target for inventors, as even poorly designed machines could make a profit. The development of large-scale machinery meant that work could no longer be carried on at home. Factories offered many advantages to investors and businessmen. They meant that wage labourers could be brought together on a single site and could take advantage of the power source provided by the steam engine. But the factory system had other advantages. The division of labour, skill acquisition, supervision and quality control were much easier to achieve in a factory. All of these developments would increase both productivity and profitability and were therefore of great benefit to the owner.

It was the technological developments in the cotton industry, outlined earlier in this chapter (see pages 62–64), that provided the biggest boost to the development of the factory and factory production. Specialist factory production allowed the Lancashire cotton industry to reduce its production costs in real terms by two-thirds between 1780 and 1812. This further increased demand and led to growth rates of 12 per cent between 1780 and 1790 so that by 1800 cotton accounted for 25 per cent of all exports by volume, whereas in 1780 it had been just 2 per cent. Cotton masters showed a far greater willingness to embrace change and new technology and it was this that allowed the rapid transformation to a factory-based system in the last quarter of the eighteenth century. Not only did the factories allow a clear division of labour with specialist spinners and weavers but there even developed specialist spinning and weaving towns. It is therefore hardly surprising that the system was adopted by other industries even if, as in the case of the woollen industry, it was at a much slower rate. As a result, a factory system gradually developed (see Source J).

SOURCE J

Andrew Ure, writing in 1835, describing the factory system

The term Factory System, in technology, designates the combined operation of many orders of work-people, adult and young, in tending with assiduous skill a series of productive machines continuously impelled by a central power. This definition includes such organizations as cotton-mills, flax-mills, silk-mills, woollen-mills and certain engineering works; but it excludes those in which the mechanisms do not form a connected series, nor are dependent on one prime mover. Of the latter class, examples occur in iron-works, dye-works, soap-works, brass foundries. The factory in its strictest sense, involves the idea of a vast automaton, composed of various mechanical and intellectual organs acting in uninterrupted concert for the production of a common object, all of them being subordinated to a self-regulated moving force.

> **How useful is Source J in explaining the growth of the factory system?**

Lancashire, in particular, became the cotton-textile centre with production also in Derbyshire and Lanarkshire. The advantages that it possessed allowed the cotton trade to develop with the West Indies and the southern states of the USA. At the same time, transport developments allowed it to access raw materials and reduce transport costs, while the Lancashire coalfield provided the power for steam engines once water power declined in importance.

> **ACTIVITY**
>
> Make a list of the ways in which the factory system changed the economic development of Britain.
>
> Which do you think was the most significant impact? Explain your answer.

Developments in transport: canals, railways and steamships

As we saw in the previous section (pages 64–66), improvements in transport were vital for the economy to expand. They would allow greater supplies of raw materials to be brought to factories and the transportation of finished products to a wider and larger market.

Canals

Although canals had started to be developed in the period up to 1780, it was the 1790s that saw what has been described as 'canal mania'.

Table 2.6 Acts passed for river navigation and canals

Year	Number of Acts	Year	Number of Acts
1750–54	3	1785–89	6
1755–59	7	1790–94	51
1760–64	3	1795–99	9
1765–69	13	1800–04	6
1770–74	7	1805–09	3
1775–79	5	1810–14	8
1780–84	4		

> **ACTIVITY**
>
> What does Table 2.6 tell us about the development of the canal network?

As a result, the amount of goods that could be transported increased dramatically (see Table 2.7 on page 70).

Table 2.7 Calculations made by a group of contemporary engineers in 1800

Transport	Tons
Pack horse	One-eighth
Stage wagon on soft road	Five-eighths
Stage wagon on macadam road	2
Barge on river	30
Barge on canal	50
Wagon on iron rails	8

ACTIVITY

Find points to support each of the following views:

• 'Canals were crucial to early industrialisation.'

• 'Canals had a limited impact on industrialisation.'

Canal sites became important places to locate factories and their importance in moving goods is clearly seen in cities such as Birmingham, which has more miles of canals than Venice. In particular, it was their ability to carry vast amounts of coal at a cheap rate which, allied to the development of the steam engine, encouraged industrial development. By 1800 a network of canals crossed England linking major towns and cities with coalfields (see Source K).

SOURCE K

Robert Southey, *Espriella's Letters from England*, 1800

What is the view of the author of Source K about the contribution of Brindley to the 'transport revolution'?

England is now crossed in every direction by canals. This is the district in which they were first tried by the present Duke of Bridgewater, whose fortune has been greatly increased by the success of the experiment. His engineer, Brindley, was a man of real genius for this particular type of work who thought nothing but locks and levels, perforating hills, and floating barges upon aqueduct bridges over unmanageable streams. When he had a plan to form, he usually went to bed, and lay there working it out in his head till the design was completed. It is recorded of him that being asked why he supposed rivers were created, he answered after a pause – to feed navigable canals.

Railways

However, though canals were the important transport method for the first part of the period, it was railways that would dominate the latter part. They would create a revolution in land transport and communications. There had already been early railways where carts were mounted on wooden rails and pulled by horses, particularly in quarries and mines to move loads over short distances. However, two important developments would dramatically change the situation. Firstly, wooden rails were replaced by wrought iron in the eighteenth century. But it was the development of the steam engine and the ability to create steam locomotion that would really transform the situation. Although early trials were disappointing, with low speeds of 4 mph and regular breakdowns suggesting that rail travel was not an alternative to road, improved models emerged in the 1820s. It was the opening of the Stockton to Darlington line in 1825 that revealed the real potential of railways as the price of coal dropped by more than 50 per cent because railways were cheaper, faster and could carry larger loads. In 1830

George Stephenson built a line between Liverpool and Manchester. This line used twin tracks meaning that trains could run more frequently and he was soon followed by other railway engineers such as his son, Robert Stephenson, and **Isambard Kingdom Brunel**.

However, construction was not cheap with costs on average £40,000 per mile. To raise funds railway companies sold shares. These were often bought by the middle class and although some routes were not profitable the major ones did bring in large profits for the shareholders, but without the availability of capital from the middle class and their willingness to invest it is unlikely there would have been the growth in the network. It was the 1840s that witnessed the greatest investment and although there was a collapse at the end of the decade another period of boom followed in the 1860s. In the years between 1825 and 1875 some £630 million was invested in railways, a sum far greater than any other industry and leading to a network that covered much of the country (see Table 2.8 on page 72).

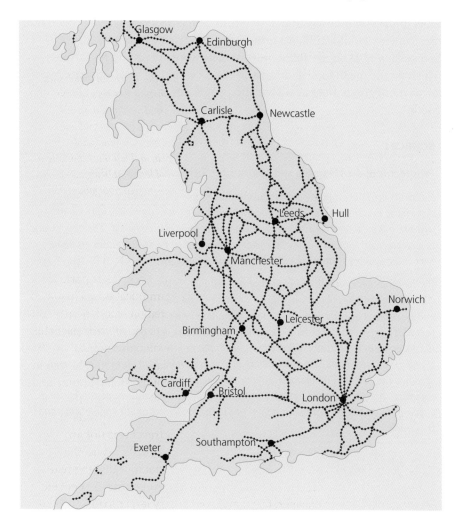

KEY FIGURES

George Stephenson (1781–1848) was a civil and mechanical engineer and has been described as 'the father of the railways'. He built the first steam locomotive to carry passengers on a public line, the Stockton to Darlington railway, in 1825. He also built the first public railway between cities to use locomotives. This was opened in 1830 and ran between Liverpool and Manchester. Stephenson also developed the standard gauge for railway tracks that is used across much of the world.

Isambard Kingdom Brunel (1806–59) was a mechanical and civil engineer. His achievements covered many aspects, building dockyards, the Great Western Railway, steamships and a large number of tunnels and bridges for the rail network.

Figure 2.2 Map showing the rail network in 1852

Table 2.8 Mileage of railway construction

Year	Mileage	Year	Mileage
1832	39	1841	14
1833	218	1842	55
1834	131	1843	90
1835	201	1844	810
1836	955	1845	2816
1837	544	1846	4540
1838	49	1847	1295
1839	54	1848	373
1840	–	1849	16
		1850	7

ACTIVITY

The impact of railways on the life of Britain was far reaching. Do you think they had a greater impact on economic life than social life?

Explain your choice.

Although rail transport had a profound impact on both the economic and social life of the country (see Sources L and M), it is difficult to isolate the exact impact on industry and agriculture. Some historians have argued that the economy would still have grown at a rapid rate without them. Yet Sources L and M suggest that new markets were opened up for farmers which would mean food shortages in towns would be less frequent. Prices fell as more goods were available and people now had a greater choice of goods.

SOURCE L

Prospectus of the Liverpool and Manchester Railway Company, 1824

Railroads are now proposed to be established as means of conveyance manifestly superior to existing modes. The railroad scheme holds out to the public not only a cheaper, but far more expeditious conveyance than any yet established. The importance, to a commercial state, of a safe and cheap mode of transit for merchandise, from one part of the country to another, will be readily acknowledged.

What according to the author of Source L were the advantages of the development of the Liverpool to Manchester railway?

By the projected railroad, the transit of merchandise between Liverpool and Manchester will be effected in four or five hours, and the charge to the merchant will be reduced at least one-third. Here, then, will be accomplished an immense pecuniary saving to the public, over and above what is perhaps still more important, the economy of time. It will afford stimulus to the productive industry of the country; it will give a new impulse to the powers of accumulation, the value and importance of which can be fully understood only by those who are aware how seriously commerce may be impeded by petty restrictions, and how commercial enterprise is encouraged and promoted by an adherence to the principles of fair competition and free trade.

SOURCE M

Railway News, 1864

In the grey mists of morning, we see a large portion of the supply of the great London markets rapidly unloaded by these night trains; fish, flesh and food, Aylesbury butter and dairy fed pork, apples, cabbages and cucumbers and we know not what else, for the daily consumption of London. No sooner do these disappear than at ten minutes' interval arrive other trains with Manchester packs and bales, Liverpool cotton, American provisions. At a later hour of the morning, these are followed by other trains with the heaviest class of traffic – stones, bricks, iron girders and steel pipes.

> Compare and contrast the views of Sources L and M about the impact of the railway.

Steamships

It was not just internal transport that was revolutionized by the development of the steam engine, but also international trade. Steam power was also applied to ships. When engines were made more efficient and ships did not have to carry so much coal, then steam ships were able to carry goods across the world. The great age of international steam ships was after 1850, but by the end of our period the balance had shifted from ships using sails to ships powered by steam. This led to a significant growth of overseas trade in the second half of the nineteenth century.

Raw materials: iron and coal

Industrial development was driven by the growth of three staple industries. We have already looked at the cotton industry; the other two were iron and coal. Cotton, iron and coal were the raw materials of the growth that took place in the period after 1780, with coal fuelling the new factories and later the new modes of transport, while iron was used in the manufacture of machines, in construction and for domestic goods.

Iron

The iron industry witnessed a growth in the period after 1750, but it saw an even more dramatic growth in the period between 1780 and 1820, so that by 1806 Britain was exporting iron and it was contributing 7 per cent towards the national income. Unlike the cotton industry, iron production was already based on large-scale enterprises and used a domestic raw material. What was crucial in its development was the replacement of charcoal by coal following the development of the blast furnace of **Abraham Darby** in 1709. This allowed a blast of air to be applied to the coke to raise the temperature so that the iron ore could be smelted (see Source N).

KEY FIGURE

Abraham Darby (1678–1717) developed a method of producing pig iron in a blast furnace using coke rather than charcoal. The furnace was used for the first time in 1709.

Read Source N. Using
your contextual
knowledge, how
important for the
development of the
iron industry and
industrial growth was
Darby's innovation?

ACTIVITY

Using the information on
pages 73–4, how do you
explain the growth in
iron production as
shown by Table 2.9?

Table 2.9 Production of iron
1620–1854

Date	Annual output of pig iron in tons
1620	35,000
1700	20,000
1740	20,000 (30,000 tons imported)
1780	70,000
1806	250,000
1823	455,000
1854	3,070,000 (Imports largely end)

What does Source O
tell us about the
importance of iron in
industrial
development?

SOURCE N

Abraham Darby II's account of his father's iron works at Coalbrookdale

*About the year 1709 Abraham Darby came into Shropshire in Coalbrookdale. He
here cast Iron Goods in sand out of the Blast furnace that blow'd with wood charcoal.
Sometime after he suggested the thought that it might be practicable to smelt the Iron
with pit coal. Upon this he first try'd with raw coal as it came out of the Mines but it did
not answer. He not discouraged, had the coal, coak'd into cynder, as is done for drying
Malt, and then it succeeded to his satisfaction.*

This was the most significant change in the industry, but its adoption was
slow, in part because it was not until rising timber prices made coke
smelting more economically viable, but also because Darby was reluctant
to share his knowledge. However, the use of the Watt and Boulton steam
engine from around 1775 rather than water power was a major catalyst in
the growth of production, and this process was further helped by Henry
Cort. Cort took out a patent in the mid-1780s for a puddling and rolling
process that used ordinary coal to produce wrought iron products. The
impact of these changes can be seen in the levels of production in Table 2.9.

The growth of railways only added to the demand and as the table shows
production soared while prices fell, but as a song of the 1820s made clear
iron was being used for a variety of purposes (see Source O).

SOURCE O

Canal Song of the 1820s from Birmingham, 'Humphrey Hardfeatures'
Description of Cast Iron Inventors

Since cast iron has got all the rage,

And scarce anything's now made without it;

As I live in this cast iron age,

I mean to say something about it.

There's cast-iron coffins and carts,

There's cast-iron bridges and boats,

Corn factors with cast-iron hearts,

That I'd hang up in cast-iron coats.

We have cast-iron gates and lamp posts,

We have cast-iron mortars and mills too; And our enemies know to their cost

We have plenty of cast-iron pills too.

We have cast-iron fenders and grates,

We have cast-iron pokers and tongs, sir;

And we shall have cast-iron plates,

And cast-iron clothes, ere long sir.

Coal

Over the same period coal output rose from 17 to 48 million tons. However, not only was coal an important industry in its own right, but it was also important to a large number of other industries and processes (see Source P).

SOURCE P

George Stephenson comments on the importance of coal

The Lord Chancellor now sits upon a bag of wool; but wool has long ceased to be emblematical of the staple commodity of England. He ought rather to sit upon a bag of coals, though it might not prove so comfortable.

What does Source P tell us about the changes in the British economy in the period after 1750?

Its growth and importance become even clearer in Table 2.10.

Coal was used for a variety of purposes including manufacturing and in the metal industry, transport and to drive the very pumps that kept the mines free of water. However, its initial growth had been in the domestic market and particularly in London once a cheap and ready supply of wood or charcoal had diminished. The construction of terraced houses with back-to-back fireplaces, with the smoke going up through a chimney built in the dividing wall, helped in the growth of London during the sixteenth and seventeenth centuries. Coal was about half the price of other fuels in London even in the seventeenth century, and the cost of other fuels meant that it was worth transporting it from the coalfields of the North East. The development of the northern coalfields meant that the North had access to some of the cheapest fuel and as many of the iron ore deposits were close to coalfields it further encouraged its consumption in that industry. The ability of the coal industry to meet the increasing demand meant that industrial production was not held back. Industries that needed direct heat or relied on steam to power machines were supplied. More mines were opened and more men were employed, particularly as the work was labour intensive with little mechanization until much later. Although there was little scope for technical advancement in the industry, some changes were introduced that did help increase production. The use of **pit ponies** reduced the cost of coal as **barrowmen** were replaced by boys to supervise the ponies and they could be paid at a much lower rate. Developments in the iron industry meant that cast-iron tubes were available, which could be used in shafts making it possible to sink mines to a greater depth, and the development of the cast-iron rail meant that there were greater economies in underground transport. There were also improvements in ventilation and the development of the **wheeled corf** which could run on rails and be brought up the shaft without being unloaded further reduced costs. However, the process of extracting the coal remained much the same, with only 2 per cent of coal being extracted mechanically as late as 1900, and the only way production could be increased was by employing more men, with over 216,000 employed in the industry by 1850.

Table 2.10 Output of coal, 1700–1854

Year	Output in millions of tons
1700	2.9
1750	5.2
1775	8.8
1800	15
1815	22
1830	30.3
1854	64.7 (first official figures)

KEY TERMS

Pit ponies Ponies that worked underground in the mines hauling coal.

Barrowmen Men who hauled wagons of coal.

Wheeled corf A wheeled wagon or basket used for bringing coal out of the mines.

Growth of markets: domestic and international and growth of free trade

The eighteenth and early nineteenth centuries witnessed an extension of Britain's markets both domestically and overseas. This was due to a number of reasons, including the rising population, which created demand, improved and cheaper transport facilities, which meant goods were more widely available and at cheaper prices, and a growing empire which supplied cheap raw materials and provided a further market for finished goods. Some historians have even argued that the period from 1750 witnessed a consumer revolution that further stimulated production.

The development of markets

Before the industrial changes of the period most trade had been local, particularly agricultural goods, with farmers reliant on selling their produce at local markets. However, the development of the railways in particular meant that fresh produce could reach markets further away as described in Source M (see page 73). Growing markets meant that business flourished and the profits generated were often used to fuel further expansion or investment in other industries.

Arguments for and against free trade

Unlike many European countries, Britain also had the advantage of free trade within the country, particularly once the use of turnpike roads with their tolls began to decline. This can be compared to France, where the ending of internal tariffs had to wait until **Napoleon Bonaparte**. The absence of tariffs in Britain meant that inefficient producers were not protected from competition, while the consumer gained as prices were not kept artificially high. This policy, known as free trade, was promoted by economists such as **Adam Smith** and **David Ricardo**. Smith argued that industrial development and trading should be left to develop naturally, without government intervention. The government's sole purpose should be to create the conditions in which trade could flourish.

However, this idea clashed with the previous policy of **mercantilism**, whereby there were tariffs on some goods. This may have benefited domestic industry that did not face competition. The Navigation Laws of the seventeenth century controlled the trade between Britain and its colonies so that the colonies supplied Britain with raw materials while Britain supplied the colonists with finished products. The government had also granted the sole trading rights to some companies, such as the **East India Company**. Finally, to prevent other states benefiting from British expertise the government had banned the export of some machinery and had forbidden skilled craftsmen to emigrate. Most importantly for the ideas of Smith and Ricardo, it appeared as if this policy had been successful as the British Empire had expanded and Britain was now the world's leading trading nation, replacing the Dutch.

The impact of the Napoleonic Wars on the arguments for Free Trade

Although some leading politicians such as **William Pitt the Younger** were convinced by the arguments of the free-traders, the war with France in the late eighteenth century and the **Napoleonic Wars** of the early nineteenth century meant that the debate about the benefits for the economy of free trade were shelved. However, the war did much to change opinion with many realizing that free trade would lessen the likelihood of conflict as nations developed trade links with each other (see Source Q).

SOURCE Q

Richard Cobden, speech at Manchester, 15 January 1846

I see in the free trade principle that which shall act upon the moral world as the principle of gravitation in the Universe – drawing men together, thrusting aside the antagonism of race and creed and language and uniting us in the bonds of eternal peace. I believe the effect will be to change the face of the world, so as to introduce a system of government entirely distinct from that which prevails. I believe that the desire and motive for large and mighty empires; for gigantic armies and navies will die away when man becomes one family and freely exchanges the fruits of his labour with his brother man.

It was also argued that Britain, as the first industrial nation, did not need the protection of tariffs. In fact, on the contrary it was argued that the abolition of tariffs would allow the importation of cheap raw materials which would lower the cost of manufactured goods and therefore further boost demand. It was argued that this would be particularly beneficial for industries such as textiles and iron which were becoming increasingly reliant upon the export market.

Growing support for free trade

Many of the lower class were converted to free trade as not only did they see improved employment prospects as demand for goods increased, but they were also persuaded that the cost of food would decline once the hated **Corn Laws** were removed. Moves towards free trade did occur. Even before the wars with France, Pitt had signed a treaty with the French reducing tariffs, but war put this on hold. After the war, the Board of Trade was dominated by supporters of free trade and the 1820s saw a series of measures that reduced tariffs on some imported goods to 10 per cent from a staggering 40 per cent. Laws on the export of machinery, the emigration of skilled workers and the Navigation Laws were all relaxed. Even the Corn Laws were placed on a sliding scale. However, it was the recession of 1837 that brought

KEY FIGURE

William Pitt the Younger (1759–1806) was the son of William Pitt the Elder (Earl of Chatham) who had been Prime Minister in the 1760s. When Pitt was appointed Prime Minister in 1783 he was only 24. He left office in 1801, but returned in 1804 and continued until his death in 1806. His rule was dominated by the French Revolution and wars against France. He was an outstanding administrator who raised taxes to pay for the war and took harsh measures against radicals.

How useful is Cobden's speech in Source Q as evidence for the benefits of free trade?

KEY TERM

Napoleonic Wars (1803–15) Napoleon fought a series of wars against the European powers of Britain, Austria, Russia and Prussia, as well as in Spain and Portugal. Throughout the period the British were the only power who, at some point, did not make peace with France. The wars came to an end following Napoleon's defeat at Waterloo in 1815, but he had already been weakened by a long struggle in Spain and Portugal and war against Russia.

the whole issue of free trade back to the surface, with the demand for free trade supported by the manufacturing interest, many of whom had gained the vote as a result of the 1832 Great Reform Act (see page 99).

Trade recessions, particularly that of 1837–42, converted many manufacturers to free trade. Others argued that if tariffs with the USA were removed it was likely that the USA would reciprocate. As they were the main supplier of raw cotton it would lower the cost of cotton for manufacturers, making the British industry more competitive, securing the jobs of many workers. At the same time, it would boost exports of the finished product to the USA. It was therefore hardly surprising that towns such as Manchester and Liverpool became the centre of the free trade movement. The Anti Corn Law League, a powerful organization aiming to end the duty on imported corn, was founded in 1838 and this reflected a growing belief in the principle of free trade.

The Anti Corn Law League and Free Trade

The League was led by the industrial and commercial middle class who saw the benefits their businesses and firms would gain from free trade and the overall gains that could be made by the economy. The League focused on the Corn Laws as they were seen as the great symbol of protectionism, keeping the price of corn and bread artificially high solely for the benefit of landowners. The attack on this was symbolic in another sense; it represented an attack by the new industrial class on the old landowning aristocracy, a battle between two ideologies. The Corn Laws became more and more indefensible as through the first half of the 1840s the Prime Minister, **Robert Peel**, removed or reduced tariffs on most goods through his free trade budgets of 1842 and 1845. By the end of 1845 tariffs had gone from 500 items and in 1846 the symbol of protectionism finally went when the Corn Laws were repealed. The repeal was a triumph for the new industrial order over agriculture, even if it led to the fall of Peel's government as many Conservative landowning MPs voted against it. Cobden defended the repeal in a later speech (see Source R).

SOURCE R

Richard Cobden, speech, 1870

To pay for that [imported] corn, more manufacturers would be required from this country; this would lead to an increased demand for labour in the manufacturing districts, which would necessarily be attended with a rise in wages, in order that goods might be made for the purpose of exchanging for the corn brought from abroad.

> **Summarise in your own words the message of Source R.**

Events would appear to prove Cobden right; the repeal did set Britain on the road to what historians have described as 'mid-Victorian prosperity' and the continued growth of the economy after 1850.

SUMMARY DIAGRAM

Why was there a rapid growth of industrialization after 1780?

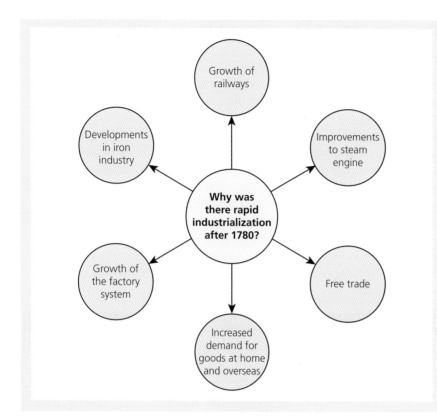

ACTIVITY

Re-read pages 76–79.

Write an explanation as how and why free trade would be beneficial to the British economy in the nineteenth century.

ACTIVITY

For each of the factors shown on the summary diagram briefly explain how they brought about rapid industrialisation.

 # Why, and with what consequences, did urbanization result from industrialization?

Although Britain was already heavily urbanized, with some 15 per cent of its population living in towns by 1750, the period from 1750 to 1850 witnessed a dramatic growth in towns, particularly those associated with the industries of the industrial age. By 1800, 25 per cent of Britain's population lived in urban settlements. This figure had reached 54 per cent by 1800 and some 80 per cent by 1880. Most of this was because of the changing occupational structure of the country. Despite some terrible living and working conditions that resulted from this rapid growth, the standard of living rose with most workers able to earn several times the subsistence level. There was also an increase in the average height, which suggests an improvement in nutrition and, perhaps surprisingly given some of the conditions, in health. Literacy also improved, as it paid to be able to read and write.

The growth of towns and its impact on living conditions

There is much controversy over population growth and its relationship to the economy. The experience of developing countries suggests that rising population may not result in industrialization and may hinder economic development, but this does not appear to have been the case in Britain. It would appear that the initial increase in population was a stimulus to the growing economy and that industrial development was sustained by increasing employment opportunities as industry expanded and agriculture became more productive. This view appears to be supported by the distribution of the population growth. There were significant differences between industrial counties, such as Lancashire and the West Riding of Yorkshire, Warwickshire and Staffordshire, which grew rapidly and the more agricultural regions of the south (see Table 2.11 below).

ACTIVITY

What can we learn from Table 2.11 about the growth of towns in the period from 1800 to 1851?

Table 2.11 Population growth of selected towns (000s)

Town	Pre-1801	1801	1811	1821	1831	1841	1851
Blackburn	6	12	15	22	27	37	47
Manchester	30	75	89	126	182	235	303
Leeds	24	53	63	84	123	152	172
Salford	8	14	19	26	41	53	64
Stockport	5	17	21	27	36	50	54
Coventry	15	16	18	21	27	31	36
Leicester	13	17	19	26	41	53	61
Swansea	4	7	9	11	15	20	25
Worcester	11	11	14	17	19	27	28
Norwich	39	36	37	50	61	62	68

The rise in population meant that there was a labour surplus which was used to further industrial expansion. The growth in population also meant that there was an abundant supply of cheap and mobile labour, which led to a decrease in production costs. This labour also provided an increase in markets, which with the decrease in costs was often able to buy the new industrial goods. Thus, population growth linked to employment and industrial growth (see Source S).

SOURCE S

How valid is Young's view in Source S about the link between population growth and industrial growth?

A. Young, *Political Arithmetic*, 1774

Why have the inhabitants of Birmingham increased from 23,000 in 1750 to 30,000 in 1770? Certainly because a proportional increase in employment has taken place; wherever there is a demand for hands, there they will abound. Thus where employment increases, the people increase; and where employment does not increase the people do not increase. Away my boys – get children, they are worth more than they ever were.

Living conditions in towns

The rapid population and industrial growth led to the typical industrial landscape of mines, factories and mills set against a backdrop of rows of often poorly built terraced houses. Unskilled labourers crowded into tenement buildings and cellars for which they paid low rents. Back-to-back housing with little privacy sprang up in many of the great industrial towns, with builders looking to cram in as many as 70 to 80 dwellings per acre. Housing standards remained poor for the casual and unskilled labourer as it was uneconomic for the speculative builder to build high-quality homes. As a result, many of the city dwellers had to contend with bad housing, filth and bad water. But people flocked to them because they offered employment. Edwin Chadwick in his Sanitary Report of 1842 noted how much more unhealthy it was for a labourer to live in a city. A labourer's child was twice as likely to die before they reached the age of five in the city of Liverpool than in the rural county of Rutland. Three children out of every twenty died in Britain in the 1840s before the end of their first year and in some of the areas of tenement blocks the figure was as high as one in four. In Sheffield and Manchester more than half the children born in the 1830s failed to reach the age of five. It is perhaps therefore surprising that the industrial cities continued to grow at the rate they did, but this may be explained by migration to them and a high birth rate due to early marriage.

> **ACTIVITY** 🔁
> How significant was the work of Chadwick?

Edwin Chadwick

Edwin Chadwick (1800–90) was a social reformer who played a significant role in reforming the Poor Law in 1834 and later in bringing about major changes in urban sanitation and public health. He was particularly influential in the period from 1832 to 1854. He was employed by the Royal Commission to inquire into the operation of the Poor Law and in 1833 became a full member of the Commission, helping to draft the final legislation. This was followed by his appointment as secretary to the Poor Law Commissioners in 1834 but he struggled to work with his superiors. However, with the outbreak of typhus in 1838 he convinced the Poor Law Board that an inquiry was required, using, for the first time, doctors to look at conditions that might cause ill health. He edited the work they produced and in 1842 published, at his own expense, *A Report on the Sanitary Condition of the Labouring Population of Great Britain*. The report led to government establishing a Health of Towns Commission to recommend legislation. His report also led to the Public Health Act of 1848, the first time the government had taken responsibility for the health of its citizens. He became a commissioner of the Metropolitan Commission of Sewers and of the General Board of Health. In 1884 he became the first President of the Association of Public Sanitary Inspectors.

All of this would suggest that the conditions for workers were very poor, and this is reinforced by studies into the standard of living. Certainly there is no firm evidence to suggest that there was an improvement in the standard of living of workers in the period from 1750 to 1820. In fact, not only were living conditions poor but there were still harvest failures, the problems caused by the French and Napoleonic Wars and the rising population, all of which would suggest that the standard of living was likely to have fallen rather than risen in this period. However, in the period after 1820 it is possible to see an improvement, particularly by the 1840s as real wages do seem to have increased and even more so after 1850. The average earnings of workers grew only slowly in the period to 1750 and then slightly more rapidly to the end of the century. This is reflected in their patterns of consumption, with no change in the period to 1759, but growth in the period to 1798, followed by a return to stagnation at the start of the nineteenth century, improving at the end of the period before taking off after that, with a substantial rise in the real wages of industrial workers in the 1850s and 1860s.

ACTIVITY

To what extent did the standard of living change in the period from 1750 to 1850?

Although the rapid population growth in the industrial towns and cities made many social problems worse, such as overcrowding, poverty and high death rates, and were clearly evident in many of the working-class areas, industrial cities did inspire awe. Those interested in commerce saw them as symbols of progress (see Sources T and U).

SOURCE T

Extract from a British newspaper, *The Morning Chronicle*, 22 October 1849

This city – this great capital of the weavers and spinners of the earth, the Manchester of the power loom, the Manchester of the League, our Manchester – is but a thing of yesterday. A man, only a few years dead, recollected the people crowding to admire the first tall chimney built in Manchester, and had seen the Liverpool coach set forth at six in the morning, in good hope of reaching its destination not very long after six o'clock at night. Considerably within two thirds of a century, the scattered villages of Manchester, Salford, Hulme, Pendleton, Chorlton and two or three others, became the vast cotton metropolis which has lately succeeded in swaying the industrial and commercial polity of England.

SOURCE U

Compare and contrast the views of Sources **T** and **U** about the impact of industrialization on cities.

Extract from a weekly magazine, *The Chambers Edinburgh Journal*, 1858

Manchester streets may be irregular, and its trading inscriptions pretentious, its smoke may be dense and its mud ultra muddy, but not any or all of these things can prevent the image of a great city rising before us as the very symbol of civilization, foremost in the march of improvement, a grand incarnation of progress.

Such reports offer a much more optimistic view of industrial change and suggest that there were benefits, even given the appalling conditions. However, for the working class crowded into below-standard housing it is unlikely they would have had the same view. For them, most evidence suggests that at best there was a modest rise in wages at the end of the period, but that needs to be contrasted with environmental deterioration, lower standards of public health and a change in working arrangements that disrupted traditional patterns. Even if there was an improvement in levels of real wages the question of the standard of living should probably not be judged solely in terms of wages. The greatest beneficiaries of industrial change were the middle and upper class, then the skilled workers whose jobs were not threatened by mechanization.

ACTIVITY

Make a list of the problems faced by workers in the new industrial towns. Which do you think was the most serious problem? Explain your choice.

SOURCE V

An engraving of an industrial town by Roth, c.1880

What can we learn from Source V about conditions in industrial cities? How far does this source support the view of Sources T and U?

Working conditions: child labour, hours, pay and safety

Although an increasing number of workers were employed in the new factories, it should not be forgotten that, at least at the start of our period, there was still a significant number working as domestic servants and in the fields. There is little doubt that industrialization brought change to the working life of many. Factories demanded that there was discipline. Factory owners had invested heavily in machinery and therefore wanted to keep them working all the time. This required a shift system and workers who worked regular and unvarying hours, unlike the cottage system where they could work what hours they pleased. As mass production increased, factory owners increasingly demanded that workers worked longer hours. This was in contrast to pre-industrial society where there were fewer distinctions between work and home life. Work was home life through the year with more hectic activity at harvest and haymaking and similarly work in the cottage industries would be more intense when a job had to be completed for market or the agent was due to collect finished goods. In many activities absence from work had been institutionalized with some workers earning enough to be able to keep 'St Monday' for leisure.

The development of factories required a new form of discipline for workers. Time became a crucial issue for factory owners and some installed a 'clocking-in' system, often sacking those who failed to arrive on time. Owners also had to ensure that tasks were completed efficiently and this led to the introduction of fines for drunkenness, poor quality work and excessive talking.

Women and children

Industrialization, particularly in the textile industry, brought women and children, sometimes as young as five, into the factories, but they were also employed in coal mines and other developments. By 1833 women and children made up two-thirds of the workforce in the textile industry; and even when the number of children began to fall in the 1840s they were replaced by women rather than men. Most of the work done by women, and certainly by children, was unskilled and wages were usually between one-third and one-sixth those of men. Long hours were the norm until the 1844 Factory Act (see Table 2.13), but if conditions and hours were bad in the northern factories, they were even worse further south, particularly among the seamstresses in London, or among those organized on a workshop basis making things such as boxes, paper bags and toys.

Children had been an essential part of the economy for families even before the Industrial Revolution, particularly in rural areas where they helped with agriculture, and even in the cottage wool industry, both spinning and carding. In the domestic system they had worked under the supervision of their parents, but in the factory the family unit broke down. The Industrial Revolution made their use more systematic and widespread. They were particularly valued in the cotton industry as they were nimble, could go under machines to pick up loose cotton and had a delicacy of touch (see Source W).

ACTIVITY

Copy and complete the following table on life for workers before and after industrialisation.

Life before industrialisation	Life after industrialisation

Using the information in the table, explain to what extent industrialisation brought change for the workers.

What can we learn from Source W about why children were employed in textile mills?

SOURCE W

J. Aitkin, *A Description of the Country from Thirty to Forty Miles Around Manchester*, 1795

Children are soon very dexterous at connecting broken ends with prepared cotton at the rollers, their small fingers being more active and endued with a quicker sensibility of feeling than those of grown persons, and it is wonderful to see with what dispatch they can raise a system, connect threads, and drop it again into work almost simultaneously.

For many owners the most important traits were the ease with which children could be disciplined and the low wages they could be paid. Moreover, the population growth meant that there were plenty of young hands available. It was calculated by Andrew Ure in 1835 that boys in the Lancashire cotton mills earned 24.5p per week, while adult males were paid £1.13. Children in general earned between one-third and one-sixth of adults.

Much attention has been given to the exploitation of child labour by the factory system, particularly the use of 'pauper apprentices'; that is the children who were removed by the **Poor Law Guardians** to work in factories so that they were not a burden on the poor rate. Many of these finished up working very long hours with harsh discipline, no education or recreation time and inadequate food. As a result, many were unhealthy and even deformed as a result of keeping their limbs in unnatural positions for long periods (see Source X).

KEY TERM

Poor Law Guardians
Poor Law Guardians were responsible for the administration of poor relief in their areas, which were made up of a group of parishes.

SOURCE X

Report of the Board of Health at Manchester, 1796

The large factories are generally injurious to the constitution of those employed in them, even where no particular diseases prevail, from the close confinement which is enjoined, from the debilitating effects of hot or impure air, and from want of the active exercises which nature points out as essential to childhood and youth, to invigorate the system, and to fit our species for the employments and duties of manhood.

← **How typical is the view in Source X about the impact of factories on the health of workers?**

Evidence suggests that the worst conditions were experienced early on in the period and that improvements were made as the period progressed.

Industrial expansion led to the building of factories without regulation or even the belief that it was needed. As a result, there was no provision for ventilation, or sanitation. Meanwhile, there were no safety regulations, with machines often devoid of protection, which led to horrific injuries (see Source Y).

SOURCE Y

Sanitary Conditions of the Labouring Population of England, 1842

The accidents which occur to the manufacturing population of Birmingham are very severe and numerous, as shown by the registers of the General Hospital. Many are the consequence of the want of proper attention to the fencing of machinery, which appears to be seldom thought of in the manufactories; and many are caused by loose portions of dress being caught by the machinery, so as to drag the unfortunate sufferer under its power. The shawls of the females, or their long hair, and the aprons and loose sleeves of the boys and men, are in this way, frequent causes of dreadful mutilations.

One class of accidents is very frequent in Birmingham – severe burns and scalds. So numerous are these cases, particularly the former, that in the General Hospital two rooms are devoted to their reception. A great number of these accidents we know to have arisen from the children having been left without proper superintendence; and many are caused by the custom of wearing loose linen pinafores, which are drawn with the current of air into the fire.

It was not just horrific injuries that were a problem, children were often exhausted by the work they did or suffered illness as a result of the conditions (see Source Z).

(see Source Z).

SOURCE Z

Quarterly Review, 1866

The boys were kept in constant motion throughout the day, each carrying from thirty to fifty dozen of moulds into the stoves, and remaining long enough to take the dried earthenware away. The distance thus run by a boy in the course of a day was estimated at seven miles [11 km]. From the very nature of this exhausting occupation children were rendered pale, weak and unhealthy. In the depth of winter, with the thermometer in the open air sometimes below zero, boys with little clothing but rags, might be seen running to and fro on errands or to their dinners with perspiration on the foreheads, after labouring for hours like little slaves. The inevitable results of such transitions of temperature were consumption, asthma and acute inflammation.

> **Compare and contrast the views of Sources Y and Z about the suffering of those working in factories.**

But it was not in just factories that conditions were poor, it was the same in mines where children and women would work in darkness pulling carts or opening ventilation doors. However, it is equally important to note that even on farms conditions were bad with children working in wet and cold conditions in gangs that travelled from farm to farm.

Impacts on different social classes

The changes we have considered did not affect each class in the same way. One of the simplest ways to see how different classes were affected is to look at the average real income per person. This is calculated by dividing the total income of each class per year by number of people in that class. This figure is then converted to real income by dividing it by the cost of a subsistence basket of goods. Table 2.12 shows how many subsistence baskets a person could buy each year, that is the minimum needed for survival, what might be called bare-bones subsistence.

> **ACTIVITY**
>
> Industrial change had a major impact on the lives of children. For each of the following issues, explain how they were affected:
>
> - education
> - safety
> - hours at work
> - sanitation.

> **ACTIVITY**
>
> What can we learn from Table 2.12 about the standard of living of the population in the period from c1700 to c1870?

Table 2.12 Average real income per person (multiples of subsistence income). Source: Robert C. Allen, 'Revising England's Social Tables Once Again', *Working Papers in Economic and Social History*, Number 146, 2016

	1688	1759	1798	1846	1867
Landed	30.92	45.42	53.57	49.97	50.98
Bourgeoisie	20.58	14.74	37.16	32.43	51.39
Lower middle	5.26	5.19	8.40	12.74	7.25
Farmers	3.80	4.50	6.89	10.91	11.96
Workers	3.27	3.27	4.39	4.37	6.21
Cottagers and paupers	1.02	1.02	1.17	1.98	2.43
Average	**4.90**	**5.16**	**7.77**	**9.43**	**11.07**

The table shows that over the period of industrial change the average consumption more than doubled. All of the social classes gained, but the table shows that the gains were not uniform with workers making no real gain in the first part of the period, but seeing a much improved position after 1850.

The landed class

Throughout the period, the **landed classes** did well. At the start of the period they were able to consume 30 baskets and that rose considerably in the first part of the period before becoming stable. However, it must be remembered that they did not spend this income on subsistence baskets, but would have bought more expensive goods or used the surplus income to invest in their estates or in the new industrial enterprises. However, although their position did not decline, their relative position did. In the late seventeenth century the rent they received made up 16 per cent of the national income but by 1867 it accounted for just 5 per cent, a clear indication of the changing nature of the British economy.

The bourgeoisie

They were the second wealthiest group and although their average real income declined at the start of our period, they made considerable gains in the period from 1800 onwards. This group included people such as Sir Richard Arkwright who earned about £20,000 per year (about £1.5 million today), a figure that his son probably doubled. These were the very men who made money from business enterprises and provided most of the investment in the new industrial activities. They were drawing an income as large as that of the landowners, with Arkwright's son reputed to be the wealthiest commoner in the country.

The lower middle class and farmers

Table 2.12 shows that at the start of our period the lower middle class earned twice the amount of workers, but by the end of the period that gap had narrowed considerably, so that people such as shopkeepers and clerks were earning little more than a skilled craftsmen. Farmers, on the other hand, did well, increasing their income nearly threefold.

Workers

Given the diverse nature of the workforce, any generalizations must be qualified. The experience of different groups of workers varied during the period 1750 to 1850. The Table 2.12 suggests that for much of the period the standard of living remained roughly static, but this ignores the considerable inequality among different groups of workers. Those who worked in the expanding industrial sectors, such as engineering, ceramics and iron, did much better than those in the handicraft sectors, such as handloom weavers or stocking knitters, who experienced considerable poverty (see Source AA).

KEY TERM

Landed class A term used to describe landowners who owned sufficient land so that they could live entirely from rental income.

Read Source AA.
How valid is Carlyle's
view of the period to
1829?

SOURCE AA

Thomas Carlyle, 1829

It is the age of the machine. Nothing now is done directly, or by hand. Old modes of exertion are discredited and thrown aside. On every hand, the living artisan is driven from his workshop, to make room for a speedier, inanimate one.

At the start of the period the difference in earning between different groups of workers was minimal, but as the period progressed considerable change occurred. The handloom weavers did very well in the period from 1800 to 1825 when their income rose dramatically, but then collapsed to almost subsistence level by 1850 when they were earning 37.5p per week compared with £1.50 at the start of the century. Where machinery could replace skilled artisans there was suffering; they continued to work in their trade as that was where their skills were, but as machinery became more and more efficient so they became poorer, often ending up in suffering. Though they continued to work at their trade, the greater use of machinery reduced many to poverty. This was the fate of those involved, for example, in framework knitting and pillow lace weaving. Instead of a narrow frame that could produce a dozen pairs of stockings per week there were now machines that could produce that many in a day. Knitting frames were also not difficult to operate so those who had lost their jobs in handloom weaving moved into the stocking industry, adding to the labour pool and further depressing wages there. It was handworkers in particular who suffered as more and more industries were industrialized with the result that the average wage of the working class did not rise until the handicraft sector was replaced by factories. Alongside the handloom weavers and framework knitters, agricultural labourers also suffered. However, their wages varied from region to region, but in the south-west it was only 40p per week and in the northern counties slightly higher at 60p per week.

In contrast, the engineering boom meant that pattern-makers, fitters, smiths and millwrights in the Manchester area were earning above £1.50 per week and carding operatives were on £1.25 per week. However, perhaps one of the biggest gainers was those employed in the iron industry. By the late 1850s **furnace men**, **puddlers** and **rollers** in the more prosperous works were on between £2.12.5 and £3 per week. The wage level was even higher for 'shinglers' who took the impurities out of metals as they were on £4.75 per week.

The poor

The incomes of the poor did rise gradually during the nineteenth century, having been virtually static in the eighteenth.

The new methods of production had transformed the lives of many. The destruction of the cottage industry meant there was a massive change for labourers, be they men, women or children. This is perhaps best summarized in the Royal Commission on Population published in 1949 (see Source BB).

KEY TERM

Furnace men, puddlers and **rollers** These were all jobs done in the iron industry: furnace men were responsible for the blast furnaces, puddlers were responsible for stirring molten iron with iron oxide to produce wrought iron, and rollers rolled the iron into sheets.

SOURCE BB

Royal Commission on Population, London, 1949

The industrial and agricultural revolutions carried with them a shift from settled, traditional ways of life, in which changes came slowly, to new ways of life in which changes were liable to be frequent and abrupt. The old settled ways of life, in which ties of family and community had been strong, were passing. They were succeeded by an intense competitive struggle in which the emphasis was placed on the individual rather than the community. Opportunities for 'getting on' were multiplied, but at the same time, it became increasingly necessary to struggle to keep one's job and one's place in the community.

In your own words, explain, according to Source BB, what changes had taken place in the lives of workers since the start of the Industrial Revolution.

Life became more disciplined, as we saw in the previous section. The last section suggested that the first generation of workers in industry worked in worse conditions than their predecessors. It was the middle and upper classes who were the beneficiaries and those skilled workers whose jobs were not threatened by machines. Towards the end of the period there was some improvement for workers, but the greatest gains would come only after 1850 when the price depression in the late nineteenth century allowed workers to enjoy the benefits of industrialization.

Government responses to the consequences of industrialization

There was very little reform to either living or working conditions in the first half of the period. This meant that the poor and working class were left vulnerable to disease given the poor living conditions. Water was often contaminated and there were frequent epidemics of **cholera** and **typhoid**. Government was dominated by the rich, be they landowners or manufacturers, and they did not want to pay for improvements or force others to improve their houses. It would not be until 1842, with a report into the 'Sanitary Conditions of the Labouring Poor', that eventually a series of laws were passed to improve conditions. This saw the establishment of a General Board of Health, but despite this measures were often not implemented as local authorities had to pay for them from local taxes which they did not want to raise. With medical science also in its infancy, doctors debated the causes of disease but few offered effective answers and were certainly not aware that decaying matter led to disease. It would not be until the 1860s that Louis Pasteur was able to establish that micro-organisms led to rotting and disease.

It took the work of campaigners such as Edwin Chadwick to bring about improvements in public health. He was helped by the passing of legislation, such as the Poor Law Amendment Act of 1834 and the Municipal Corporations Act of the same year. These provided the foundations on which men such as Chadwick could build. Reports from the Assistant Poor Law Commissioners often stressed the link between poverty and disease.

ACTIVITY

Draw up a table to show how each class' standard of living was affected by industrial change. The chart should have four columns, in the first list the classes – landed, bourgeoisie, lower middle, workers, poor. In column two list the gains they made, in column three the losses and in the final column make a judgement as to whether they gained or lost.

KEY TERMS 🔑

Cholera An infectious disease contracted from infected water causing vomiting and diarrhoea and possibly leading to death.

Typhoid An infectious bacterial fever leading to spots and stomach pains.

Even after the report of 1842 into sanitary conditions the government was reluctant to act as the report had alienated a number of influential people and groups. However, pressure was maintained through the formation of the Health of Towns Association in 1844 to press for legislation. Finally, in 1848 a Public Health Board was established, but only on the basis of a renewed five-year lease and it would survive for only two terms, with Chadwick himself removed in 1854. It would take until the 1870s before substantial reform was passed.

It was not just poor health but poor food that blighted the poor. Much of the food was contaminated. The chemical alum was often added to bread to make it look whiter and therefore could be charged at a higher price. Leaves from ash, sloe or elder were offered instead of tea, while milk and beer were watered down. The old medieval laws that protected bread and ale could no longer be enforced and in 1815 when the Assize of Bread (a law controlling standards of bread production) was formally repealed it was decided that free competition was better than regulation. But, as with public health, it would not be until the 1870s when the Conservative Prime Minister, Benjamin Disraeli, passed the 1875 Food and Drugs Act that effective legislation was put in place to improve the quality of food.

Factory conditions and working hours, particularly those for children, became a central concern in the early nineteenth century. However, as Table 2.13 on page 92 shows it would be a long struggle before significant legislation to control it was passed. Not only was there opposition from factory owners, who believed that restrictions would hit their profits and damage trade, but many families welcomed the additional income the labour of children brought. There were also many who argued that factory work was good for children and helped their development, while others claimed that the work was light and easy (see Source CC).

ACTIVITY

What evidence is there that working and living conditions improved in the period? What evidence is there that working and living conditions deteriorated in the period? Do you think that overall they improved or deteriorated?

How useful is Source CC in explaining why there was opposition to reduce working hours and limit child labour?

SOURCE CC

Minutes of a meeting of the Master Worsted Spinners of Halifax as late as 1851

This meeting views with alarm the measures proposed in the House of Commons, to curtail the hours of labour in mills or factories, and to limit the ages of children employed in the same.

That the condition of those employed in worsted mills does not warrant the conclusion that the present usages of the trade are injurious to the health and comforts of this class of operatives; and that the present term of Labour (12 hours per day) is not attended with any consequences injurious to those employed, and is not more than adequate and necessary to provide for their livelihood.

That an enactment which will abridge the hours of labour, or limit the age of children employed in worsted mills, will produce the following effect:

1 *It will cause a proportionate reduction of the wages of this class.*

2   *It will materially cripple the means of those who have large and young families, who, in many instances, are the main support of their parents.*

3   *It will raise the price of goods to consumers, which will affect the home trade considerably, and will produce serious effects upon the prosperity of the district.*

4   *It will throw out of employment and the means of existence the numbers of children now beneficially engaged in worsted mills.*

Despite this opposition, concern, particularly about child labour, did grow for a number of reasons. It was led by Tory reformers such as Richard Oastler, John Fielden and Anthony Ashley Cooper, the seventh **Earl of Shaftesbury**. They expressed concern about the new factory system, while others, influenced by ethical and religious concerns, believed that it was both immoral to employ children and was exploitative. It was also felt that, away from their parents, they were not being brought up with the correct principles. It was the organization of the factory system that became the focus of publicity in the growing national press and it became a major 'interest story'. With the Whig government of the 1830s passing a large number of reforms it was perhaps not surprising that factory legislation became a topic of interest. Perhaps this change in attitude was less surprising when Richard Oastler was able to compare factory work with that of slaves on the plantations in the West Indies (see Source DD below).

> **KEY FIGURE**
>
> **Earl of Shaftesbury**
> (1801–85) Anthony Ashley Cooper, the seventh Earl of Shaftesbury, was a well-known social reformer. In 1833 he introduced the Ten Hours Act, but it was modified by the Whig government. In 1847 the Ten Hour Bill finally became legislation. He was also responsible for introducing Mining Legislation, outlawing the use of women and children underground. He also attempted to get legislation passed prohibiting the use of boys as chimney sweeps. This law was not enforced until 1864.

SOURCE DD

Richard Oastler, 'Yorkshire Slavery', *Leeds Mercury*, October 1830

Thousands of our fellow creatures both male and female are existing in a state of slavery, more horrid than victims of that hellish system of colonial slavery. These innocent creatures drag out their short, but miserable existence in a place famed for its profession of religious zeal – in the worsted mills of Bradford. Thousands of little children, both male and female, but principally female, from seven to fourteen years of age are daily compelled to labour from six o'clock in the morning to seven in the evening, with only – Britons blush as you read this! – with only thirty minutes allowed for eating and recreation. Poor infants! Ye are sacrificed at the shrine of greed.

> **How useful is Source DD in explaining the conditions in the textile mills of Bradford?**

It was argued that such hours prevented children from receiving any form of education, another issue that was becoming an important political concern. However, such articles did not mean that there were not opponents of factory reform. Table 2.13 on page 92 shows how slow it was to bring about change and even when change was achieved how much of the reform was limited.

> **ACTIVITY**
> Draw a spider diagram to show why factory legislation was passed.

Table 2.13 Government measures to improve working conditions 1800–50

Date	Act	What did it do?	Impact
1802	Health and Morals of Apprentices Act	No pauper apprentice to do night work in textile mills. Labour during the day limited to 12 hours	Not very effective as no system of inspection and penalties not enforced
1813	Owen's campaign to protect factory children	Led to establishment of a Select Committee	
1819	Cotton Mills and Factories Act	No children under 9 to work in cotton mills Working hours of ages 9–16 limited to 12 hours per day	Difficult to enforce
1831	Act to reduce hours forbade night work	No night working if under 21	Limited to cotton mills
1833	Royal Commission on Factory Reform	Investigate working conditions in mills and factories	Led to Factory Act of 1833
1833	Factory Act	No children under 9 to be employed. Children 9–13 to work no more than 48 hours per week. Those aged 13–18 no more than 69 hours per week	Inspector system begun and applied to textile mills
1838, 1839, 1840	Ten Hour Bills	Attempt to limit working for older children to 10 hours	Failed to get approval
1842	Mines Act	No children under 10 or women to work underground in coal mines	Inspection of mines started
1844	Factory Act	Minimum working age in textile mills reduced to 8. All children can work no more than 6.5 hours per day. Young persons, 13–18, and women to work no more than 12 hours per day	More inspectors appointed. Safety rules to fence off dangerous machines
1847	Factory Act	Work of women and young persons, 13–18, limited to 10 hours per day in textile factories	Long hours continue for men. Women and young persons now to work in shifts

There were attempts to bring in a ten-hour day for all workers. This failed despite the efforts of Lord Shaftesbury and it would be only in 1847 when a limited version was passed. There were also problems with the legislation that was passed. Reports from inspectors revealed that many employers were not complying with the Acts. Requirements for certification to confirm the age of the child were complex and the requirement for children to attend classes was difficult to enforce. It was also difficult to ensure those classes were of a good standard.

SOURCE EE

Andrew Ure, a Scottish doctor and dentist who specialized in research into manufacturing conditions, writing after the Factory Act of 1833

I have visited many factories, both in Manchester and the surrounding districts, and I never saw a single instance of corporal punishment inflicted on a child, nor did I ever see children in ill-humour. They seemed to be cheerful and alert, taking pleasure in the light play of their muscles. The work of the lively elves seems to resemble a sport, in which the habit gave them a pleasing dexterity. As to exhaustion, they showed no trace of it, emerging from the mill in the evening; they began to skip around and commence their little amusements like boys coming from school.

SOURCE FF

Extract from Factory Inspectors Report 1836, from the British Parliamentary Papers 1836

My Lord, in the case of Taylor, Ibbotson and Co. I took the evidence from the mouths of the boys themselves. They stated to me that they commenced working on Friday morning, the 27th May last, at six a.m., and that, with the exception of meal hours and one hour at midnight extra, they did not cease working till four o'clock on Saturday evening, having been two days and a night thus engaged. Believing the case scarcely possible, I asked every boy the same questions, and from each received the same answers. I then went into the house to look at the time book, and in the presence of one of the masters, referred to the cruelty of the case, and stated that I should certainly punish it with all the severity in my power. Mr Rayner, the certificating surgeon, was with me at the time.

> **Compare and contrast the views of Sources EE and FF about child labour following the passage of the 1833 Factory Act.**

Although children in factories were a cause for concern, little was done for exploited children outside the factories. The findings of the royal commission on factories in 1833 and 1843 and on mines in 1843 were shocking, but child labour was not abolished; educational provision was limited and there was no general agreement on even reducing working hours by two hours for those over thirteen. Young people would continue to work long hours well into the twentieth century.

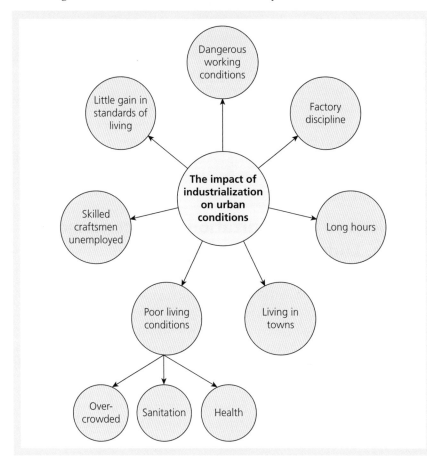

ACTIVITY

Use material from the section on government response to the consequences of industrialisation to find evidence to support the following statements:

- The government response to living and working conditions was slow.
- The government was unable to bring about change to working conditions because of opposition.
- Changes in working conditions were the result of the campaigns of individuals rather than the government.

ACTIVITY

Add details and evidence to each of the points to support each factor.

SUMMARY DIAGRAM

Why, and with what consequences, did urbanization result from industrialization?

Why, and with what consequences, did industrialization result in popular protest and political change?

The Industrial Revolution created huge tensions in society. These would become more apparent as the period progressed and particularly in the nineteenth century. To understand why these tensions did not emerge at the start of the period we need to remember that in 1790 employment in cotton mills, the major factories of the period, was less than two per cent of the working population. The growth in factories meant that much of the female population who had worked as hand spinners became unemployed, while mechanization meant children were able to take on some of the jobs previously done by men. It was the same in the countryside where agricultural mechanization led to an increase in rural poverty. It is therefore not surprising there were protests about the changes and the conditions in which people found themselves both working and living. The industrial changes also led to growing disenchantment with the political system and calls for reform. Initially the demand for political reform came from the middle-class factory owners who were making much of the wealth of the country and demanded a share in the political power with the traditional landowning classes who dominated Parliament. However, as the period progressed workers who laboured to create that wealth realized that the only way their position would change was through representation either in Parliament or through pressure groups, such as trade unions. The traditional ruling class therefore faced pressure for reform and to share power, a process that would be just starting by 1850.

Reactions to mechanization and economic change, Luddites and Swing Riots

Protest from workers was nothing new. There had been protests against enclosure in the sixteenth and seventeenth centuries, while food riots had also been commonplace at times of high prices and poor harvests. Government failure to take action led to people taking direct action or threatening unrest until the problem was resolved. Industrial change created a new situation, with workers living more closely together in large industrial towns. This made protest easier to organize and on a larger scale.

The introduction of machines threatened those who were skilled workers and led to direct action in the form of machine breaking. The Napoleonic Wars of the early nineteenth century produced further hardship. They led to dramatic price rises and periods of unemployment when soldiers and sailors were demobilized at the end of the war in 1815, which led to riots and demands for reform. This set a pattern that continued for much of the rest of the period. Riots were a particular worry for the government in the wake of the events of the French Revolution and given their lack of law enforcement agencies.

Luddites

The years around the French Revolution and Napoleonic Wars were difficult for workers. They coincided with a period of increasing mechanization that saw attacks on factory owners who tried to install machinery in mills. Known as Luddites, after Ned Ludd who had broken machines in Nottingham in 1779, the aim was to destroy machines that the workers believed were making them unemployed. The most serious outbreaks were in the lace-making regions in Nottinghamshire in 1811, which then spread to the woollen industry of Yorkshire and Lancashire in 1812–13. Although the government saw revolutionary intent behind these protests, it is more likely that it had economic causes as the height of protest coincided with the peak of the rise in bread prices. The war and the continental blockade had also disrupted employment. The initial outbreaks of machine breaking were in areas where hosiery and lace were made and these industries were heavily dependent on exports, which had been disrupted by war. Therefore, although the Luddites attacked machines that were producing inferior products that threatened the respectability of their trade, they were also defending themselves against wage cuts in a market that was shrinking considerably.

The protests were certainly well organized and became increasingly violent. Protests hit their height in 1812 with a factory near Leeds being burned down and other factories in the city seeing machinery destroyed (see Source GG).

> **ACTIVITY**
>
> Make a list of the causes of economic unrest. What do you think was the most important cause? Explain your choice.

SOURCE GG

The *Leeds Mercury*, 29 February 1812

The depredators, or to use the cant terms, Luddites, assembled with as much privacy as possible, at the place marked out for the attack and divided themselves into two parties, the more daring and expert entered the premises, provided with proper implements for the work of destruction, which they accomplished with astonishing secrecy and dispatch. The other party remained conveniently stationed to keep off intruders. As soon as the work of destruction was completed, the Leader drew up his men, called over the roll, each man answering to a particular number instead of his name, they then fired off their pistols and marched off in regular military order.

> **How useful is Source GG in explaining the Luddite threat?**

This was soon followed by the destruction of machines at nearby Cleckheaton.

Yorkshire Luddism was organized by the croppers who resisted the introduction of the gig-mill and shearing frame designed to end the monopoly of woollen cloth finishing exercised by no more than 5000 workers who could demand high wages for their skills. Many mill owners could not afford to defend their premises and so the Luddites chose their targets carefully, with the 1812 campaign culminating in the shooting dead of a prominent mill owner, William Horsfall, in an ambush near Huddersfield. Power looms were also attacked but the number of these machines was not large until the 1820s.

The authorities viewed the outbreaks as serious, sending in 12,000 troops and executing 17 Luddites in 1813. By the end of 1813 the protests had largely died down although there were a few incidents in 1814. Despite the ending of the unrest it was a clear indication that workers were able to organize themselves and when they did it was very difficult to control. With no voice in Parliament, direct action was the only way workers could be heard.

Unrest 1815–20

By 1815 the key elements for protest were again in place. Wheat prices were high and the end of the war with France led to a trade recession and unemployment as there was no longer the demand for armaments as Britain rapidly demobilized its forces. This hit the iron industry, which had expanded considerably during the war; similarly the decline in demand for uniforms hit the textile industry. At the same time, overseas trade was slow to recover and high unemployment resulted. As unemployment rose so did the supply of labour with returning soldiers. Not only were there protests against unemployment and poverty but this time they were accompanied by demands for political reform (see pages 97–100).

In 1817, inspired by the activities of John Johnson, a member of the Hampden Club (a radical political club) and a Salford tailor, a protest march of 'Blanketeers' to London was organized. This was to protest about the hardship of the handloom weavers of the north-west, but it was broken up by troops at Stockport after just seven miles (11 km). This was followed by the Derbyshire Rising led by 300 iron workers and stocking makers from north-east Derbyshire, but this was foiled by a government informer.

An upturn in the economy and the falling price of wheat in the 1820s helped to bring a decline in industrial protest. However, there were also protests in rural areas. Food riots had been widespread in the years of high prices during the 1790s and 1800s. In East Anglia most years saw ricks, or stacks of corn and straw, being attacked, cattle maimed and the destruction of farm outbuildings. The years 1816–17 and 1822 were particularly bad with attacks on farmers who paid below the going rate.

ACTIVITY

Copy and complete the table below on the threat of unrest:

Evidence that unrest was serious	Evidence that unrest was not serious

Use the information in the chart to help you decide how serious unrest was during the period.

The Swing Riots

Rural protest culminated in the Swing Riots of 1830–01, so called after Captain Swing – a fictitious character whose name was used to send threatening letters to farmers. A poor harvest was the spark for unrest in the south and east of England. Large 'open' parishes that were totally dependent on agriculture were the worst hit. Often led by the better-off and probably better-educated sector of the rural labour force, village craftsmen and specialist farm workers destroyed threshing machines. These machines threatened one of the few sources of winter work and the protestors demanded higher wages. Attacks were also made against the leaders of the local community for failing to carry out the traditional obligations of the better-off in society during a time of hardship, a clear sign of the decline in paternalism. As with the Luddites, the government was anxious; some 2000 were arrested, 500 were **transported** to Australia, 600 were imprisoned and 19 executed. However, unlike the Luddites it appears as if the Swing Riots did have an impact as the widespread introduction of threshing machines was delayed for twenty years and there were some improvements in wages. The riots would also provide part of the context for the passing of the Great Reform Act of 1832 (see page 99). However, much of the protest in the period from 1800 was centred more around political demands, culminating in the Chartist movement of the late 1830s and 1840s.

Demands for political reform

Nearly all the protests in the period before 1815 had been aimed at working conditions and harsh landlords and employers. However, after 1815 political demands were made more frequently. There had always been a radical tradition in Britain, which can be seen in the English Civil War in the mid-seventeenth century with groups such as the Levellers, who had argued for a more equal and democratic society, and radical ideas had not died out with the repression of the 1790s that followed the ideas of the American and French Revolutions. The idea that ordinary people should have some say in the running of the country was therefore still alive.

Peterloo

With the ending of the Napoleonic Wars in 1815 political discontent at home was less likely to be deterred by war and the charge that unrest was helping Britain's enemies. In 1776 a leading radical, Major John Cartwright, had written about giving the vote to all men in a secret ballot. In 1812 he met with other leading radicals and formed the Hampden Club. He then toured the country encouraging the establishment of other clubs, which were set up in many areas of the north. They also encouraged the formation of other clubs, such as the Patriotic Union Society, which was set up in Manchester. Their most notable achievement was organizing a meeting at St Peter's Field in Manchester at which the radical orator, Henry Hunt, was to speak. The meeting attracted between 50,000 and 60,000 people and seriously worried the authorities who were concerned that a riot might follow. The authorities assembled 1000 troops

ACTIVITY

Which of the following statements do you most agree with:

- Economic unrest in the period 1780–1830 was never a serious problem.
- Economic unrest in the period 1780–1830 was a threat to social order.
- The most serious economic unrest in the period 1780–1830 was the Swing Riots.

KEY TERM

Transportation The removal of those who had been convicted of an offence to a penal colony, usually Australia.

and special constables, meanwhile the magistrates ordered the arrest of Hunt. As the troops advanced to arrest him the crowd resisted and in the struggle that followed 15 were killed and 400 wounded. The struggle became known as Peterloo (after the Battle of Waterloo) and became a byword for repression.

SOURCE HH

'Manchester heroes', a cartoon by George Cruikshank. From left to right the comments read: 'Cut them down, don't be afraid, they are not armed, courage my boys and you shall have a vote of thanks, and he that kills most shall be made a Knight errant and your exploits shall live for ever in a song or second Chivey Chace' / 'Cut him down, cut him down' / 'Oh pray Sir, don't kill mammy, she only came to see M Hunt.' / 'None but the brave deserve the fair' / 'Shame' / 'Shame, shame, murder, murder, massacre' / 'shame, shame'.

> How useful is Source HH in portraying the events at Peterloo?

Spa Fields

Other protests followed, such as the meeting at Spa Fields in 1819 which was attended by 50,000. However, the radicals were deeply divided on how far democracy should go and whether there should be property qualifications for voting to ensure that voters were informed and voting was not ruined by the ignorant masses. The movement also disagreed about policies and methods and there were also regional differences.

Calls for reform 1829–32

Despite these differences some changes were brought about, particularly in the period after 1820 when it appeared as if economic stability had returned. In 1829 Roman Catholic emancipation was passed, allowing Catholics to both vote and become Members of Parliament (MPs). This opened the way for

ACTIVITY

Why do think the authorities were so concerned about the demands for political reform?

further changes and in 1832 the most significant reform, the Great Reform Act, was passed. In part, this was in response to the disturbances that had been gripping Britain in the years 1830–01, most notably the Swing Riots (see pages 96–97), with MPs concerned that any delay to reform might lead to further unrest. Their concerns seemed to be justified when initial attempts at reform failed and there were riots in Bristol, Bath, Coventry, Worcester, Warwick, Derby and Nottingham. Although the numbers involved, with the exception of Bristol and Nottingham, were not large there were concerns that the middle class might join the protests started by the lower class. The government was also worried that a political issue could result in popular violence and the danger that could bring if the issue was not resolved.

The Great Reform Act 1832

In the end the Reform Act was passed, but it was limited in scope. Although some of the most serious abuses – such as **rotten boroughs** and the lack of representation in Parliament of the new industrial towns – were tackled, the franchise was raised only from 516,000 to 813,000 out of a population of 24 million. This meant that the working class did not gain the vote, even if it satisfied the demands of the growing middle-class industrialists who did. It did, however, prevent revolution, but the lack of political gains, the limited nature of the Factory Acts (see page 92) and the passing of the Poor Law Amendment Act in 1834 led to growing working-class discontent. It resulted in the emergence of a number of groups demanding more political rights; these eventually united to form the Chartists.

The Chartists

The Chartists supported the six points of the People's Charter, which was drawn up in 1838. It demanded:
- universal manhood suffrage, with every male over 21 getting the vote
- no property qualifications on voting or being an MP
- annual elections to Parliament
- equal electoral districts
- payment of MPs
- voting by secret ballot.

The Charter was drawn up by William Lovett and presented to Parliament in May 1839. The Chartists believed that political reform was essential if living and working conditions were to be improved. The movement attracted widespread support. The petition presented to Parliament in 1839 had 1.2 million signatures, while its newspaper, the *Northern Star*, had 40,000 readers. The scale of the protest was much larger than other previous radical movements and it even spilled over into armed revolt in Newport, South Wales, when 1.5 million signed a petition demanding the release of those arrested for leading the protest. A further petition was presented to Parliament in 1842 signed by 3.3 million, but when this failed the movement went into decline. However, it revived and in 1848 a further petition with

ACTIVITY

Using the information in this section, explain why it was so difficult to achieve political reform in the period before 1832.

KEY TERM

Rotten borough A borough that although it had very few voters was still able to return an MP, often due to corruption or bribery or where a family controlled who was elected.

some 5 million signatures was presented to Parliament. The government was also concerned that a mass meeting in London would lead to revolution and brought in over 7000 troops, but it passed off peacefully. The scale of protest was unprecedented and the length of time over which Chartism was sustained was remarkable, but ultimately it failed to achieve its aims.

Why did Chartism gain large-scale support?

Chartism had developed for a number of reasons. In the short term it can be argued that disappointment with the reforms of the 1830s played a role. However, economic changes also played a significant role. Domestic workers in particular had lost out to competition from factories, from falling prices as more efficient and cheaper production undercut them and from fluctuation in trade. Factory workers faced harsh conditions, long hours, dangerous workplaces and low wages caused by a growing labour market. The period 1836–43 was also one of depression. Rises in bread prices caused considerable hardship to increasing numbers living on the edge of subsistence so it was not surprising that Chartism was able to attract support from victims of economic change (see Source II).

> **ACTIVITY**
> Construct a spider diagram to show the reasons for the emergence of Chartism.

SOURCE II

A former Chartist writing in 1856 recalling the views of a delegate to the 1839 Chartist Convention. From R. Lowery, *Weekly Record*, September 1856

> **How useful is Source II in explaining the reasons for the growth of Chartism?**

One delegate, a handloom weaver, described his hardships, lack of food, and his starving wife unable to feed her baby. There is something about the sight of our family suffering from hunger that none can judge who have not experienced it. Your judgement is deranged as your child looks up with piteous face and tears.

By the late 1830s the grievances of workers were increasing and they were becoming used to forming groups to put pressure on the government. As protests had not brought about a change in their conditions the next logical step was to reform Parliament so that the working class had a political voice and would pass measures to improve their position. This was clearly explained by the West London Boot and Shoemakers Charter Association in their appeal to the boot makers of London in April 1842 (see Source JJ below).

SOURCE JJ

The West London Boot and Shoemakers Charter Association, 1842

> **Compare and contrast Sources II and JJ as evidence for support for Chartism.**

Most of us, like too many of our class, regarded politics as something foreign to our interests. We have been content to see our trade affairs as our main interest and to see our enemies as those who seek to reduce our prices and our wages without seeing that the feelings of our employers to us is tied up with wider political matters. We have ignored the influence of the despotic government and not asked why the whole system of injustice has been allowed to go on for so long.

Origins of organized labour, trade unions and co-operative societies

Trade unions in the eighteenth century were small organizations of mostly skilled male workers. Their object was to protect their traditions and skills and maintain the prices paid for their products. People who joined trade unions were mainly those who had completed a long apprenticeship and wanted to protect their status against cheap labour from unskilled workers. The number of strikes was limited, but the craftsmen did organize and develop 'combinations' involving a considerable number of occupations.

Early trade unions and combinations

The law did not recognize any right to come together to interfere with trade or business. Such organizations were prosecuted by the businessmen who bought the craftsmen's work and traded the products. Despite this, some trades such as papermakers, print workers, plumbers, painters and shoemakers did come together. However, there was an ongoing struggle between the businessmen and their craftsmen suppliers well before **Pitt's Combination Act of 1799** and a body of law that could be used against unions of tradesmen. The main concept was that a group of people who met together to influence trade were conspiring. Between 1710 and 1800, 29 conspiracy trials of tradesmen's groups took place showing just how difficult it was for workers to come together in organized groups.

As a result, combinations often resorted to secrecy, with meetings held at night, passwords and symbols and oaths of loyalty. This raised further fears among the authorities, particularly in the 1790s when there was concern about the implication of events in France. The laws of 1799 against illegal oaths and against combinations in general did not introduce anything new but were a further guarantee against possible disorder. The trade unions became more skilful in concealing their meetings, raising funds to help members and intimidating employers and **blacklegs**.

Unions in the period after the Napoleonic Wars

The industrial changes and rapid population rise put pressure on unions trying to maintain traditional practices and guarantee prices. In 1814 the Statute of Artificers reduced apprenticeship restrictions and threatened the status of craftsmen. The Combination Act of 1799 made associations of workers and employers illegal to free up trade. However, the law became a focus for discontent and strikes occurred during and in the aftermath of the Napoleonic Wars. The number of large labour organizations increased in the second decade of the nineteenth century, but the unions faced considerable challenges from:
- new machinery that threatened the competitiveness of traditional trades
- a new unskilled workforce of women, children and unskilled workers who could be trained to use the new machines quickly

KEY TERMS

Pitt's Combination Act 1799 The Act prohibited trade unions and collective bargaining. It was passed partly in response to fears following the French Revolution, but also because the government was concerned that workers would strike during the war against France.

Blacklegs Workers who break a strike and continue to work during trade disputes.

- the ending of apprenticeship rules
- the repression of protests (see pages 97–99)
- the determination of employers to oppose unions.

Unions in the 1820s

However, where the factory system did not dominate and older trades continued, unions developed. In 1824 the Combination Acts were repealed. It was hoped that making unions legal and not open to prosecution for conspiracy would stop the strikes and unrest. Instead there was considerable growth in union activity after the repeal and in 1825 the Act was modified to exclude **picketing** as a tactic to intimidate those who wanted to work. Unions remained free to negotiate over wages, conditions and hours worked but other activities were liable to be considered as criminal conspiracies operating in restraint of trade.

These developments were followed by a period of experiment with attempts to create a national union structure from restrictive and backward-looking associations of skilled workers. What was new was the growing political awareness of skilled workers. This was aided by the radical press which spread ideas of popular participation in politics, mass movements for the reform of Parliament and the influence of individuals such as **Robert Owen** who brought new ideas of socialism to the movement.

In 1829 **John Doherty** led the organization of the new Grand General Union of Operative Cotton Spinners following attempts by the cotton spinners of Lancashire to unite and join with fellow workers in Scotland. However, despite attempts at joint action and the establishment of a fund for workers on strike, their attempts to bring about higher wages in Lancashire failed. This was because they lacked sufficient funds, found it difficult to get co-operation between the different areas and the timing was poor as the strike was during an economic downturn when demand for cotton goods was low.

Doherty also attempted co-operation between unions by forming the National Association for the Protection of Labour (NAPL) in 1829 from twenty different skilled trades, mostly in Lancashire and Cheshire, but this also failed and could not sustain an effective organization after 1833. In part, this was because much of the protest was about the threat to handloom weavers, but this did not concern other workers. This was an issue as different trades had different issues that did not appeal to other workers. There were also concerns from some that union activity was associated with violence and they did not want to be associated with it.

The Grand National Consolidated Trade Union

The greatest experiment was the Grand National Consolidated Trade Union which was established in 1834. It originated among the trades of London and was mainly an association of tailors, silk weavers and shoemakers.

It was supported by Robert Owen and had some innovative features:

- mutual support during strikes
- a fund to provide sickness benefits
- some inclusion of women
- inclusion of agricultural workers (see page 88).

Although it attracted 16,000 members, it achieved less than the NAPL and soon collapsed despite its wider hopes.

SOURCE KK

Adapted from resolutions of a conference in London in February 1834 which founded the GNCTU

No longer will the working-man be told there are 'lower orders' in society. The truth is out! We know that all men are equal in the eyes of Nature and all have equal right to the products of Nature. We call on our brethren gathered here, nobly to resolve upon such measures that seem fitted to give the working men their just rights and the full reward of their labours. We shall achieve a complete emancipation of the productive classes as full emancipation from the tyranny of capitalism.

> **How useful is Source KK in explaining why trade unions were formed?**

However, it is often seen as the forerunner of the **Trades Union Congress**. Despite this, unions continued to suffer from economic change, in particular the economic depression of the 1830s and 1840s, which was made worse by the large number of workers who depended on the manufacturing industry. The legal status of unions remained uncertain, and the treatment of the agricultural workers of Tolpuddle was a clear warning of the severe treatment that could be meted out.

> **KEY TERM**
>
> **Trades Union Congress**
> The federation of trade unions in England and Wales which represents most trade unions. It was formally established in the 1860s.

Tolpuddle

There had been considerable rural unrest in the early 1830s with the Swing Riots (see pages 96–97). Rural labourers had been faced with wage cuts and this had led some agricultural labourers in the Dorset village of Tolpuddle to form a friendly society of labourers to negotiate with the farmers. As with other unions, members swore to abide by the rules. Local magistrates were concerned by this and approached the Home Secretary who agreed to the arrest of the members and they were charged under the 1797 Act against treasonable oaths. Six of the members were sentenced to seven years' transportation – banishment to a penal settlement in Australia to work as forced labour. The sentences attracted considerable criticism and in March 1834 the GNCTU organized a mass protest against the severity of the sentences, but despite this the men were still sent. Similarly, violence in a Glasgow cotton strike in 1837 led to the trial of union leaders. The Miners' Association, formed in 1842, with 60,000 members, was unable to achieve higher wages.

It appeared that unions had failed to achieve anything of substance, but in the period after 1800 there were larger-scale organizations and their activities were more diverse with greater political awareness. Some union

> **ACTIVITY**
>
> 1 Why was it so difficult for workers to establish combinations and unions?
>
> 2 Briefly explain why the government was so concerned by the emergence of unions and combinations.

activity had been legalized and unions were not just seen in terms of conspiracies and secret oaths. Despite this, union membership was still low and unions were still largely organizations of skilled labourers who saw unskilled workers as their enemies as much as the employers. They were also challenged by other working-class groups such as the Chartists (see pages 99–100), **friendly societies** and co-operatives. It was also still unclear what they could legitimately do to persuade workers to support strikes despite the government's changing attitude towards the demand for change from workers. Despite this change in attitude union delegates were still ignored by the prime minister (see Source LL).

KEY TERM

Friendly societies
Associations of workers set up to provide insurance, pensions and savings or co-operative banking.

SOURCE LL

A letter of protest about a union delegation being ignored by the Prime Minister

The cool and very degrading manner in which the truly anxious exertions of the humble but meritorious members of the several trades in London were received this day CAN NEVER be effaced from our memories, as being in every respect so totally in opposition to the declared sentiments of Sir R. Peel that he would answer for our kind reception. Our hopes have been most miserably disappointed (the great and useless expense and serious loss of time being a minor consideration) but we at the same time most unanimously state our conviction that a deputation from Mr Hunt's Partisans would have been received with more attention and would not have been so unceremoniously dismissed (after being very uselessly detained in the wet and cold for upwards of two hours) with the cheerless and heartless message that there was no answer.

> **How useful is Source LL in explaining the difficulties in establishing trade unions?**

Government reaction to demands for change

The king's ministers in the eighteenth century had little doubt about their right, as members of the upper class, to govern. They were also convinced that the liberty of individuals was best preserved by the minimum of legislation. However, to intervene in order to preserve social stability was acceptable and part of traditional government responsibility. It was generally believed that individuals pursuing their self-interest and in competition with others would benefit all of society as it would result in cheaper goods and offer employment opportunities. Society was still very hierarchical and in particular the countryside was dominated by ideas of deference to the authority of landowners and the Church. It was not expected that workers and labourers would challenge the status quo.

Government reaction during the French and Napoleonic Wars

However, industrial change and the growth of urban settlements as well as the ideas of the American and French revolutions challenged these beliefs. It was Pitt's governments of the 1790s that faced the initial demand for change. Not only were there challenges from radicals who wanted the political system changed, but the economic conditions also favoured revolution. Poor harvests in 1792 caused wheat and therefore bread shortages and this was repeated in 1795–96 and, added to a rising population, there was ever growing pressure on resources. The concentration of workers in factory towns served only to make the threat greater. Faced by the challenge of war with France and the lack of resources to deal with domestic unrest the government responded with a series of measures designed to crush radical activity. The government used agents to influence opinion by subsidizing newspapers and loyalist associations. These included the so-called Pitt's Clubs, loyalist groups intended to rival the radical clubs that were spreading the ideas of the French Revolution. The government rushed through a series of measures to deal with the 1797 mutinies that occurred and made life difficult for reformers by allowing attacks on them locally. So-called 'Church and King' mobs attacked radicals and dissenters. There were 200 prosecutions for treason and '**Habeas Corpus**' was suspended, which allowed those who had been arrested to be held without trial.

KEY TERM

Habeas Corpus This is the process by which a person who was arrested was required to be brought before a court or they had to be set free.

Table 2.14 Government measures against unrest, 1792–1800

Date	Government measure
1792	Royal proclamation against seditious publications
1794	Arrest of leading London radicals
1794	Habeas Corpus suspended
1795	After street demonstrations and a stone thrown at the King, the government passed the 'Gagging Acts'
	The Treasonable Practices Act forbade expressing views likely to bring King or government into contempt
	The Seditious Meetings and Assemblies Act. Meetings of 50 people or more needed permission and magistrates could disperse meetings if there were 'seditious observations'
1797	Seduction from Duty and Allegiance Act
	Act against Administering Unlawful Oaths
	These were both brought in following naval mutinies
1798	Arrest of members of a radical group called the United Englishmen
1799	Act for the More Effective Suppression of Societies Established for Seditious and Treasonable Purposes
1799–1800	Combination Acts preventing workers uniting for higher wages or better conditions

Government reaction under Lord Liverpool and the Tories 1815–30

Lord Liverpool came into office in 1812 following the assassination of the previous prime minister, Spencer Perceval. His government was well aware of how Pitt and his government had responded to the radical demands. In this tradition they responded in much the same way. In order to tackle the Luddite challenge, machine breaking was made a hanging offence. The government also made use of spies and agents in a similar way to Pitt and

KEY FIGURE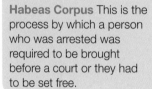

Lord Liverpool (1770–1828) Robert Banks Jenkinson was the son of an advisor of George III. He was first elected as an MP in 1790 and served as Home Secretary and Foreign Secretary before becoming Prime Minister in 1812. The first part of his rule is often described as 'reactionary' because it was characterized by repressive legislation designed to deal with the unrest that followed the Napoleonic Wars, whereas the second part of his administration in the 1820s is seen as more liberal as the economy improved.

directed the armed forces to deal with unrest. 'Habeas Corpus' was again suspended. Local authorities were given the authority to ban public meetings. These Acts were not new and revived Pitt's 'Gagging Acts'. The most comprehensive response to the demand for change was the Six Acts introduced after the Peterloo Massacre of 1819 (see textbox below). The government supported the action of the Manchester magistrates and troops and passed a number of measures in November and December 1819. The government also introduced the 1815 Corn Laws, or Importation Act. Although it was designed to ensure that the country had sufficient bread, it was seen by workers as a blatant piece of class legislation as it would keep the price of corn artificially high by preventing imports, while allowing landowners to maintain their profits. It led to riots in London and threats to Parliament from the mob.

The Six Acts

1 The Training Prevention Act made any person attending a gathering for the purpose of training or drilling liable to arrest. People found guilty could be transported for seven years.

2 The Seizure of Arms Act gave powers to local magistrates to search property or persons for weapons.

3 The Seditious Meetings Prevention Act prohibited the holding of public meetings of more than 50 people without the consent of a sheriff or magistrate.

4 The Misdemeanours Act reduced the delay in bringing those convicted of treasonous acts to trial

5 The Blasphemous and Seditious Libel Act provided stronger punishments, including banishment, for those involved in publishing writing against Church or state.

6 The Newspapers and Stamp Duties Act put a duty on journals and newspapers even if they contained just opinion not news. This hit radical publications.

ACTIVITY

What evidence is there to support the view that the government was repressive in the period 1790–1820?

These harsh measures have to be seen in the context of the economic climate (see page 96) and the fear of revolution. However, the period after 1822 when the economy recovered saw a change in government attitude. The government pursued an economic policy based more on the freedom of trade. Import duties were lowered, which encouraged trade, and the maximum duty on imported goods was set at 30 per cent. Foreign ships were allowed cheaper and easier access to British ports, which encouraged more trade in imported products. The Navigation Acts were changed to allow colonies freer trade, while trade with the newly independent countries in South America was encouraged. All of this encouraged business and stimulated the economy.

Reform under the Whigs in the 1830s

It was not just in the field of the economy that the government responded to demands for change. The 1830s in particular witnessed significant political changes. Reform was an important issue in the 1830 election, and instead of repression that had characterized the earlier periods, after many twists and struggles a Reform Bill was finally passed in 1832. It gave the vote to many of the middle class and helped to split them from the workers so that those who had some property were now represented in Parliament. However, many of the new industrial towns and cities were given representation. It meant that commercial and manufacturing interest acquired more influence even if Parliament was still under the control of landowners.

Although the government did not abandon repression as an instrument of policy, as seen with the treatment of the Tolpuddle labourers, the Swing Riots had raised the issue of rural poverty. This played a significant role in the passing of one of the most far reaching reforms, the Poor Law Amendment Act of 1834. Prior to this, those in need of help had been given relief in the form of cash or kind, known as '**outdoor relief**'. However, the cost of this had been rising as the population grew and therefore in 1834 the Poor Law Amendment Act was passed. This required those who could work and needed help to enter the **workhouse**. However, workhouses were designed to be so unappealing that few would go there unless they were absolutely desperate. This brought down the cost of relief, but created problems in industrial areas where the authorities were unable to cope with the numbers needing help in times of depression. The Act was also seen as inhumane as families were split up in the workhouses and conditions were often appalling.

The other major issue continued to be the price of corn. The Corn Law of 1815 had been modified, but by the 1840s it was one of the few commodities still protected by tariffs. The Prime Minister, Sir Robert Peel, had abolished or reduced duties on many good in his budgets of 1842 and 1845, providing a further stimulus to the economy, but the Corn Laws still remained. However, in 1846 they were also repealed. Although Peel himself believed in free trade, the issue split his party and eventually led to his downfall. The reasons for the repeal are an area of controversy. Some historians have argued that Peel was pressured into repeal by the Anti Corn Law League, a middle-class pressure group of industrialists who saw the advantage for workers of cheap food. Others have argued that Peel himself was convinced of the benefits of free trade for the economy, while others have said that it was the **Irish famine** that was the reason they were repealed. It was a symbolic moment as it represented a move away from the dominance of the landed interest to industrialists.

Governments appeared to be becoming more responsive to the demands of the people. They were beginning to take action regarding conditions in factories and the health of the people (see pages 89–93). However, these changes were slow in coming about and it would be the twentieth century

(see pages 89–93)

KEY TERMS

Outdoor relief The giving by local authorities of poor relief in the form of money, food, clothing or goods to those who needed it without them having to enter an institution.

Workhouse Parishes were required to set up places where poor people would have to work to earn money. In 1782 parishes had been allowed to join together to build and maintain workhouses and the 1834 Act made sure that by 1868 all parishes were in unions that had a workhouse.

Irish famine Potatoes were the staple food of most of the Irish peasant population. However, a potato blight in 1845 which destroyed the crop led to mass starvation and emigration.

ACTIVITY

Find evidence to support each of the following statements:

• The government reaction to demands for change was repressive.

• The government made concessions only when there was economic stability.

• The government was unwilling to reform because of concerns about revolution.

• The government was more responsive to demands for change in the period after 1830 than in the period before.

before all workers got the vote. The government was also still willing to use force and troops as the Chartists discovered at Newport and in their demonstrations in London (see pages 99–100). Yet the state was gradually widening its role and taking on greater responsibilities as would be seen in the later nineteenth and twentieth centuries, culminating in the establishment of the Welfare State, but that would be one hundred years later.

(see pages 99–100)

SUMMARY DIAGRAM

Why, and with what consequences, did industrialization result in popular protest and political change?

Response of the workers to industrialization	Group
Destroy machines	Luddites, Swing Riots, Blanketeers
Marches/demonstrations	Peterloo, Spa Fields
Demand the vote	Chartists
Organize combinations	Grand General Union of Operatives, GNCTU, Tolpuddle
Riots	Events before Great Reform, Act of 1832 – Nottingham, Bristol

Response of government to industrialization	Evidence
Legislation (repression)	Suspend Habeus Corpus
	Six Acts
	Ban combinations
Legislation (reform)	Reform Act 1832
	Poor Law Amendment Act
	Repeal of Corn Laws
Force	Troops against Luddites
	Peterloo

Chapter summary

The years from 1750 to 1800 had provided the initial boost to the industrialization process, but by the end of the eighteenth century factory production was still the exception rather than the rule, with only the textile industry seeing more large-scale mechanization. It was the period from 1800 to 1850 that saw the growth of an industrial economy, as industry replaced agriculture as the main source of national wealth. However, the move from an agricultural to an industrial society was not straightforward. There were periods of trade recessions and unemployment as well as major changes to the working and living patterns of many. This all led to periods of protest and social unrest,

when the workers complained about their living and working conditions that resulted from the economic changes. Initially, the government had been fearful of these protests and, in part because of the revolution in France and fear of its spreading, had responded harshly. However, as the nineteenth century progressed, the government gradually responded to the demands of the workforce and took on new responsibilities, passing legislation to control working hours and conditions, as well as living conditions. It was a slow process and there were still times when the demands of an increasingly politicized workforce were not met, as with the Chartists at the end of the period. Yet by 1850 workers had gained some recognition through unions and were starting to see some of the benefits as living standards for them began to rise.

Refresher questions

1 What changes did the agricultural revolution bring to farming?

2 What were the reasons for the rise in population 1750–1850?

3 How did investors raise money for industrial enterprises?

4 What was the importance of technological developments in the textile industry?

5 Why did the factory system develop?

6 What was the impact of the factory system on workers?

7 How did the development of the coal and iron industries help industrial growth?

8 What were the benefits of free trade?

9 In what ways did industrialization affect working and living conditions?

10 Why were women and children employed in factories?

11 In what ways did workers benefit from industrialization?

12 Why was there opposition to a reduction in working hours?

13 What did the Luddites and Swing Rioters want to achieve?

14 Why did workers demand the vote?

15 What attracted workers to support Chartism?

16 Why was there opposition to trade unions?

17 In what ways did the government respond to the demands of the workers?

 # Study skills

Paper 1 guidance: Sources

Evaluating sources using source content and provenance

Once you are sure what the source is saying about the issue in the question (not just what the source is saying, generally) you need to think what questions you need to ask yourself about its provenance (that is who wrote it, when it was written, where it was written and why). This means considering first of all what the evidence actually is. Is it a letter; is it a report; is it a record of a conversation; is it a speech; is it a memoir, is it a diary; is it a newspaper article?

The danger is that you will just assume that all diaries are reliable because the person involved in the historical events writes them; or all newspaper articles are unreliable because the journalists want to sell papers; or all records of conversation are useless because the person might not remember the exact words. Try not to generalize about evidence of this type but instead look at the particular source.

After looking to see what the source is, ask yourself some key questions:

- Why was it written? For example, if it is a speech, why was it delivered?
- Who is the intended audience? A diary or a letter will have a different audience from a public report or a newspaper.
- When was it written? Something written in the middle of a historical development, like the early years of industrialization in the 1760s when it is not clear what will happen, is very different from something written later when the outcome is known, for instance.

- How typical is it? For example, if a factory owner writes that he wants to improve conditions in factories, is this a usually held view by someone of that class?
- How useful is this source as evidence, even if you don't think it is 'true' or 'unbiased'? It might be, for instance, that a source is very supportive of the government for its response to Luddite protests. This might not be justified but is the source still useful as evidence for a widely held view that the government was repressive in the period 1812–20?

 ## Activity

Look at the four sources that follow and fill in the table below in answer to the following question: 'How far do the Sources A–D support the view that the Luddites were revolutionary?'

Source	What is it?	When was it written?	Why was it written?	Is it typical?	Is it useful?
A	A letter	1812 at the start of the Luddite activity	To issue a warning to a factory owner	Yes, he claims to have information that the factory uses shearing frames	Yes, as it is supposedly written by Ned Ludd
B					
C					
D					

Which do you think the most useful source here is? Explain your answer.

Most useful source	Explain why

SOURCE A

Part of a Luddite warning letter to a Huddersfield factory master, 1812

Sir,

Information has just been given in, that you are the holder of those detestable shearing frames, and I was desired by men to write to you, and give you fair warning to pull them down, that if they are not taken down, I shall detach one of my lieutenants with at least three hundred men to destroy them, and that if you have the impudence to fire at any of my men, they have orders to murder you and burn all your Housing.

We will never lay down our arms until the House of Commons passes an act to put down all machinery hurtful to the Commonality, and repeal that to the frame breakers – but we petition no more, that won't do, fighting must.

Ned Ludd

SOURCE B

A newspaper, the *Leeds Mercury*, reports on the destruction of machinery,
29 February 1812

*The depredators, or to use the cant terms, Luddites, assembled with as much privacy
as possible, at the place marked out for attack and divided themselves into two
parties, the more daring and expert entered the premises, provided with proper
implements for the work of destruction, which they accomplished with astonishing
secrecy and dispatch. The other party remained conveniently stationed to keep off
intruders. As soon as the work of destruction was completed, the Leader drew up
his men, called over the roll, each man answering to a particular number instead of
his name, they then fired off their pistols (for they were armed) and marched off in
regular military order.*

SOURCE C

A local militia captain in Oldham explains his views about the unrest to the
Home Secretary (Letter from William Chippendale to the Home Secretary,
22 May 1812)

*Of the disturbances which have taken place in this County, of the peculiar character
and desperate cast of those wretches who have been the fomentors of them and of the
object to which their diabolic efforts are directed I have lately become acquainted with
a Member, and one of no common activity, of the Secret Revolutionary Committee of
Royton, a place in which every inhabitant (with the exception of not more than five or
six) are the most determined and revolutionary Jacobins.*

SOURCE D

The major in charge of military operations reports to the Home Secretary
(Report from General Maitland Prescot to the Home Secretary, 23 May 1813)

*It gives me great satisfaction on considering the whole of the situation of this District
(County of Chester), and after weighing in my mind everything that has actually
occurred since I came here, to be able to state to you my decided conviction that
those who may be concerned in any real revolutionary object, are by no means in
so considerable number as is generally credited by many; and believing as I do their
numbers to be small, I am equally convinced their plans and objectives, such as they
may be are crude and indigested. I have no doubt that their great supporter was fear. I
do not believe that dissatisfaction will get any head, or that real mischief will increase to
any extent, provided a vigilant eye be kept over them.*

Comparing and contrasting two sources

In the previous chapter (pages 52–53) you were given advice on how to
compare two sources and a table that you could use to help you approach
such a question.

The example on page 112 shows a completed table using Source B and C
from pages 58 and 59.

Source	Points on which sources agree	Points of each source that show this	Reasons as to why sources might agree (Provenance)	Points on which sources disagree	Parts of each source which show this	Reasons as to why the sources might disagree (Provenance)
B	Improved farming methods Individual – in this instance Bakewell played a key role in introducing selective breeding	'improved on the husbandry of his neighbours' He merits particular notice	Written by A. Young, he supported the new ideas	Improvement by selective breeding Introduced new ideas	The principle is to gain the best, whether sheep or cow He hath in this part of his business many ideas which I believe are particularly new	Date written and purpose to record what he saw in his travels
C	Improved farming methods Individual – in this instance Townshend played a key role in bringing in the Norfolk rotation through the use of turnips	It is probable that this eight years was that of his improvements round Raynham But to be the father of the present great foundation of Norfolk husbandry is an honour that merits the amplest eulogy	Written by A Young, book designed to promote improved farming methods	Improvement by using Norfolk husbandry methods of four-course rotation Introduced some new ideas, such as turnips but not marling	There is reason to believe that he actually introduced turnips in Norfolk But the idea that he was the first who marled there is erroneous	Written later and with the purpose of promoting improved methods of farming

The key to a good answer would be a point by point comparison of the two sources. In this instance, both sources are in overall agreement that improvements were taking place in agriculture so it would probably be a good idea to begin with points of similarity. The answer could begin by explaining that both sources stress the importance of individuals in promoting improvements and that they were responsible for bringing in specific methods. You could support this with reference to both the sources and commenting on how Arthur Young would focus on this as he was keen to promote new ideas in farming. However, you could then go on to show they differ with B focusing on animal husbandry, whilst C focuses on crop rotation. Therefore, each source focuses on different elements of the agricultural revolution. This might be explained by the dates, with crop rotation possibly starting later.

Once you have made a point by point comparison which includes a consideration of the provenance of each source and use of some contextual knowledge, you would then make an overall judgement about their views on improvements in agriculture.

Paper 2 guidance: Essay questions

Writing an introduction

Having planned your answer to the question as described in the previous chapter (pages 53–55), you are now in a position to write your crucial opening paragraph. This should set out your main line of argument and briefly refer to the issues you are going to cover in the main body of the essay. The essays will require you to reach a judgement about the issue in the question and it is a good idea to state in this vital opening paragraph what overall line of judgement you are going to make.

It might also be helpful, depending on the wording of the question, to define in this paragraph any **key terms** mentioned in the question.

Consider the following question:

> 'Improvements in transport were the main reason for the rapid growth in industrialization after 1780.' How far do you agree?

In the opening paragraph of an answer to this question you should:
- identify the issues or themes that you will consider – these might be mechanization, the development of steam power, improvements in transport, growing demand
- state your view as to which of the factors was the most important.

This type of approach will help you to keep focused on the demands of the question rather than writing a general essay about industrial growth after 1780. It might also be helpful to occasionally refer back to the opening paragraph.

This approach will also ensure you avoid writing about the background to the topic, for example explaining developments that had taken place before 1780, which has no relevance to the question set. Another mistake is to fail to write a crucial first paragraph and rush straight into the question. Readers appreciate knowing the direction the essay is going to take, rather than embarking on a mystery tour where the line of argument becomes apparent only in the conclusion.

The following is a sample of a good introductory paragraph:

> The growth of industrialization depended a lot on the improvements in transport. Without better roads and canals and shipping, it was harder to get raw materials to workshops and factories. Better communications increased the goods taken to markets for sale and thus increased money for reinvestment. However, there were other key factors that have to be taken into account and compared with the importance of transport, such as population growth, the availability of capital, technical innovation and a favourable attitude by government towards economic growth. It may be that better communications were more a result than a cause of rapid industrialization.

Avoiding irrelevance

You should take care not to write irrelevant material as not only will it not gain marks, but it also wastes your time. In order to avoid this:

- look carefully at the wording of the question
- avoid simply writing all you know about the topic; remember you need to select information relevant to the actual question, use the information to support an argument and reach an overall judgement about the issue in the question
- revise *all* of a topic so that you are not tempted to pad out a response where you do not have enough material directly relevant to the actual question.

Consider the following question:

'Economic change was never seriously threatened by popular protest.' How far do you agree?

The following is a sample of an irrelevant answer to the question above:

> Chartism was a well-organized working-class protest movement. The Chartists were angry that the working class had not been given the vote in 1832, the crushing of the trade unions and the introduction of the New Poor Law in 1834. It developed in centres of the old decaying industries such as textiles and stockings, with the handloom weavers providing the backbone to the movement. The Chartists drew up a Charter containing their six points or demands. These included adult manhood suffrage, vote by ballot, equal electoral districts and the payment of MPs. Although they attracted a lot of support in the period from 1838 to 1848 support then died away.

Although the Chartists might be seen as part of the popular protest against industrialization, the paragraph at best offers some background as to whether they were a threat when it considers its appeal to those in the 'old decaying industries'. Much of the answer is focused on their demands and these are not linked to the idea that they were too radical to threaten the government. There is no real attempt to link the material to economic change as the six points were political and the answer would need to show that through political reform they wanted to bring about economic change. The answer is not completely descriptive but analysis is only implied and then not focused on the actual question.

LONG ANSWER QUESTION PRACTICE

The focus of this section has been on avoiding irrelevance and writing a focused vital opening paragraph. Using the information from the chapter, write an opening paragraph to two of the essays below, ensuring that you keep fully focused on the question. It might also be helpful to consolidate the skill developed in the last chapter by planning the answer before you start writing the paragraph.

1 'Industrial growth in the period to 1780 was limited to the textile industry.' How far do you agree?

2 How important was the iron industry in economic development in the period after 1780?

3 'The railways played a more important role than canals in the growth of industry in the period after 1780.' How far do you agree?

4 To what extent did industrial change lead to a decline in living conditions for the working class?

The short questions

It is very important to write analytically in both the essay questions and also the shorter questions that ask for explanation. The short question is not asking you to describe events or developments but is asking you to explain causes or consequences. For higher level marks you need to distinguish, too, between the relative importance of causes to show that you have thought about which might be more convincing.

Looks at these two extracts from answers. One describes and one explains.

Explain the importance of the steam engine in industrialization.

Extract A

The steam engine was invented by Thomas Newcomen. The original engines were used to pump water from mines and it was not until the end of the eighteenth century that the technology of Newcomen was modified by Watt and Boulton. Watt patented a steam engine that reduced the amount of fuel needed to power the engine. When Watt went into partnership with Boulton they then produced an engine that was cheaper and more reliable. A later modification created rotary movement so that the engine could be used to drive machinery. When Watt's patent ended in 1800 other firms began to produce the engines so that the number available grew rapidly.

The extract simply describes the changes and modifications that were made to the steam engine. There is little attempt, other than by implication, to link the material to the actual demands of the question.

Extract B

In the early period of industrialization the steam engine played only a minor role, pumping water from mines. It was only with the development of rotary motion that its full potential could be realized as it allowed steam power to drive machinery. The steam engine became even more important in the period after 1800 as Watt's patent expired and others made considerable improvements to his design. Not only did steam power revolutionize industry by powering machines, which increased productivity and the range of jobs that could be done mechanically, but it also had an impact on agriculture with the development of steam ploughs and threshing machines, but also in transport with the development of railways, which would transform the carrying of goods.

The second extract not only avoids telling the story but makes a distinction between long- and short-term causes and begins to argue about the relative importance of the engine over time.

EXPLAIN QUESTIONS

Using the information from the chapter, write an opening paragraph to two of the short essays below, ensuring that you keep fully focused on the question.

 1 Explain why there was a growth in the coal industry in the period from 1780 to 1850.

 2 Explain the importance of canals in industrial growth.

 3 Explain why there was opposition to industrial change.

 4 Explain the impact of industrialization on working conditions.

CHAPTER 3

Liberalism and nationalism in Germany, 1815–1871

Before 1789, 'Germany' was a geographical expression, not a country and consisted of over a thousand states. After 1815, this had reduced to 39 separate states but the chance of there being a unified Germany seemed remote. Austria dominated central Europe and surrounding powers were unlikely to accept a new Germany. Attempts at unity in 1848 had failed. However, by 1871 the whole situation had changed and there was a powerful new state dominated not by Austria, but by Prussia. This had been achieved by Prussian military and economic growth and by the adept diplomacy of its leading statesman, Otto von Bismarck. This chapter deals with the causes and consequences of the Revolutions of 1848 and the events and developments which led to the creation of the German Empire in 1871 through the following questions:

★ What were the causes of the Revolutions in Germany in 1848–49?

★ What were the consequences of the 1848–49 Revolutions?

★ What were Bismarck's intentions for Prussia and Germany from 1862 to 1866?

★ Why was the unification of Germany achieved by 1871?

KEY DATES

1806	Napoleon ends Holy Roman Empire	1863	Alvensleben Convention
1813	War of Liberation	1864	War between Denmark, Austria and Prussia
1815	Treaty of Vienna	1865	Convention of Gastein
	German Confederation formed	1866	Austro-Prussian War
1819	Carlsbad Decrees	1867	North German Confederation
1832	Hambach Festival		Luxembourg Crisis
1834	Zollverein formed	1869	Hohenzollern Candidature
1848–49	Revolutions in Germany	1870	Franco-Prussian War
1850	Humiliation of Olmütz	1871	Creation of the German Empire
1862	Bismarck becomes Minister President of Prussia		

What were the causes of the Revolutions in Germany in 1848–49?

In 1848 and 1849 nearly all of Europe except for Russia and Britain experienced major revolutions. Key elements were middle-class discontent about the lack of effective parliaments. In Germany there were also hopes for a new German nation which would bring together those who shared the German language and culture. The revolutions were also driven by economic discontent and popular unrest.

KEY TERM

Holy Roman Empire This is the name given to the lands of central Europe that owed allegiance to an overall emperor. There was little in the way of central government in this medieval union of princes and cities, which had its origins in the coronation of Charlemagne in 800, and in practice the lands were independent. Since the fifteenth century the emperor had been the rulers of Austria, the Habsburg royal family. It was formally dissolved by Napoleon Bonaparte in 1806.

The impact of Metternich's system on the states of Germany after 1815

Before 1806 the German-speaking states of central Europe had been in a loose union called the **Holy Roman Empire**, whose rulers were the Emperors of Austria. After 1815 Austria again led a German union but the control imposed on Germany was much greater. The major revolutions that broke out in Germany in 1848–49 were caused by a desire to overthrow the restrictions on German political and intellectual life imposed by Austria and its principal minister Prince Metternich after the overthrow of Napoleon in 1815 and the Congress of Vienna. Metternich was determined to stifle what he considered to be the main threats to Austria and to the rule of the European monarchs: liberalism and nationalism.

ACTIVITY

Make sure you know what is meant by the following concepts:

- Nationalism
- Liberalism.

Write brief definitions of these terms.

Prince Clemens von Metternich

Prince Clemens von Metternich (1773–1859) was the son of a minor noble in the Rhineland. Like his father he became a diplomat, rising to be the Austrian ambassador to Napoleon's France in 1806. He became Foreign Minister in 1809 in the wake of Austria's defeat by Napoleon. He favoured keeping the peace with France but did join the British-led coalition against Napoleon in 1813 when negotiations for a general peace failed. He worked to keep the coalition together and played a leading role in the Vienna negotiations after the war, acquiring Northern Italy for Austria and dominating Germany. He took a leading role in European diplomacy after 1815 and supported harsh measures to suppress unrest in both Austria and in other parts of Europe, opposing new ideas. He did not foresee the revolutions in Austria which forced him from power in 1848 and he lived in exile in Britain until his death in 1859.

Germany by 1815

Before 1789 Germany was a patchwork of different states, not a unified country. German as a language was spoken in many regions of central Europe but there was little to unify the different states other than language. And even then there were distinct regional variations. There were over a thousand different states, some large and some small. There were no republics and apart from some smaller areas ruled by leading churchmen, princes ruled most states. Ordinary people had little participation in government. There was an overall authority over most of what became Germany called the Holy Roman Empire. This was traditionally headed by the Emperor of Austria who also ruled considerable areas of land that were not Germanic – for example Hungary, the modern-day area of the Czech Republic and Slovakia, and part of modern-day Poland. The larger states were Saxony, Prussia and Bavaria. Their traditions were very different. Prussia, as was the case with much of northern Germany, was Protestant. Bavaria, as with much of southern and parts of eastern Germany, was Catholic. Some states had developed armies and governmental organizations and strong economies; others were little more than cities or small rural areas with miniature administrations.

The coming of the French Revolution and the rise of Napoleon Bonaparte transformed Germany. Prussia and Austria, the largest military states, were unable to prevent conquest by France. This began during the Revolutionary Wars (1792–1801) and was continued by the wars waged by the French ruler Napoleon who became Emperor of France in 1804. His armies dominated central Europe and he was able to abolish the Holy Roman Empire in 1806. He ruled some of Germany directly and some by setting up puppet rulers. This unified Germany to a considerable extent and led to modernization. The new German kingdom was subject to the more modern system of law and government that the French Revolution had brought to France. Prussia had to modernize after its defeat by Napoleon in 1806. Though it remained independent, it was dominated by France until 1812. Napoleon did not want to overthrow an established monarchy like Prussia and did not have the resources to occupy it in a way that he did the smaller states of western Germany. Austria was defeated by France in 1805 and again in 1809 and lost its dominance over Germany.

However, overambition caused Napoleon's downfall. He was unable to defeat Britain; he could not control Spain and he unwisely invaded Russia in 1812. In this campaign he endured considerable losses and in a series of battles in 1813–14 was driven out of central Europe and forced to abdicate in 1814.

The victorious nations – Austria, Russia, Prussia and Britain – were anxious not to see further influence of revolutionary ideas and to keep France contained. This meant ensuring that Germany was more stable and

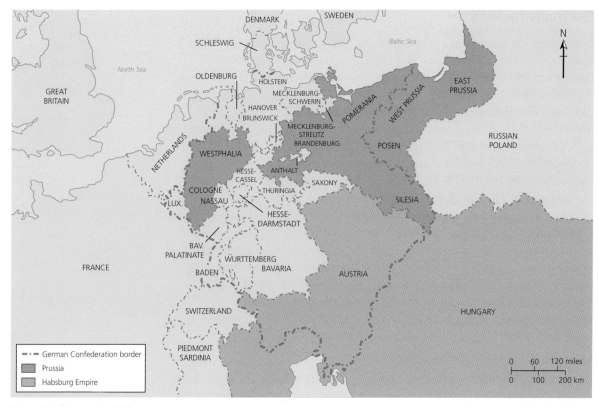

Figure 3.1 Germany in 1815

ACTIVITY

Reread the section starting on page 119 and compare and contrast Germany in 1789 and Germany in 1815. List changes and list what remained the same.

KEY TERMS

Constitution A set of rules by which a country is run.

Diets The name given to the assemblies of parliaments of the German states.

less open to attack. Prussia was expanded as a result of the peace conference at Vienna 1814–15 and given lands on the Rhine to prevent a further French invasion. The large numbers of German states that had made French invasion possible were amalgamated into just 39. The authority of the monarchs in these states was strengthened. The dominant power was Austria who was the head of a new German Confederation (the 'Bund').

Metternich and Germany

The chancellor or chief minister of Austria from 1821, Prince Clemens von Metternich, had played an important role in ensuring the defeat of Napoleon, and was committed to maintaining the authority of the monarchs and resisting the forces of change – especially nationalism and liberalism. Nationalism went against Austria with its large multinational empire dominating Germany. Liberalism, which aimed to give more people a say in government, went against the idea that only monarchs ruled and their only responsibility was to God, not to their subjects.

The states of the Bund had mostly adopted **constitutions** and had elected **Diets** but the power of these assemblies was very limited and only in the

South German state of Baden was there a very **liberal** constitution. It was easy for Metternich to ensure that the assemblies could not challenge the power of the rulers and he later forced censorship and political repression on them.

As Austria was the leading military power and the largest state in the Confederation, Metternich had considerable influence over its members. The rulers of Austria, Russia and Prussia had agreed in what came to be known as the Holy Alliance to resist any change in Europe and maintain the dominance of the monarchs, the ruling aristocracy and Church. There was to be no spread of nationalism and no introduction of parliaments, voting or free discussion. The subjects were to obey and respect their traditional masters.

However, Metternich faced forces in Germany that had been influenced by the new ideas of the French Revolution of liberty and equality. He also faced a new interest in nationalism – of a German state that would take in German speakers and reflect German ideas and culture. These ideas were alien to the outlook of an aristocrat like Metternich who saw himself as part of an international culture dominated by educated and enlightened nobles like himself who knew best what their rulers and their subjects needed. He looked back to the ordered world of the eighteenth century, while many, especially younger people in the German states, wanted to look forward to a new world of greater national unity and independence.

Metternich resorted to repression to maintain his 'system'. Abroad, he supported joint action by the great powers against any change to the Vienna settlement. Within Germany there were harsh laws against free expression. In 1819 the pro-monarchist playwright Kotzebue was assassinated by a student. Metternich called representatives of the larger German states together at Carlsbad and pushed through decrees controlling the press, supervising universities and setting up a central commission at Mainz to investigate and suppress revolutionary secret societies. In 1820 the Bund agreed to limit the topics that elected assemblies in individual states could discuss and also to confirm that armed force might be used in the case of individual states supporting revolution.

KEY TERM

Liberal Early nineteenth-century liberals believed that there should be elected assemblies to which governments should be accountable; and that states should not be allowed to ignore the rights of their citizens. These rights included freedom of expression and opinion, freedom to trade, freedom from arrest without charge and punishment without a lawful trial.

SOURCE A

Press Law of the Carlsbad Decrees, 1819

Publications that appear in the form of daily papers or as [periodical] issues, may not be conveyed to print in any German Confederal State without the foreknowledge and prior approval of the state authorities. If publications give any Confederal state cause for legal complaint, this complaint should be settled against the author or publisher of the publication.

All published writings appearing in Germany must be furnished with the name of the publisher and, insofar as they belong to the class of newspapers or periodicals, also with the name of the editor. Published writings for which this rule is not observed may not be circulated in any Confederal state and must, if such takes place in a secret fashion, be confiscated immediately upon their appearance, and the disseminators of the same, must receive an appropriate fine or prison sentence.

How far does Source A support the view that Metternich's control of Germany was tyrannical?

Clemens von Metternich, *Political Confession of Faith*, 1820

Union between the monarchs is the basis of the policy which must now be followed to save society from total ruin…

The first principle to be followed by the monarchs, united as they are by the coincidence of their desires and opinions, should be that of maintaining the stability of political institutions against the disorganized excitement which has taken possession of men's minds…

Let [the Governments] in these troubled times be more than usually cautious in attempting reform and change, to the end that good itself may not turn against them – which is the case whenever a Government measure seems to be inspired by fear.

Let them be just, but strong; beneficent, but strict.

Let them maintain religious principles in all their purity, and not allow the faith to be attacked and morality interpreted according to the social contract or the visions of foolish sectarians.

Let them suppress Secret Societies, that gangrene of society.

How useful is Source B in explaining why Metternich wanted to impose censorship and political control on Germany?

The censorship in Germany was widespread and extended from newspapers and pamphlets to works of history and literature. Schiller's famous play *William Tell*, written in 1804, was censored after 1819 because it showed the Swiss hero defying Austrian authority. Even Baden, which had a liberal constitution, dared not allow freedom of expression. The universities were purged of radical teachers and students. The King of Prussia had wanted to be more liberal but was forced by Austrian pressure and his fellow princes to enforce the repressive laws. Police opened mail, searched homes, used spies and informers.

In 1830 there was more unrest following news of a revolution in France, and Metternich responded by pressing Prussia and the larger states to agree to the Six Articles, which applied to the whole Confederation from 1832. These limited the rights of the diets or assemblies in constitutional states and reinforced the authority of the rulers. They also explicitly made the overall laws of the Confederation able to dominate individual state laws and stipulated that federal law superseded individual state law, thus further limiting the ability of individual states to pass liberal measures or limit rulers' power. The Ten Articles of 5 July 1832 prohibited unauthorized political organizations, meetings, appeals and festivals.

However, the resources available to the repressors were not those of modern dictatorial states. Radical thought was driven underground but not destroyed. Monarchs sometimes resisted conservatives – for example the King of Prussia refused the demands of conservative ministers to suppress all craftsmen's and workers' organizations. It was not possible to prevent national feeling or to suppress all liberal ideas. The revolutionary spirit could not be eradicated and in 1848 a wave of revolutions in Germany and the Austrian Empire forced Metternich to flee to Britain and ended his 'system'.

How effective was Metternich's system?

Metternich attempted to hold back change by using the influence of the most powerful of the members of the Bund to force the German states to apply censorship and police action against nationalists and liberals. However, this proved futile in the end because his system did not offer anything very positive to the people of Germany.

- The memories of Napoleonic rule remained strong and offered an alternative of a more unified and more liberal Germany.
- Early nineteenth-century censorship could not stop the spread of ideas even if they had to be read cautiously and secretly.
- The development of the German economy in the period to 1848 brought about change that the Metternich system could not easily control. Railways and factories brought greater urban growth and a changing workforce that undermined the traditional world of the eighteenth century that Metternich wished to maintain.
- The development of German culture in this period – painting, poetry, literature and especially music – that censorship did not control had the unforeseen result of encouraging a sense of German identity and nationalism.
- Austria was associated through Metternich with repression, and hostility to national hopes and aspirations. This undermined the Bund and ultimately led to the emergence of a Prussian-led Germany in 1871.

> **ACTIVITY**
>
> Reread the section on Metternich. Find material which justified each of the following statements:
>
> - 'Metternich was a responsible conservative who succeeded for a long period in bringing stability to Germany.'
> - 'Metternich imposed an outdated system on Germany which ignored its best interests and was doomed to fail.'
>
> How justified do you think both of these statements are?

SOURCE C

A cartoon of Metternich's flight from Vienna, 1848

> **What point is the cartoon in Source C making about Metternich's failure?**

The influence of liberal ideas and the emergence of a middle class

In the half century after 1815 the population of German-speaking Europe grew by 60 per cent from 33 to 52 million. The fastest growth was in areas where there was technological and economic change. This change did not transform Germany into an industrial society, but manufacturing and internal trade did grow. The road network went from 15,000 km in 1820 to 53,000 km in 1850. Canals expanded and the first railway was opened in 1835 and by 1848 there were 2000 km of track. Steam power also grew. There were 400 steam engines in 1834 and 1200 in 1850. Population grew rapidly in the cities and this in turn encouraged more intensive arable farming with a 40 per cent increase in cash crops from 1815 to 1850. The easing of traditional trade barriers within Germany meant greater trading and more wealth.

These changes led to a growing middle class. The country remained overwhelmingly rural with 72 per cent of people working on the land even by 1848. However, there were significant developments in key areas. The professions – for example, lawyers, doctors, teachers, lecturers, surveyors – expanded rapidly in the late eighteenth and nineteenth centuries. There was a growth in business activity and manufacturers, traders, shippers and the businesses associated with economic activity such as bailiffs, farm managers, insurers, bankers. There was also a considerable growth in culture and education – the numbers involved in professional music, theatre, art, literature and publishing grew. There were 16,000 students in higher education in Prussia in 1820 and this increased to 30,000 by the end of the 1830s and 100,000 by 1850.

There was also the development of the state bureaucracies. Though the nobles dominated the higher ranks, the administrations of the states were open to educated middle-class Germans.

The importance of this growth was that the ideas of liberalism and nationalism spread. The most receptive audience for ideas about political, social and economic change were the middle-class urban dwellers with the education to absorb new thinking. They were also receptive because of discontents.

The German middle class were often frustrated at the lack of opportunity in states whose higher offices were dominated by the traditional nobility. They resented the control that the rulers backed and encouraged by Metternich had over freedom of speech. The worst combination was the existence of constitutions and diets (parliaments) which allowed limited control by elected representatives over governments and their policies and restricted discussion. The censorship imposed by Metternich was particularly unpopular with well-educated middle-class Germans. The economic growth was not enough to provide sufficient jobs for graduates and opportunities in state service were limited by noble privilege. Thus, there was growing discontent especially by the 1840s.

The desire for liberalism was not confined to the middle classes of Germany. It had been seen in revolutions in Spain and Italy in 1820; in France in 1830; in the movement for reform of Parliament in Britain which led to the reform of Parliament in 1832. German liberals did not all have the same aims but there were some unifying features:

● A belief in progress and opposition to the power of rulers and reactionary aristocrats and clerics.
● A belief in representative parliaments that would represent the interests of the people.
● A belief that there were natural rights for citizens against censorship, arbitrary imprisonment and oppression by rulers.
● A belief in freedom of individuals to prosper and be independent.

For Metternich the criticisms of the traditional rule of princes were international.

SOURCE D

A letter from Metternich to the Emperor, 1841, gives an unfavourable view of opposition in Germany

In all four countries, France, Germany, Italy and Spain, the agitating classes are principally composed of wealthy men, trying to gain personal advantage for themselves. They are paid officials, men of letters [writers], lawyers and those involved in education. Their aim is to improve their position in society.

What does Source D show about Metternich's view of nationalism?

However, this view did not take into account the amount of discussion of liberal ideas that went on among students, in chambers of commerce, in state assemblies and in debating societies. It also did not take into account that many liberals were businessmen, manufacturers, merchants and craftsmen.

In addition, it did not take into account the expansion of nationalism among the German middle classes. This did not always take the form of agitation to create a united Germany, but was often focused on promoting a sense of German identity and culture. For example in 1832 there was a festival at Hambach to promote nationalism. Those attending consisted of 29 academics, 57 students and 100 shopkeepers, merchants and manufacturers. The widespread interest in what was a golden age of German music, literature and art went beyond the agitators identified by Metternich.

SOURCE E

A student, Arminius Riemann, at the Wartburg Festival of 1817 speaks bitterly of disappointed hopes after the defeat of Napoleon by German troops in 1813

Four long years have passed by since the Battle of Leipzig defeated Napoleon. The German people then built up lovely hopes. They have all been frustrated! Everything has turned out to be disappointing. Much that is great and splendid could have happened but has not taken place. Many fine and noble feelings have been treated with mockery and contempt. Only one prince has honoured his word [to grant a constitution] and in his free land we are celebrating the festival of the Battle.

SOURCE F

A speech delivered during the Hambach Festival in 1832 by a lawyer, Philipp Siebenpfeiffer, who had helped to organize the event

Look at Sources E and F. Compare and contrast these sources on the condition of Germany.

Fatherland – freedom – yes! A free German fatherland – that is the meaning of today's festival. These are the words that have echoed like thunder throughout all the German territories, rattling the bones of all traitors to the German national issue, yet encouraging all true patriots. May Germany rise again from the debris under which time's force and the nobles' treachery have buried it.

And the day will dawn when Germans from the Alps and the North Sea, from the Rhine, the Danube and the Elbe rivers, will embrace as brothers; when all the suffocating regulations and tolls, all the symbols of division, obstruction and oppression will vanish. This is the spirit of today's festival, the spirit of the renaissance of our fatherland.

The greater the interest in German culture, the more was the desire for freer discussion and an end to the domination of Metternich. Though not all nationalists were liberals, there was a distinct overlap. This was to result in revolutions throughout Germany in 1848 and the establishment of a national parliament at Frankfurt.

This parliament had 336 members. In all, 80 per cent of them were university educated; 20 per cent were civil servants; 15 per cent were teachers; 16 per cent were lawyers; and 4.5 per cent were journalists and writers. Though only 10 per cent were businessmen, this may have been because most businesses in Germany were small and their owners could not afford to be away dealing with higher politics. The predominance of the educated middle classes in this key political development showed how important this class, even though a minority of Germans, had become in promoting a new more liberal and united Germany by 1848.

ACTIVITY

Reread the section above and list in order of importance the effects that the growth of the middle class had on Germany 1815–1848.

Compare your list with others in the class to see if you agree on the main consequences of this development.

The growth of nationalist ideas

Before 1789 there was little support for a united Germany and loyalties to individual states or regions were strong. German speakers were widely diffused through central Europe. There were religious differences between north and south and east Germany. Many educated Germans thought of

French as the language of civilization. There were many dialects and ethnic groups in the Holy Roman Empire and the Germanic world. What changed was the influence of the occupation of Germany by the French during the Revolutionary and Napoleonic period. This brought greater unity of law and administration to large areas of Germany. It saw a period of reform and modernization in Prussia. It also saw the resistance to French occupation that was to inspire later generations of nationalists. Student volunteers were formed into a company of volunteers by the Prussian officer **Adolf von Lützow**. They took the name 'Frei Korps' and were also known as 'the Black Troopers'. With their black uniforms and death's head insignia they acted as shock troops in the struggle against the French in the so-called 'War of Liberation' in 1813.

However, they were never numerically significant in the war against the French and there was no mass nationalist rising. Many Germans fought in, rather than against, Napoleon's armies, and the Battle of Leipzig was fought mainly by regular Prussian troops. The student soldiers, however, acted as an inspiration for nationalist student movements that arose after 1814.

Nationalism in the sense of a belief in a united Germany was not a mass movement but there were strong intellectual influences on the educated middle class. German philosophers like Herder, Fichte and Hegel wrote about the unique character of the German 'Volk'. Hegel was a great admirer of the Prussian state. There were those, too, who argued for a new German state. These included the poet Ernst Arndt who wrote of a 'Fatherland'. The most enthusiastic support for these ideas came in students' unions called Burschenschaften. The movement urged physical strength and athletic exercises and there was a strong vein of hostility to foreign influences and anti-Semitism.

The festival at the Wartburg in 1817 was to celebrate the sixteenth-century religious reformer Martin Luther as German national hero. It was here that the ruler of Saxony had protected Luther from being arrested and tried for his challenge to the Catholic Church.

Metternich and the princes repressed nationalism but it had strong if limited support and another festival – this time at Hambach in 1832 – which saw more countermeasures from the authorities. In the 1840s there was another wave of anti-French feeling with fears of French influence in Germany with nationalist groups holding illicit meetings and nationalist songs like 'Die Wacht am den Rhein' (the Guard of the Rhine) and 'Deutschland über alles' (Germany over all) becoming well known.

A more benign form of nationalism was the development of a strong German culture in the arts. The arts had thrived in eighteenth-century Germany but as part of a wider European culture. However, literature and poetry in the first half of the nineteenth century showed the beauty of the German language, especially when set to music by composers such as Schubert and Schumann. German opera and symphonic music became

KEY FIGURE

Adolf von Lützow (1782–1834) was a professional soldier from a military family. He fought against the French in 1806 and became an ardent opponent of Napoleon and a Prussian nationalist. He fought as a volunteer against the French in 1809 and was wounded. He was allowed to form a force of guerrilla fighters known as the Frei Korps or the Black Troopers. His troops were badly defeated in 1813 and disbanded in 1814. He continued to serve in the Prussian army.

world renowned. Weber and Wagner explored Germanic legends and folklore. The development of Berlin showed the power of German architects and the paintings of artists like Caspar David Friedrich had a distinctly German theme of romantic forests, ruined chapels and wintry landscapes. The Brothers Grimm explored folk tales and fairy stories.

Probably this cultural development was far more important in promoting a sense of pride in German-ness than the patriotic societies and the political groups.

Wanderer above the Sea of Fog, 1818, by Caspar David Friedrich

This painting in Source G has been seen as representing troubled times. How would you use knowledge of Germany in 1818 to support this view?

ACTIVITY

Reread the section on Nationalism. Find evidence to support the views below:

- German nationalism was most significant in the arts and should not be exaggerated as a movement for change.
- German nationalism was a powerful and important movement by 1848.

Which do you think is more convincing and why?

KEY TERM 🔑

Sorbs or Wends By the mid-nineteenth century there were about 165,000 of these Slavonic people with their own language, customs and culture living in the border areas between modern-day Germany and Poland.

SOURCE G

By 1848 there had been a significant growth in awareness of German identity but there was no consensus about a future German state. The problem lay in defining a possible new 'Germany'. Would it include Austria, the most important state in the Confederation of 1815 even though its Emperor ruled over a host of Eastern European nationalities? Those who believed so thought in terms of a 'Grossdeutschland' (greater Germany). Or would a new Germany consist only of the purely German states? There was a problem, too, with this 'Kleindeutschland' (smaller Germany) as Prussia had taken lands from Poland at the end of the eighteenth century and also included Slavonic elements like the **Sorbs or Wends**. Thus a 'small Germany' would still encompass lands of very different traditions and religious beliefs. It would be difficult to establish the boundaries of any new Germany and such a state would not easily be accepted by the surrounding powers, especially France.

To move from a general interest in and admiration for all things German to actually creating a new Germany seemed a remote possibility even by 1848 and only the dream of a minority. Most German speakers retained their loyalty to their individual states and the overwhelmingly large rural population had a limited interest in nationalism in any form.

The impact on Germany of the Zollverein

The economic disunity caused by a whole network of customs barriers in and between the different states seemed to reinforce the political disunity in 1815. Taking goods from one part of Prussia to another at the start of the nineteenth century could involve paying 63 different customs duties. Germany had huge numbers of customs posts and economic progress was severely hindered by a lack of internal free trade. As part of a general modernization, Prussia removed its internal customs barriers in 1818. Because its territories were separated and other states lay between the Rhine and its main eastern lands, it negotiated agreements with the intermediate states to remove barriers in 1819. This led to other Germanic states forming commercial unions. A general agreement was made between the Prussian union and the other unions in 1834 and was known as the **Zollverein** (customs association or union). This was a significant event.

- Austria was excluded so its leading role in the German confederation was weakened. It would not have been possible to include the vast amount of non-German lands in the Austrian Empire in the customs union. Most other German states were linked in an economic agreement but Austria was not.
- The leader in establishing this customs union was Prussia, which established the possibility that Prussia might take the lead in greater German unity.
- The freer trade encouraged greater prosperity, especially in Prussia whose industries, trade and road and rail networks grew
- The ending of customs restrictions encouraged the growth of railways, which acted as a unifying factor between the German states.
- Greater prosperity encouraged both urban growth and the growth of the German middle class.

KEY TERM 🔑

Zollverein This means customs (zoll) union or association (verein). A customs union is an area in which members trade without paying tariffs or payments when goods are moved from one area to another.

SOURCE H

An English observer in the 1840s writes about the Zollverein

The Zollverein by directing capital to internal in preference to external trade has had a great influence in improving the roads, the canals, the means of travelling, and the transport of post – in a word giving additional impulse to inland communications of every sort. On every side beneficial changes are taking place. Railways are being constructed in many parts of the German territory – steamboats are crowding the German ports – everything is being transported with greater cheapness and rapidity. Saxony has profited most, being more advanced in manufacturing than most of the German states. To her it has opened up a market of 26 million consumers.

How useful is Source H for showing the impact of Germany of the Zollverein?

ACTIVITY

Marx thought that revolutions were brought about by economic change. Discuss from the basis of your study of history how important you think economic factors have been in bringing about wider changes.

The Zollverein did not produce political unity in itself. Within Germany there remained suspicion of Prussia, especially in the Catholic south, which saw the largest state in this economic union as militaristic with a different Protestant religion. However, it did establish greater economic unity and there was a body set up to regulate customs called the Customs Parliament, which included most of Germany and not Austria, and so undermined the Austrian-led Confederation.

Social and economic problems in the 1840s and their importance for the revolutions of 1848–49

The 1848 revolutions were brought about not merely by middle-class Germans desiring greater unity and liberalism but also because of the discontent of workers and peasants brought about by economic hardship and social resentment.

Long-term social and economic problems

There were long-term trends that threatened to bring discontent in Germany.
- Resentment against the censorship and controls of the Metternich system.
- A growing middle class, increasingly well educated and influenced by ideas of liberalism and nationalism.
- Moves towards greater economic unity which encouraged more desire for more political unity.
- More national awareness in terms of the arts and culture which encouraged more people to think in terms of German unity.

However, given the limited number of urban dwellers and the predominance of rural life and the power of the states to enforce the Metternich system, these trends alone would not have been likely to result in political revolution. What changed the situation in the 1840s was the growth of economic and social problems resulting from population growth.

The population growth since 1815 had put pressure on agriculture. While it opened up more opportunities to sell produce, it meant that many people left the countryside and moved to towns. More available labour created opportunities for larger factories and extended workshops. However, this changed the nature of employment. In place of the close relationship between small employers and traditional craftsmen where master and men worked together and there was a paternal ethos where employers felt a duty to look after the welfare of their workers, there was more distance between employers and their workforce. Greater trading opportunities increased the desire for profits and, as with many countries that saw greater industrial and economic growth in the first part of the nineteenth century, there were problems with working conditions. Hours were often long, and cheaper female and child labour was exploited. Though not massively industrialized, German did see changes to its workforce. The greater availability of labour had a depressing effect on wages.

In addition, rising populations meant that there was a rise in prices. Especially after 1845 there was quite rapid inflation. Living standards suffered and discontent grew. In some slum areas of Berlin in the 1840s, 2500 men, women and children lived in 400 rooms in great tenement blocks. Unemployed men could be classified as beggars and put to work on treadmills in special workhouses.

The rise in technology and larger workplaces also hit traditional crafts. Much of industry before 1815 had been conducted on a small scale in the home. Textiles had been particularly important and the handloom weavers were the backbone of the industry. With more use of power looms and larger units, the domestic weavers suffered a decline.

Life was hard not only for many workers and craftsmen but also for peasants. There had been many who had left the land in the 1840s either for cities or to emigrate to the USA. Rents were high and many aristocratic landlords were ruthless in exploiting their workers or taking over common land to make profits from the growing internal trade.

Radicalism

The problems of the 1840s were the background to a new interest in political ideas. Radicals saw a new system based on the pursuit of money and undermining the conditions of workers. The most famous was the Rhineland journalist Karl Marx who condemned the exploitation of the **proletariat** by the new capitalist class and was angry at the decline of traditional trades, arguing that new production methods alienated the worker from what he produced, making workers merely exploited wage slaves in a capitalist system.

The dependence on markets also meant that more were liable to periods of unemployment and hardship. The emerging doctrine of **socialism** attacked the whole business system, arguing that profit was the result of exploitation and denying the workers the just price for their labour. The only remedy was to overthrow the entire system and give political power to the workers.

Short-term economic problems

An immediate crisis was caused by poor corn harvests in 1846 and 1847 and also by a potato blight that affected Germany and other parts of Europe, especially Ireland. Potatoes were not only a cash crop but a major part of rural diets. The famine produced by these failures caused widespread starvation and unrest. Corn prices rose by 50 per cent and this meant that workers in cities paid a much higher proportion of their wages simply to survive. On top of this came a trade recession in Europe generally, which meant wage reductions and layoffs.

The situation by 1848

A toxic mix had emerged by 1848 of rural and urban hardship, resulting in alcohol and subsequent domestic abuse, unemployment, poor housing and

KEY TERMS

Proletariat Karl Marx, the theorist of Communism, gave this term to the industrial working class that had emerged from the industrial revolution and the growth of large-scale factories.

Socialism This is the political belief that the state should own the major means of production and should be run for the benefit of those who produce, not those who own land and factories or businesses or make themselves rich through investing money (capital). Their profits are seen as a result of exploiting workers.

health. Political ideas like socialism and democracy fed on this discontent in the same way that middle-class grievances led to the greater interest in ideas of constitutional government and nationalism.

These economic and social problems were not unique to Germany. Much of Europe experienced:

- a rising industrial workforce facing the threat of unemployment, low wages and poor living conditions in expanding cities
- an agricultural population under pressure from rising population and not having enough work or land
- a rising middle class resentful of aristocratic domination and inadequate social opportunities – either to gain employment in state government or in business
- memories of the French Revolution and ideals of liberal representative government for the middle classes, the overthrow of royal and aristocratic power and more democracy for the ordinary people.

The outbreak of revolution in France in 1848 was the cause of widespread revolution in Europe. In Germany the different discontents came to a head and resulted in a major challenge to the settlement of 1815.

ACTIVITY

Draw up a table showing different causes of the 1848 Revolution in Germany in one column; in a second column briefly explain the importance of each cause; in the third column 'mark' the importance of the factor on a scale of 1 to 6 with 6 being the most important. In the final column explain your 'mark'.

SOURCE I

How useful is Source I for explaining why there was revolution in Berlin in 1848?

This journalist wrote about living conditions among the poorest workers in Berlin. From Heinrich Bettzeich, *The Physiology of Berlin*, 1846

They had nothing. Not a bed nor a table, without firewood, clothes, shoes or stockings, no work, no money, no potatoes, no prospects, no consolation, no charity. Hope only of the workhouse or a miserable death in the poor house – only rags and straw and dirt and vermin and hunger, hunger howling in their entrails.

SUMMARY DIAGRAM

What were the causes of the Revolutions in Germany in 1848–49?

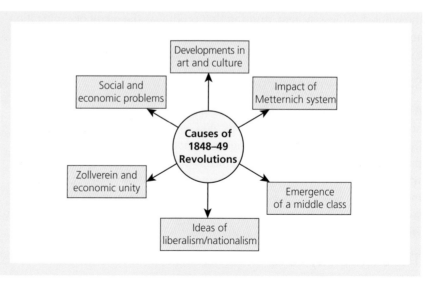

ACTIVITY

Briefly explain how each factor brought about the 1848–49 Revolutions.

What were the consequences of the 1848–49 Revolutions?

The revolutions of 1848 were serious but did not succeed in their aims of establishing a new Germany. The older rulers returned in the wake of military suppression of revolutions. However, in the longer term the revolutions had major consequences.

A summary of events 1848–50

The news of the overthrow of the French monarchy in a revolution of 1848 led to unrest in Germany. The first states affected were those of the south where there was more of a liberal tradition. The King of Bavaria was unpopular and there had already been unrest in that state. A series of local revolts broke out in Germany reflecting different discontents. Peasant unrest was widespread with attacks on landowners and tax officials. There were some revolts inspired by socialist ideals and a desire for a republic. In many states there were calls for more powers to be given to the assemblies. In Austria there were disturbances that led to the fall of Metternich and his flight to Britain in March. In Prussia the so-called 'March Days' occurred. Widespread demonstrations led to the killing of over 200 demonstrators by troops. The Prussian king Frederick William IV gave way under pressure and accepted many demands.

Unrest forced similar concessions in other German states. The unrest took on a new dimension with the meeting of delegates from various German states in late March to arrange for a new National Constitutional Assembly at Frankfurt. The initiative came not from Prussia but from the minister of the small state of Hesse-Darmstadt, the liberal Heinrich von Gagern. The hopes of the spring were not, however, realized. Divisions soon appeared among the revolutionaries and a conservative reaction developed. The middle classes began to fear popular unrest. In Austria the power of the Emperor was restored by loyal troops. When the revolutionary impulse subsided, the Prussian king was able to regain control and troops restored royal authority in October. The Tsar of Russia who had not been faced with revolution gave his support to the restoration of Habsburg control in Eastern Europe. Austria was strong enough to prevent a new German union and by 1850 the old German Confederation was restored and many of the liberals were exiled or imprisoned. Popular unrest had been repressed. Revolutionaries like Marx had been driven out of Germany. The authority of landlords, factory owners, police, army and traditional rulers had been restored.

KEY TERMS

Bill of rights A legislative guarantee to citizens of a country that their liberties will be respected and that they will not be subject to arbitrary rule.

Franchise The right to vote in elections.

KEY FIGURES

Ludwig I of Bavaria
(1786–1868) was King of
Bavaria between 1820 and
1848. A patron of the arts
and passionate about
Greek culture, he was a
prolific builder. Initially
liberal he became more
conservative after 1830. He
alienated conservatives by
his relationship with the
actress Lola Montez (Eliza
Gilbert) and also faced
popular unrest in 1844 and
1848, when he abdicated.

**Frederick August II of
Saxony** (1797–1854) was a
progressive young prince.
He was regent from 1830,
with his father introducing
reforms to Saxony. He
became king in 1836 and
continued a reforming
policy. He appointed liberal
ministers in 1848 but
dismissed them in 1849.
Angry crowds forced him
to flee until he was restored
to power by Prussian and
Saxon troops. He was
killed by falling in front of a
horse in 1854.

**Frederick William IV of
Prussia** (1795–1861)
reigned as King of Prussia
from 1840. He was a keen
builder and improver and
developed Berlin. He had a
belief in the traditional role
of king and aristocracy and
refused to accept the offer
to be Emperor of Germany
in 1849. He restored
monarchical authority after
the Revolution of 1848 but
was not a dictator and
accepted a new
Constitution, which lasted
until 1918 in Prussia.

The initial responses of the German states to the 1848 Revolutions

The speed of events in February and March 1848 accounts for the sudden collapse of resistance by the states to the forces of change. Faced with pressure from elected assembly and from many middle-class and respectable officials and professionals, the rulers abandoned hopes of crushing the revolts by armed force. They were conscious that it would not be possible to rely totally on military power without a very considerable loss of life. They were also conscious of the fate of the French king Louis XVI who was executed by his own people in 1793 during the French Revolution.

There was more of a liberal tradition in the smaller states of South Germany and these were the first to make concessions. On 27 February 1848 a meeting of citizens in Baden demanded a **bill of rights** and even greater powers for the assembly, already one of the most liberal in Germany. Similar meetings were adopted in Württemberg, Hesse-Darmstadt, Nassau and other German states. Strong popular support for these movements forced rulers to give in to many of the so-called March Demands. There was more resistance in Bavaria where royal troops suppressed demands, but here both conservatives and liberals opposed the king **Ludwig I** because of his unpopular mistress Lola Montez and he abdicated. Previous developments such as the granting of liberal constitutions in the South and the particular unpopularity of the King of Bavaria helped to explain the initial response in the South.

In the North, the disturbances also produced change without initial resistance from the established governments. Not all of the German rulers were despotic in outlook. The King of Saxony **Frederick August II** accepted change peacefully in 1848. The Saxon government resigned in March 1848 after demands for change. The liberal Karl Braun introduced the abolition of censorship, the reform of the **franchise**, reform of the judiciary, the regulation (i.e. public recognition) of clubs, societies, associations; having the army to swear an oath on the Constitution. Not until May 1849 were there violent clashes in the capital Dresden. In Prussia, King **Frederick William IV of Prussia** had no wish to be a military dictator and was distrustful of military power and conservative advisors. Here, too, there were initial concessions.

Probably crucial was the sudden collapse of Metternich's control. When Austria went into revolution, the mainstay of princely power in Germany was removed. Some of the smaller states did not have the resources to repress their populations and when the Prussian monarch made concessions, others could hardly resist.

The immediate changes that the Prussian king accepted were the creation of a middle-class Civic Guard to maintain order; the calling of a new assembly to draw up a new constitution that would reduce the power of the monarchy and allow for more representative government; and an acceptance of German nationalism.

SOURCE J

The revolutionary Karl Schurz was a student in Bonn in 1848. He joined the revolution but fled in 1849 to the USA where he later became a senator. His *Reminiscences* (1907) were published after his death

Great news came from Vienna! The fall of Prince Metternich! The students organized themselves as the armed guard of liberty. In the great cities of Prussia there was a mighty commotion. Not only Cologne, Coblenz, and Trier, but also Breslau, Königsberg, and Frankfurt-am-der-Oder, sent deputations to Berlin to entreat the king. In the Prussian capital the masses surged upon the streets, and everybody looked for events of great import.

While such tidings rushed in upon us from all sides like a roaring hurricane, we in the little university town of Bonn were also busy preparing addresses to the sovereign, to circulate them for signature, and to send them to Berlin. On the 18th of March we too had our mass demonstration. A great multitude gathered for a solemn procession through the streets of the town. The most respectable citizens, not a few professors, and a great number of students and people of all grades marched in close ranks, enthusiasm without bounds broke forth. People clapped their hands; they shouted; they embraced one another; they shed tears. In a moment the city was covered with black, red, and gold flags, and not only the Burschenschaft, but almost everybody wore a black-red-gold cockade on his hat. [Red, black and gold were the German national colours.]

> **How useful is Source J for explaining the reaction of the German states to the initial disturbances in March 1848?**

SOURCE K

In this Berlin cartoon of March 1848, the Prussian King Frederick William IV is shown, supported by the army, shutting out demands from his middle-class subjects for a new constitution

> **Compare and contrast the attitudes to revolution shown in Sources J and K.**

The collapse of the Frankfurt Parliament

The idea of a **Constituent Assembly** or Vorparlament for the whole of Germany was a radical idea but stood little chance of success. Its 800 members met with high hopes in the St Paul's Church in Frankfurt in May 1848 but the experiment ended in May 1849 without achieving a new German state. There are a number of factors that are often said to account for this.

SOURCE L

The Frankfurt Parliament, painted in 1848

> **How far does Source L suggest that the Frankfurt Parliament was a significant body?**

An unrepresentative body

The first is the unrepresentative nature of the membership of the assembly with the educated middle-class professionals predominating and limited representation from both manufacturing and trading interests and the landed proprietors and peasants – even though over 70 per cent of Germans were not bourgeois urban dwellers. Far from offering decisive action, the assembly members spent a lot of time on detailed legalistic discussions and it was not until October that a draft constitution for Germany was produced, and a bill of rights proposed. By this time the revolution had lost impetus and had become divided.

Divisions

The second is that there was no fundamental agreement on what the new German state would be. Some advocated a greater Germany including Austria and some of its empire but not Hungary. The Catholic South had more in common with Austria than the Protestant North. The other solution was a smaller Germany excluding Austria, but that would mean the dominance of Prussia. Prussia's lands made up two-thirds of a reduced Germany and it was not universally trusted or admired in Germany. By October it was accepted that the Kleindeutsch solution would be adopted but again by that time a reaction against change had set in.

Limited appeal

The third explanation is that the assembly offered little for the mass of Germans, especially the peasants, and that the Revolution lacked popular support. The middle-class delegates supported property rights. Even the abolition of feudal dues was to be accompanied by compensation to the owners. There was little acceptance of demands for state intervention to protect workers or protective tariffs to avoid cheap foreign farm imports that the peasants and landowners wanted.

Overreliance on Prussia and its army

The fourth explanation is based on the overreliance of the assembly on Prussian military power in a dispute with Denmark. The Danish king had wanted to incorporate the provinces of Schleswig and Holstein into Denmark. The German Confederation opposed this but had to rely on the Prussian army.

However, the main reason was that the assembly had been part of a wave of enthusiasm for change in March and April 1848. Through the summer of 1848 there had been increasing divisions within the German states between the middle-class moderates and those who wanted to make more decisive social and political changes. The loss of impetus allowed conservative elements to become stronger and to advocate ending the revolutions by force. The monarchs had not lost the loyalty of their armed forces, which remained strong. When the time was right the forces of monarchism began to regain control. In October there was a reaction in Prussia with a virtual royal coup as troops occupied the capital. The new assembly in Prussia was dissolved. In Saxony the reform cabinet was dismissed in 1849, which led to bitter fighting in Dresden, the capital, between more radical revolutionaries and the armed forces of both Saxony and Prussia, which brought the revolution to an end. The Habsburg monarch reasserted its control not only of the Germanic lands in Austria but also over Hungary, Poland and its Slav territories by the use of military force supported by the Tsar of Russia. The revolutionaries of 1848 were not determined or united enough to resist these changes, which were mirrored in many of the other German states.

The crucial turning point for the Frankfurt Assembly was the refusal in March 1849 of King Frederick William IV of Prussia to accept the position of emperor of a new united Germany. Famously he said that he would not accept 'a crown from the gutter', i.e. offered by the people. Prussian military power was not adequate to deal with a challenge from Austria over the dominance of Germany. Conservative pressure, too, led him to put the interests of the Prussian monarchy before the difficulties and expense of being a new German emperor.

Faced with a more powerful Austria, increasing divisions, the violence in Dresden and the limited agreement on major policy issues, the Frankfurt Assembly looked increasingly weak. It had announced a new constitution in

ACTIVITY

In a table list all the reasons you can find in the section starting on page 136 and your own research for the failure of the Frankfurt Assembly. Give each one a mark of between 1 and 6 (1 = not very important, 6 = very important). Create an essay plan in response to the following question: Assess the reasons for the failure of the Frankfurt Assembly.

March 1849 but it was never put into practice. The assembly dissolved itself in May. Radical members carried on in Stuttgart until June when troops finally dissolved it and suppressed resistance in Baden.

> **What accounts for the different view of the role of the Prussian monarchy in Sources M and N?**

The importance of the reassertion of Austrian power and the humiliation of Olmütz

The key to events in Germany lay with developments in the Austrian Empire. The overthrow of Metternich had resulted in the monarchy making concessions. Famously the Emperor had said 'tell the people I agree to everything'. Faced with revolution in Italy, Hungary and unrest in the German and Slav lands, the scale of unrest was too much and too sudden to be met with force. A radical constitution was accepted and a Constituent Assembly called. Unrest was so acute that the Emperor was forced to leave Vienna in May 1848.

The recovery of Austria

However, even by the summer there were indications of recovery. Risings in Italy were put down and Austria defeated nationalist forces under the King of Piedmont at the battle of Custoza. The Constituent Assembly that met in June in Vienna was divided and ineffective and there was little agreement between German speakers and other nationalities such as the Czechs. Imperial forces crushed an attempt to create an independent Czech state in June.

The break away by Hungary found little support among the German revolutionaries. Radical unrest in Vienna was finally crushed by the Austrian army under its commanders Windischgrätz and Jelačić in October 1848. The moderates were divided from the radicals by a new constitution offered in March 1849. In Hungary, Austrian forces aided by Russian troops used overwhelming force to defeat an independence movement with a final victory at Vilgos in August 1849.

A break with the weakness of the past was made when Emperor Francis abdicated and was replaced by the young Crown Prince Franz Josef who remained Emperor for the rest of the century. Conservative forces, especially the army, had restored Habsburg power. A crucial element had been the support of Russia whose Tsar Nicholas I was a firm believer in **absolute monarchy**.

The return of Austrian domination

Thus by the summer of 1849 Austria was strong enough to be able to resume her domination of Germany.

- It had strong and victorious armies which had defeated nationalism in the Czech lands, Poland, Hungary and Italy.
- It had the military support of Russia and its powerful army and reactionary ruler.
- It faced a divided Germany whose main attempt at the creation of a rival German state had failed.
- Its only possible rival was Prussia, but the Prussian armed forces were not strong enough to resist Austrian pressure.
- Prussian conservatives would not have supported any conflict with Austria and the Prussian king was not a dominant or decisive figure.

The result of this was a national humiliation for Prussia. In the aftermath of the revolutions, Prussia had not entirely tried to put the clock back but rather to gain nationalist and liberal support. In April 1849 there was a Prussian constitution. Absolute rule was not imposed but the new constitution was very favourable to the conservative landed classes. The lower house of parliament was elected by a **three-tier system** that gave landowners and the richer middle classes much more influence than less affluent elements. A third of the representatives were elected by only the wealthiest and most powerful 5 per cent. In any case, the parliament had limited power. The royal government was not responsible to parliament, and there was an upper house of nobles whose consent was also necessary for any laws. However, there was some measure of constitutional rule. As well as maintaining a constitution, some in Prussia did not want to end all progress towards greater unity, but wanted to ensure that Prussian conservative interests would be dominant in any new association of German states.

KEY TERMS

Absolute monarchy This is rule by a monarch who is free to pursue any policy and has no responsibility to any elected assembly or to their people. Absolute monarchs often claimed they had been chosen by God and were responsible only to God.

Three-tier system Each district was divided into three classes of voters according to the amount of tax paid. Generally the richest (Class 1) were around 5 per cent, the next richest (Class 2) were 13 per cent while the majority (82 per cent) were Class 3. Elections were held in the open and only men aged over 21 could vote. Each class in each electoral area chose a third of electors who in turn voted for the deputies of the parliament. So the richest 18 per cent voted for two-thirds of the electors while the bulk of the population opted for one-third. This undemocratic system persisted in Prussian elections until 1918.

An advisor to Frederick William IV, **General von Radowitz**, aimed to link the hopes of the German middle classes more to the Prussian state by a union with Saxony and Hanover. This would be different from the proposed Kleindeutsch policy of the Frankfurt Parliament in that the states were dominated by political conservatives and monarchists. It would share the conservative three-tier franchise of Prussia rather than the more democratic constitution of the Frankfurt Assembly. As it was the best hope for national unity, some 150 former Frankfurt deputies agreed to it at a meeting at Gotha. Under pressure from Prussia and its armies some 28 states joined the Erfurt Union by the end of August 1849. During the period of negotiations, Austria had been preoccupied with suppressing the movement for Hungarian independence. However, it opposed the Union. The Austrian government put pressure on Saxony and Hanover to leave the Union and supported conservative opposition in Prussia. The conservative constitution of the Union was opposed by democrats in Germany and the princes ceased to support it. A conference of German princes voted to delay establishing a constitution for the Union. Austria instead re-established the old Confederation or Bund under its leadership.

Relations between Prussia and Austria worsened to the point of a likely war. Russia backed Austria in opposing the Union. Conservative groups in Prussia swung the King towards abandoning the Union but the impression was given that Prussia had given way to Austrian pressure at a conference at the town of Olmütz on 29 November when Prussia announced that it had demobilized its forces and accepted the restoration of the Bund and, thus, an end to the Erfurt Union. The hopes of the Frankfurt nationalists for a Prussian-led independent Germany were ended. There was little that Prussia could do to oppose Austria given the more powerful Austrian forces and its support from Russia. The climbdown became known as 'the Humiliation of Olmütz' and was seen as a mark of shame for Prussia.

By 1850 an intelligent observer might have concluded the following:
- German nationalism by itself would not be enough to create a new Germany.
- A new German state would emerge only if Austrian power could be defeated or overcome.
- Conservatives in Prussia would not support a new state if it was associated with liberal ideas.
- Russian influence would be an obstacle to a new German state.
- Prussia was powerful enough to impose economic leadership on other states, but its army could not risk a conflict with Austria, especially if Austria was backed by Russia.
- There was still, after the defeats of 1848–49, a desire for a more unified Germany among the German middle class.
- Prussia remained the most likely state to bring about greater unification.

The importance of economic developments after 1849 and the Zollverein

Between 1850 and the eventual establishment of a Prussian-dominated German Empire in 1871 there were a number of important developments that changed the economy and society in Germany. The tensions of the 1840s gave way to what have been seen as 'the quiet years'. This is true politically, as the upheavals of 1848 and 1849 were not repeated. However, there was a period of rapid economic change. The ending of restriction from traditional trade guilds in Prussia meant the growth of free enterprise. It was easier to set up factories and by 1860 there were 2000 industrial enterprises employing more than 50 workers. There was a virtual revolution on the land as feudal obligations and serfdom were finally ended with 640,000 Prussian peasants being free from control and able to farm independently. This not only increased food supply but it gave industry a much-extended internal market. German industry and trade benefited from a general European prosperity in the 1850s as well as having internal free trade of the Zollverein. Internal trade in Germany doubled between 1850 and 1857. Railways doubled in the 1850s from 5800 km to 11,300 km.

Almost all economic statistics in the period show rapid growth. Steam engine capacity went from 260,000 units of horsepower to 850,000. Pig iron production increased from 229,000 to 529,000 tons. Cotton production increased from 900,000 spindles to 2.2 million.

The key driving force behind industrial growth was textiles. The shift from small-scale workshop production to mass production based on steam power was seen not only in larger states like Austria and Prussia but also in the South, in Baden, Württemberg and Bavaria. This in turn generated demand for increased coal production, which saw a rapid expansion. Technical change encouraged the growth of pig iron smelted by coke. Using coke instead of charcoal increased the scale of production and the quality of the iron.

The demand for more machinery and technical improvements encouraged a growth in engineering. Precision tools developed which meant there could be mass production of interchangeable parts. With this growth came the development of greater engineering knowledge and education, and a growth in skilled workers. Thus by the 1860s Germany had developed its economy because it had key elements needed for economic growth, namely:

- a supply of labour because of ongoing population growth
- free internal trade
- improving transport – railways, better roads and steamships as well as canals and navigable rivers
- governments sympathetic to free enterprise
- technical skills
- raw materials
- a stronger internal market with a free peasantry.

> **ACTIVITY**
>
> Test your understanding of key terms by describing what each of the following means:
>
> - Zollverein
> - Kleindeutsch
> - Grossdeutsch.

In addition there was growth in the German financial sector with banks willing to lend money and support enterprises. There was also an increase in paper money – there was 50 times more paper money in circulation by 1860 than there had been in the 1840s. This helped consumer industries and facilitated trade.

There is little doubt that economic growth encouraged national unity. Easier transport, the movement of workers, the greater interchange of products between different regions all broke down the barriers between different regions that had been such a feature of eighteenth-century Germany. The growth of interest in nationalism shown by the membership of the National Society and also of various specialist all-German associations of engineers, lawyers, gymnasts, musicians, businessmen, workers and political groups showed that regional divisions were breaking down.

Economic change also had a considerable effect on German society. There was the growth of a distinct class of industrial workers that Marx called the proletariat. This had doubled between 1848 and the 1860s to a million. Whole towns or urban districts had become 'working-class' areas. They had interests in common that crossed state boundaries. Workers in textile factors in, say, Bavaria, had common concerns with those in Prussia. This should not be exaggerated – there were 2.2 million independent craftsmen and shop owners in the 1860s and the majority of Germany remained rural. However, German society was rapidly changing.

Many saw that economic developments might eventually produce a united Germany. By 1860 this was seen as most likely to be Kleindeutsch because it would emerge from the Zollverein which continued to exclude Austria. Thus much has been claimed for the Zollverein as a cause of later unification.

However, there are some objections to this argument.
- The Zollverein was one element in bringing about growth but it was not the only element. It had been in existence since the 1830s, but rapid industrialization occurred only in the 1850s and 1860s.
- Austria was outside the Zollverein and still experienced economic growth. The idea that Prussia grew while Austria stagnated is not true. Austrian textile production more than doubled in the 1850s. Its rail network expanded from 1620 km to 5400 km. Its imports doubled and its exports tripled. Steam power tripled and iron production doubled. All this occurred when Austria was outside the Zollverein.
- Also, there was no certainty that the members of the Zollverein would support a political union when Prussia was so dominant and would amount to two-thirds of any new Kleindeutsch German state. This was vividly shown in 1866 when Prussia finally went to war with Austria and the Zollverein states sided with Austria (see page 129).

ACTIVITY

Make notes on pages 141–142 under the heading 'Economic developments in Germany 1849–1866' using sub-headings and bullet points.

The Zollverein helped to build Prussian economic power and influence but it was by no means certain that it would develop into anything more than an economic union.

SOURCE O

A liberal newspaper in 1857 writes about the links between economic and political unity

There is an intimate connection, in Germany, between the national economic development and the need for national political development. The commerce and transportation of a country demand one code of law, one national legislation, one defence policy to protect trade. These needs have been satisfied in other countries, but not within Germany. A common code of law, common legislation for the whole of the country, remains a pious wish, unlikely to happen, and our traders are defenceless abroad.

> How far does Source O support the view that economic unity was likely to bring greater political unity in Germany in the 1850s?

Long-term	Short-term
Monarchical states	Failure of Frankfurt Parliament
Need to compromise/modernize	Feudalism removed
Economic developments and	Parliamentary Government in
Prussian recovery	Prussia
Austrian economic and	Revolutions crushed
financial problems	Overthrow of Metternich
Austro-Prussian rivalry	Austrian recovery
Capitulation of Olmütz 1850	

SUMMARY DIAGRAM

What were the consequences of the 1848–49 Revolutions?

3 What were Bismarck's intentions for Prussia and Germany from 1862 to 1866?

In 1862 a dominant figure emerged as Minister President (premier) of Prussia. Otto von Bismarck was to dominate European diplomacy until 1890 and his leadership is a vital factor in the unification of Germany in 1871. He had little sympathy for liberalism or nationalism. His background as a Prussian aristocrat or **Junker** made him concerned only with the interests of Prussia and its monarchy. He was realistic to the point of cynicism and had little time for abstract ideas or ideals. Yet he took the cause of German nationalism further than any of the idealistic nationalists of 1848. He made highly effective use of changing circumstances and also of Prussian economic and military power and was one of the very greatest diplomats in European history.

KEY TERM

Junker The term for a Prussian landed aristocrat, often seen by the use of the word 'von' (of). Bismarck's full title was 'von Bismarck-Schonhausen'.

Why was Bismarck appointed as Minister President of Prussia in 1862 and what were his attitudes to liberalism and nationalism?

Bismarck came to power because of a political crisis in Prussia. In 1858 illness and mental breakdown made it impossible for Frederick William to continue to rule Prussia. His brother William became regent and subsequently king. This began a so-called new era with new reforming policies. Among these was the reform of the army. **Albrecht von Roon** was appointed Minister of War in 1859. When Austria had gone to war against France in Italy in 1859, the Prussian army was mobilized. However, the mobilization had shown weaknesses in organization and war readiness. Von Roon's task was to reform Prussia's army. He proposed creating a larger force by adding 23,000 men. This would mean creating 49 new regiments and also developing a more professional force. Prussia had relied a lot on a substantial part-time reserve force called the Landwehr or citizen soldiers. Von Roon wanted to separate this from a larger fully professional full-time force.

His proposals met with a great deal of resistance in Prussia's parliament – the Landtag. Liberal deputies regarded a professional army with suspicion after its role in suppressing the revolutions of 1848–49. They objected to the costs and also to the downgrading of the citizen soldiers of the Landwehr whom they saw as a safeguard against any future attempt to use the army to impose absolute rule. They used their votes to block expenditure to pay for the army reforms. In May 1862 the opponents of reform gained a majority in the Landtag.

This was a crucial time. If Prussia were to be able to challenge Austrian domination it needed an improved army. It could not be a great power without a professional and well-equipped military force. The economic changes had given it the potential for influence, but as the Declaration of Olmütz showed it would be under Austrian domination without military reforms. The clash between parliament and the King's government was a serious one. If the Landtag could block spending then it could dominate policy. But if the King overrode parliament and ignored the constitution then it could mean a recurrence of revolution and a reliance on brute military force.

It was a dangerous time and needed a strong personality. Von Roon summoned Bismarck from Paris with the famous telegram '*Dépêchez-vous. Periculm in mora*' ('Hurry up' in French; 'Danger in delay' in Latin). William thought that Bismarck might well bring revolution and civil war but nevertheless appointed him Minister President in September 1862 because of his reputation among conservatives and the advice of von Roon that he had the strength of purpose and unyielding character to force through the vital military changes.

Bismarck was an extreme character, but this was seen as a make or break situation. Give in and Prussia would become a weak power dominated by liberals who wanted a new nation state but without the military force necessary to achieve it. Standing up to parliament meant risking the end of the monarchy and a bloody struggle between conservatives and liberals.

Bismarck put the issue clearly to the budget committee of the Prussian parliament (Landtag) on 19 September 1862:

'Prussia must build up and preserve her strength for the advantageous moment which had already come and gone many times. Under the Treaty of Vienna, Prussia's borders were not ensuring the healthy existence of the state. The great questions of the day were not settled by speeches and parliamentary majorities – that was the mistake of 1848 – but by blood and iron.'

This was a key statement. Prussia had lost the opportunity to lead a new conservative union in 1850 (see page 140). It lost the opportunity of taking advantage of Austria's war against France in 1859. It could not go on with its territories separated from each other by other states. The revolutions of 1848 had shown the limitations of mere discussions. Economic strength and military action were the key to Prussia's development. There was nothing here about German nationalism and there was a scorn for 'speeches and parliamentary majorities' which indicated precious little respect for constitutional politics. Instead there was a brutal realism – what is known as '**realpolitik**'. What lay behind this was a cold calculation. After observing the events of 1848 and 1849 Bismarck did not think that the parliamentary opposition or the middle-class liberals would take their opposition beyond speeches, meetings, articles and general indignation.

His view is summed up in an exchange with William I, which appears in Bismarck's memoirs. The King is supposed to have said 'They will cut off your head – and mine afterwards!' Bismarck is supposed to have replied 'And so …? We will all die sooner or later. Can we perish more honourably than I fighting for your majesty's cause and your majesty fighting for his God given rights?' For Bismarck the cause was Prussia not Germany; for the monarchy, not for the constitution.

KEY TERM

Realpolitik Politics that considers not ideals or aspirations but takes a hard look at national interests.

SOURCE P

Otto von Bismarck: letter to the Prussian prime minister von Manteuffel, 1856

Because of the policy of Vienna [the Congress of Vienna, 1815], Germany is clearly too small for us both [Prussia and Austria]; as long as an honourable arrangement concerning the influence of each in Germany cannot be concluded and carried out, we will both plough the same disputed acre, and Austria will remain the only state to whom we can permanently lose or from whom we can permanently gain … I wish only to express my conviction that, in the not too distant future, we shall have to fight for our existence against Austria and that it is not within our power to avoid that, since the course of events in Germany has no other solution.

How useful is Source P for showing Bismarck's intentions towards Austria?

Field Marshal Helmuth von Moltke writes about the war with Austria in 1866

The war of 1866 [between Prussia and Austria] was entered on not because the existence of Prussia was threatened, nor was it caused by public opinion and the voice of the people; it was a struggle, long foreseen and calmly prepared for, recognized as a necessity by the Cabinet, not for territorial aggrandizement, for an extension of our domain, or for material advantage, but for an ideal end – the establishment of power. Not a foot of land was exacted from Austria, but she had to renounce all part in the hegemony of Germany… Austria had exhausted her strength in conquests south of the Alps, and left the western German provinces unprotected, instead of following the road pointed out by the Danube. Its center of gravity lay out of Germany; Prussia's lay within it. Prussia felt itself called upon and strong enough to assume the leadership of the German races.

> Compare and contrast the view of war with Austria in Sources P and Q.

Bismarck's influence on Prussian politics and the importance of his relations with William I and the Prussian Landtag in promoting the growth of Prussia

Bismarck's solution to the problem of lacking funding for army reform was to devise what he called the 'gap theory'. The constitution was said not to have envisaged a breakdown of government so rather than having a 'gap', which prevented the normal running of the state, the government could collect taxes without parliament's consent. This was a piece of rather desperate constitutional theory to disguise what amounted to bypassing parliament and resorting to a dictatorship. Bismarck was not an elected leader: he relied totally on royal power. The constitution was being ignored and the very basis of any sort of parliamentary regime undermined. Though there seemed to be little alternative, Bismarck did not have the full commitment of William I or his Queen, who hated him. It was not a situation that could go on indefinitely and without some successes it was unlikely that Bismarck's term of office would last.

A cartoon of Bismarck in Parliament, 1870

> What is the point that the cartoonist in Source R is trying to make? How would you use knowledge of Bismarck's relations with parliament to assess the validity of this evidence?

SOURCE S

Bismarck explains his view to the Landtag, 27 January 1863

The constitution upholds the balance of the three legislative powers [i.e. the king's government headed by Bismarck, the Upper House and the Lower House] with respect to the budget. None of these powers can force the others to give way. The Constitution therefore points the way to compromise. If compromise is thwarted in that one of the three powers wishes to enforce its own views in a doctrinaire way, compromise will be impossible and conflict will take place. The life of a state cannot stand still so conflicts become a question of power. Whoever has the power goes ahead with his views, for the life of a state cannot remain still even for a moment.

> **How does Source S show that Bismarck believed more in 'realpolitik' than constitutions? Compare this with Source T below.**

SOURCE T

Bismarck, shown with part of a traditional Prussian spiked military helmet on his head, is holding the Constitution of Prussia and saying, 'I can't rule with this'. From the satirical magazine *Kladderadatsch*, 1863

The protests of the liberals were ignored. Bismarck fought hard to strengthen the wavering support of the King. The army reforms went ahead. In the end this was a turning point. It confirmed Bismarck in power so that the first critical moves towards unification could be taken in 1863 and 1864. It allowed for the development of the army which in the end was the vital element in the unification by the defeat of Austria in 1866 and the subsequent defeat of France in 1870 (see below). It confirmed that there was a new if brutal realism at work in Prussian leadership which was to ensure victory even if at a cost. It also confirmed that liberal and parliamentary development in Prussia was to take second place to the needs of the army and that Prussian growth was to be dominated by conservative monarchism.

The domestic dispute confirmed Bismarck's authority and permitted him the freedom to pursue vital elements of foreign policy. Crucial was the insistence that William I did not attend a conference proposed by Austria to reform the German Confederation. Much against his inclination, the King agreed. Bismarck did not want Prussia to follow any initiative from Austria. His long-term aim was to end the Austrian-dominated Confederation, not to reform it.

The second major initiative was his decision to co-operate with Russia in suppressing unrest in Poland. Both Prussia and Russia had taken Polish lands when the Polish state collapsed and was divided among its neighbours at the end of the eighteenth century. In 1863 the Poles under Russian control went into revolt. In the Alvensleben Convention Prussia agreed to joint action to suppress Polish resistance. Though this proved unpopular and Bismarck had to backtrack and simply agree to be neutral and not to aid the Poles, it established good relations with Russia, something that was to be of vital importance in the diplomacy of the 1860s and the move towards unification.

What was the importance of Bismarck's relations with and policies towards Denmark and Austria 1864–66?

In June 1862 Bismarck met the British statesman Disraeli in London. According to Disraeli, Bismarck said 'As soon as the army has been brought to a condition to inspire respect, I shall seize the first pretext to declare war on Austria, dissolve the German Bund, subdue the minor states and give national unity to Germany under Prussian leadership.' How far Bismarck had a plan and how far he had a general aim and used circumstances when they arose has been a matter of historical debate (see Extension box at the top of page 149).

Bismarck: Master planner or improviser?

There has been a historical debate about the importance of Bismarck and whether he was a master planner who envisaged the direction that a new Germany would take, or whether he was merely an improviser who had some general objectives but no very clear idea how to put them into practice. Older historical studies tended to see Bismarck very much as a master planner.

According to H.A.L. Fisher's influential book *A History of Europe* of 1935:

'Only the most elaborate military and diplomatic preparations could ensure the success of German unification. The titanic figure of Bismarck … envisaged from the first the conditions of the German problem and allowed no scruple of conscience to interfere with the execution of his plans.'

The historian A.J.P. Taylor, in his book *Bismarck: The Man and the Statesman*, 1955, saw a much less clear-cut plan:

'By 1863 he came to realize that European politics could not be forced into a pattern by a man of ruthless will.'

For some historians, like Otto Pflanze (1963), even though he did not have a detailed plan he had 'a strategy of alternatives' and his skill was choosing the right one and setting up a situation that allowed him to choose. Some see him, like the biographer J. Steinberg (2012) as 'a political genius'. Some like E. Feuchtwanger (2002) see him using 'the circumstances and pressures' of his time.

Bismarck's own memoirs paint a picture of an all-knowing far-sighted statesman pursuing a goal.

ACTIVITY

Using information in this chapter, including primary sources, and any additional reading, find evidence for each of these views:

- 'Bismarck had few set ideas about how to unify Germany but just improvised and responded to events.'
- 'Bismarck had a clear vision for increasing Prussia's power over a united Germany.'

Which do you think is more convincing and why?

The Schleswig-Holstein issue

Opportunity arose in a quarrel with the kingdom of Denmark over the provinces of Schleswig and Holstein. The Danish king ruled these two border areas as duke and they were part of the German Confederation. They had a mixed German- and Danish-speaking population. In 1863 the King of Denmark died, leaving no direct heir. His throne was inherited by Christian of Glucksberg – but his claim to Schleswig and Holstein was disputed. German nationalists thought that Frederick of Augustenburg had the rightful claim. But the Danish king who ascended to the throne in November 1863 annexed the Duchies. The feeling in the Bund was to take action to install Frederick as duke and keep the Duchies part of the Confederation. However, Bismarck did not want to see any victory by the Bund, which he wished to destroy, not strengthen. He persuaded the Austrians to take joint military action against Denmark. In January 1864 there was an invasion by Austria and Prussia. A peace conference failed and fighting resumed in June. The two Duchies were occupied by Austria and Prussia.

However, there was no agreement on their future. Bismarck wanted to annex them to Prussia. Austria wanted to install the Duke of Augustenburg to keep them in the Bund as self-governing states. In 1865 the two countries finally agreed by the Convention of Gastein to divide the Duchies. Holstein would be run by Austria and Schleswig by Prussia. However, Prussia and Austria would have joint sovereignty over both Duchies.

The issue of the succession to the Duchies was incredibly complex. The British foreign secretary, Lord Palmerston, claimed that only three people understood the issues – one had died; one was mad and the third – himself – had forgotten. The importance of the dispute and the military action that followed can be summarized:

- The authority of the Bund was undermined. Instead of joint German action, the issue was decided by an agreement between Prussia and Austria alone. The Bund's favoured candidate was not installed.
- Prussia gained Schleswig in practice, if not in terms of law.
- Prussian forces showed themselves brave and successful against the Danes and Prussian patriotism was stirred by the war and the victory in April 1864 at Dybbøl in Denmark. (The ease of Prussian victory is often overstated; the Danes had formidable defensive positions at Dybbøl where the main battle took place and some powerful artillery and warships. The fighting was bitter and there were some severe casualties on both sides.)
- The great powers of Europe stood aside and allowed Prussia and Austria to gain lands – the lesson was drawn by Bismarck that intervention in future conflicts was not likely.
- The war provided justification for further military expansion and showed the potential of the use of force.
- The opportunity for conflict over the Duchies was created if Bismarck wanted to provoke a war with Austria.

SOURCE U

Bismarck writes to the Prussian ambassador in Paris after the Danish War in 1864

You believe that there is some hidden virtue in German public opinion, parliaments, newspapers and the like which might support or help us in a policy of creating a German union. I consider that a radical error. Our strength cannot proceed from a press or parliamentary policy but only from our position as a great military power. I consider at the moment our correct policy at present is to have Austria with us. But whether the moment of separation comes and on whose initiative it will come, we shall see. I am by no means averse to war – quite the reverse.

How useful is Source U in showing that Bismarck was planning a war with Austria as a result of the Danish War?

War with Austria

The war with Austria was the major turning point of Bismarck's leadership. Since the 1850s he had understood that the military defeat of Austria was the key to Prussian expansion and dominance of Germany. The administration of Schleswig and Holstein could provide the excuse for war, but other factors led him to hope that Prussia could be successful.

- Economic and industrial expansion had given Prussia a strategic rail network that could be used for transporting troops quickly, and a superior weapon – the needle gun. This was a breech-loading rifle, which fired more rapidly and accurately than the Austrian weapons. It was developed as a result of German engineering skills and manufactured in factories using standardized parts and modern techniques.
- The army reforms had begun to create a more professional Prussian force and there was an effective military leader, Helmut von Moltke, who understood the principle of assembling and concentrating forces quickly and decisively. The experience of modern war in the Danish conflict was also useful.
- Austria could not count on allies. Its traditional links to Russia had been weakened because it had not supported its former ally during the **Crimean War** that Russia fought against Britain and France in 1854–56.
- Relations between Russia and Prussia had been improving and Bismarck did his best to ensure French neutrality by talks with the French leader Napoleon III, hinting at possible compensation for France if it stayed out of a future war between Prussia and Austria.
- Austria itself had been weakened by a war fought in Italy in 1859 when its forces had been defeated by France and it had lost control of most of its valuable Italian lands in 1861.
- Industrially, Austria was less developed than Prussia, but rather than general economic weakness being a factor it was the limited railway links to Austria's border with Germany that was a key factor.

Bismarck had managed to get an alliance with Italy in 1865 which took advantage of the war between Austria and Prussia the following year to try to regain the province of Venetia which had remained Austrian in 1861. However, the bulk of the German states supported Austria. Bismarck had ignored their wishes in 1864 over Denmark and Prussian military expansion was distrusted.

In 1866 Bismarck successfully forced Austria into war. He encouraged agitation in Holstein against Austrian rule; he demanded control of all military forces in the Duchies and proposed plans for a new canal through the Duchies – the Kiel Canal to link the Baltic Sea and the North Sea. On 9 June 1866 Prussian forces entered Holstein.

The war that Bismarck provoked in 1866 was not a foregone conclusion. It was a considerable risk. Austria was not a weak power. A long war might well have brought foreign intervention. It would also have brought to a head opposition at home. William I was unhappy at waging war against a fellow Germanic monarch and was conscious that most of the rest of Germany was against Prussia. Everything hung on a rapid victory.

Largely because of Austrian military incompetence and the rapid movement of German forces into Bohemia, this was what Prussia achieved.

KEY TERM 🔑

The Crimean War (1854–56) was a war between Britain, France and the Ottoman Empire on one side and Russia on the other. France and Britain were eager to prevent Russian expansion into the Ottoman Empire. The war was fought in the Crimean peninsula. Austria did not support Russia despite the help it had received in 1849. A series of costly battles led to a British and French victory which excluded Russian warships from the Black Sea and destroyed the Russian naval base at Sebastopol.

The war lasted only seven weeks and there was a decisive battle at Sadowa (or Königgrätz) on 22 July 1866. The Prussians, even though their forces overall were smaller, had managed to get 221,000 troops to the front to fight 206,000 Austrians. The outcomes of this determined the fate of Germany.

SOURCE V

The Battle of Sadowa, 1866

What impression does Source V convey? Do you think it was likely to have been produced by the Austrians or the Prussians?

What was the importance of the outcomes of the Austro-Prussian War of 1866?

The war saw the end of Austrian domination of Germany. The Austrian Empire re-orientated itself eastwards and took on Hungary as an equal partner in 1867, creating the Austro-Hungarian Empire. Together the Austrian Germans and the Hungarian Magyars dominated the eastern European subject races of the Empire and accepted the loss of power in both Italy and Germany.

The Peace of Prague signed in August 1866, which Austria signed with Prussia, was deliberately lenient. There were no victory parades, no annexations of Austrian land. Venetia in Italy was given to Italy, despite Austrian military successes against the Italians. The German Confederation was dissolved, but Austria otherwise remained intact. Bismarck did not want to add any Catholic or non-German territories and he wanted to keep the option of future diplomatic relations with Austria.

SOURCE W

Bismarck's advice to William I prior to the war with Austria, 1866

We have to avoid wounding Austria too severely; we have to avoid leaving behind in her unnecessary bitterness or desire for revenge. We ought to keep the prospect of becoming friends again. If Austria were severely injured, she would become the ally of France. Acquiring Austrian lands such as Austrian Silesia or Bohemia would not strengthen the Prussian state. Vienna cannot be ruled by Berlin as a mere dependency.

> **How useful is Source W for assessing Bismarck's diplomatic ability?**

Austria's allies in Germany suffered more than Austria itself. Prussia annexed Schleswig and Holstein, Hesse-Cassel, Hanover, Nassau and Frankfurt. Four million Germans became Prussian subjects. Frankfurt was forced to pay a large fine to Prussia. The King of Hanover was expelled and his fortune confiscated. The expanded Prussia became the largest and most dominant state in a new confederation – the North German Confederation.

The Southern states did not lose territory, nor did they pay compensation for opposing Prussia, but they were drawn into alliance with Prussia. If Prussia were attacked then the forces of Southern Germany would be placed under Prussian control and the South would lose its independence.

The greatest outcome of the war was the creation of the Kleindeutsch state that the revolutionaries of 1848 had so desired, though it had been created in a way that they had certainly not wanted. This was given a new constitution which was extended to the whole of Germany in 1871.

The new German confederation was a federal state. Each of the states kept its separate governments, except for those that had been annexed. They had their own laws and own rulers and own assemblies. They raised local taxes and provided local services like education.

The overall authority for the North German Confederation was the Prussian king, who was the permanent president of the Confederation and his government – i.e. Bismarck. The new government controlled key areas of defence, trade and foreign policy. Laws affecting the whole confederation were to be made in the new parliament. The upper house or Bundesrat consisted of representatives from each state. These were sent (not elected) according to size. Prussia, the largest state, sent 17 out of 43 representatives. Saxony sent 4 and most other states simply sent 1. The lower house – the Reichstag – was elected by **universal male suffrage**.

This seemed progressive, but it was a means of ensuring that the middle-class liberals who so opposed Bismarck were weakened rather than strengthened. In any case, the Reichstag had limited powers. The lower house had control of the federal budget, but most of this was devoted to military spending. This was too vital an aspect for Bismarck to let out of his

KEY TERM

Universal male suffrage
The right of all adult men to vote.

control, so there was to be no vote on this until 1872. Any measure passed by the Reichstag needed the approval of the upper house and the President of the Confederation, so the rights and responsibilities of the elected part of the constitution were very limited.

A domestic outcome of the war with Austria was a swing in opinion away from liberal opposition to giving greater approval to Bismarck's virtual dictatorship since 1862. In the elections to the Prussian Landtag in 1866 conservative and pro-Bismarck supporters increased their vote while the liberal deputies were reduced from 253 to 148. The enthusiasm for Prussia's rapid victory and the creation of a new Germany was so great that a new party – the National Liberals – was created which supported Bismarck's policy. Together with the main conservative party – the Free Conservatives – Bismarck had a working parliamentary majority. Significantly, the disputes over the military budget were put to one side by an **Indemnity Bill** in which parliament gave retrospective legality to Bismarck's undermining of the constitution since 1862. In retrospect it was the death of any hopes for a liberal Germany and the victory of 'blood and iron'.

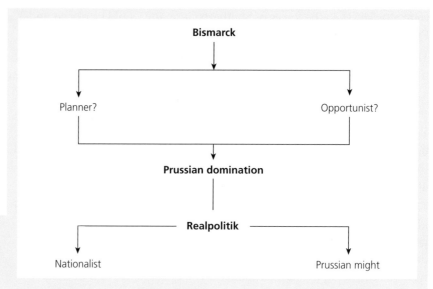

 Why was the unification of Germany achieved by 1871?

The change from 1848–50 to 1867 was remarkable. In place of a weak and divided national movement unable to dislodge Austria from its position of dominance over an ineffective German confederation, a new Germany had emerged backed by a strong Prussian army and a well-developed and expanding industrial economy. The Kleindeutsch state was largely

Protestant and led by its strongest component, Prussia, headed by a statesman of considerable insight whose gambles had paid off. However, German unification as such was far from complete. Any more union with South Germany would bring opposition from France. There was also the danger of a war of revenge by Austria despite the lenient peace of Prague. At home, industrial development had brought problems of urban slums and social discontent. The huge change in the balance of power in central Europe meant that it was of vital importance to pursue careful diplomacy with the other European powers. Also the growing nationalist feeling in Germany had been aroused by the successes of 1864 and 1866, but it was not in Prussia's interests to go further. Like many successful statesmen, Bismarck in 1867 had to face the implications and perils that his victories had brought. The result was even greater unification by 1871.

How well did Bismarck pursue diplomacy with France?

France was the key to Bismarck's diplomacy. Since Napoleon's defeat in 1815 French power had revived. Napoleon' s nephew Charles-Louis Napoleon (Napoleon III) had come to power as president of the Republic proclaimed in 1848 and made himself emperor in 1851. France had a powerful army and had defeated Austria in the war of Italian unification in 1859. Napoleon III saw himself as a key figure in European diplomacy and saw Germany as an area of special interest. He and Bismarck had met in 1865 at Biarritz. This was more than a casual discussion and there had been diplomatic contacts between Prussia and France prior to the meeting. What was actually said is obscure because of a lack of official record. Bismarck hoped to secure French neutrality in any war with Austria. Napoleon wanted Prussian support in an attempt to please Italy by persuading Austria to hand over Venice and the Veneto, which it had retained after the unification of Italy in 1861. He also hoped for some sort of compensation for any expansion of Prussia that might take place and to ensure that the expansion did not include South Germany.

Napoleon III

Charles-Louis Napoleon Bonaparte, born 1808, was the son of Napoleon's brother, who was made king of Holland. Educated in Germany, he spent his youth in Italy where he became a passionate supporter of nationalism. He and his mother Hortense, the daughter of Josephine Bonaparte by her first marriage, were forbidden to live in France after 1831 and he plotted against the French king, Louis Philippe, leading risings at Strasbourg in 1836 and Boulogne in 1840. He was imprisoned until 1845 when he escaped. In 1848 he returned and was elected president of the new Republic in 1848. He took full power in December 1851 and became emperor in 1852. He pursued vigorous policies of economic expansion, railway building and the rebuilding of Paris. Abroad he fought the Crimean War and the war of Italian unification. He built up the French army and aimed to be the key statesman of Europe. He suffered a setback in attempting to establish a Mexican empire and saw Bismarck expand Prussia without his consent. By 1870 he was moving towards a more liberal empire with a new constitution. He overestimated French military strength in 1870 and was defeated by the Prussian army and captured at Sedan in September 1870, which ended his rule. He died in exile in Britain in 1873.

The war of Italian unification, 1859

Austria ruled Northern Italy but the Italian state of Piedmont under its prime minister, Cavour, wanted to end Austrian dominance. In 1858 Cavour made an agreement with the French emperor Napoleon III for a joint war against Austria. Piedmont would gain Northern Italy in return for France gaining Nice and Savoy. The war was fought in 1859 but the heavy losses of the battles at Magenta and Solferino led to an armistice. Piedmont gained Lombardy but Venice and the province of Venetia remained Austrian until 1866 when the Prussian victory led to Austria giving Venetia to the new Italian kingdom which had been created in 1861 after the war of 1859.

The meeting was amicable but not very decisive. In fact, France was not likely to enter any war between Austria and Prussia and probably thought of its role as a mediator after prolonged fighting which would increase its prestige and influence. Bismarck had nothing much to offer France in terms of compensation for allowing Prussian expansion because German opinion would not have stood for any grant of Prussian territory.

In the end, France did remain neutral, Prussia was left free to defeat Austria and Italy did gain the Veneto. However, relations between Prussia and France deteriorated. For France, the speed of the Prussian victory in 1866 was unexpected. If the war had lasted longer it is likely that the French would have had more opportunities to mediate or to use their influence. As it was, Napoleon could do little to change events that had moved so rapidly. The whole balance of power in central Europe had been changed without any French input, and in place of a divided Germany which might have been influenced by France, there was a major new power dominating Germany.

The Luxembourg Crisis 1867

Napoleon had lost a lot of his bargaining power and Bismarck was not going to offer much in the way of compensation. This was made very clear in the Luxembourg Crisis. Luxembourg was a small state on the border of France,

Belgium and Prussia. In 1815 it was agreed that it would be linked to the kingdom of the Netherlands and its considerable fortifications would be manned by a garrison of Prussian troops, which would act as a barrier against France. In 1867 a financial crisis led to the French offering to buy Luxembourg, a move that Napoleon III hoped and perhaps expected that Bismarck would support. However, German opinion was so opposed that even Bismarck could not merely agree to that. It seemed to Napoleon that Bismarck had gone back on his agreement at Biarritz, but there had been no formal treaty. There was a real threat of war as Prussia opposed any French takeover but an international agreement at London resolved the crisis. Prussian troops were withdrawn but France did not get any 'compensation' in Luxembourg. Napoleon III was a ruler who depended on prestige and diplomatic victories, so this was a humiliation. For Bismarck it was major cause of concern. The South German states were vulnerable to France. A resentful France might ally with these states and even with Austria against Prussia. The only hope for security would be to bring South Germany into the Confederation and to end any military threat from France. However, the French army was seen as the most powerful in Europe. Bringing in largely Catholic states to the Confederation would be to cause divisions. Also the South German states were more liberal than Prussia. A larger Germany would also cause anxiety for its neighbours, Russia and Prussia, and even for Britain.

There was no easy solution to this problem and it is not certain that Bismarck was committed to expansion. He had little interest in nationalism as such and had made it clear that the time was not 'ripe' for further growth.

The importance of the Hohenzollern Candidature in the outbreak of war between France and Prussia in 1870

Bismarck had consolidated the Prussian-dominated North German Confederation and consolidated and added to Prussian territories. A weakened Austria was in no position to oppose this growth of Prussia. Britain had accepted the changes, even the acquisition by Prussia of Hanover with its links to the English crown. Russia had stayed out of the developments of the 1860s. However, France was resentful. The Catholic states of South Germany might be influenced by France. They had been forced in 1866 into military alliances with Prussia and had shown their resentment by voting against Prussia in the Zollverein assembly where all German states met to discuss economic matters. In the elections in Bavaria, Württemberg and Baden anti-Prussian candidates had done well, showing hostility to Bismarck. It was not impossible for France to ally with a fellow Catholic state, Austria, and there was a danger that Russia might change its mind because of the changed situation in central Europe and the emergence of a strong and more united Germany. Success had not brought security.

Bismarck may or may not have planned a war with France, but it was an option and he was willing to take advantage of circumstances that arose in 1868 to give him the opportunity for a military solution.

In 1868 the Spanish queen Isabella was overthrown in a revolution. Rather than establishing a republic, the new government looked for a foreign royal family to provide a ruler. One candidate was Prince Leopold von Hohenzollern-Sigmaringen, the nephew of William I of Prussia. He was married to a Portuguese princess so had some links to Iberia.

If a Prussian prince had become king of Spain, France would be bound to feel surrounded by Prussia – so this was a dangerous development. Neither William nor Leopold was enthusiastic but Bismarck pressed them to accept. Did he plan to provoke France into war? Did he hope that it would provoke a hostile French reaction and anti-German feeling that would drive South Germany away from France? Did he simply want to provoke a situation that might be of benefit to Prussia – perhaps confirming to Austria and Prussia that the French were unreasonable?

SOURCE X

Bismarck writes to the Prussian ambassador to Bavaria, 26 February 1869

Violent events would bring about further German unity. To assume the mission of bringing about a violent catastrophe is another matter. Arbitrary interference in the course of history had never achieved anything except to shake down unripe fruit. That German unity is not yet a ripe fruit is obvious. We can put the clocks forward, but time does not mover any faster.

> **Using your knowledge how reliable is Source X for Bismarck's view of future unification?**

- By March 1870 French military growth was a matter of concern. Napoleon was equipping his forces with modern rifles and field guns; he had built up a reserve of a million men and was negotiating with Austria.
- South Germany was showing distinct signs of hostility to Prussia. There was no guarantee the enforced military alliance with Prussia would be honoured or that South Germany might not prefer alliance with France and Austria.
- The growth of national feeling in Prussia and its military development meant that there would be little point in waiting for a future war. There were detailed war plans, transport was available for getting troops to the French frontier and the Prussian forces had new rifled heavy artillery developed by the Krupp armament firm.

However, other elements drove Prussia into war. In France a new foreign minister, the Comte de Gramont, was appointed, who was much more hostile to Prussia. An error by a clerk in Spain gave him opportunity to protest. The Spanish parliament (Cortes) had been dismissed before it had endorsed the candidature of Prince Leopold. Had the Cortes agreed, then it would have been difficult to withdraw. As it was this gave the chance for France to protest and for Prussia to rethink. The candidature was withdrawn. That might have resolved the crisis but for a meeting between William I and the French ambassador Benedetti on 13 July 1870 at the German spa town of Ems.

The Ems Telegram

Benedetti passed on a request that never again would a Hohenzollern candidate be supported as king of Spain. The King politely refused. The King reported the conversation which had not been aggressive to Bismarck. Seeing his opportunity, Bismarck edited the telegram to indicate an arrogant demand made by France refused by Germany unwilling to be told what to do.

In both France and in Germany, public opinion ran high and the war that had been brewing since the acceptance of the candidature in March 1870 now became inevitable. A tide of German nationalism ensured that the South German states would respect their military obligations to Prussia. A tide of French nationalism pushed Napoleon III into war.

Summary

It was a major achievement for Bismarck to enter the wars against Denmark and Austria without foreign intervention and to keep France out of German affairs. However, it did come at a price. Napoleon III could not be expected to accept the major change in central Europe without any compensation for or consultation with France because his whole regime depended on his prestige and the restoration of France as a leading European power. Bismarck might have bought Napoleon off by allowing him to purchase Luxembourg but he was prevented by the forces of nationalism in Germany, which he had himself unleashed. It became difficult for him after 1867 because no option was 'the right one'. He could not after 1867 get on good terms with France. He could not allow the situation to drift because of the danger that France would unite with Austria and South Germany against him. However, war was a dangerous option. Even if Prussia and the German Confederation won, France would remain an enemy and could not be contained for ever.

> **ACTIVITY**
>
> **A mock trial**
>
> Debate: who was more responsible for the war of 1870, Napoleon III or Bismarck? Hold a trial. Both rulers prepare a defence, helped by their 'team'. The prosecutors, helped by their teams, prepare a list of questions intended to show the guilt of both rulers. The jury, i.e. the class, decides.

The reasons for the Prussian victory in the war with France 1870–71

An outline of events 1870–71

The German forces under Moltke moved rapidly to the frontier. Within days of the start of the war on 28 July 1870, 300,000 troops had been assembled. However, the initial attacks were costly and there was no immediate decisive battle as there had been against weaker Austrian forces at Sadowa in 1866. The battles of Worth and Spicheren, 5 and 6 August, were costly. The French commander Bazaine decided to fall back on their fortifications at Metz. There were two more encounters as Prussian forces attacked them. These took place at Gravelotte on 18 August and St Privat-la-Montagne. The French did not follow up the initial repulse of the German attacks and fell back on Metz. A relief force under Marshal MacMahon was sent to break the siege. The French forces were defeated and fell back on Sedan, another frontier fortress. Moltke brought 150,000 troops rapidly into battle.

The bombardment and capture of Sedan on 1 September 1870 was not only a major victory in the sense of inflicting greater casualties on the French (17,000 to the German 9000) but it had the spectacular result that Napoleon III, who had been with his forces, was captured.

The French continued the war as a republic. Marshal Bazaine held out at Metz while the Germans besieged the fortress, but large German forces laid siege to Paris where a government of national defence had been formed.

The French were far from giving in. They fought a **guerrilla war** in north France with irregular units attacking German forces, leading to reprisals. Another substantial battle was fought at St Quentin in January 1871. There was bitter fighting in the Vosges region.

However, the French could not break the siege of Paris or inflict a decisive blow.

The French government had withdrawn to the south and decided under the leadership of veteran politician Adolphe Thiers to seek peace terms. The Treaty of Frankfurt saw Germany gain the provinces of Alsace and Lorraine, acquiring the city of Strasbourg and the fortress of Metz. France also agreed to pay a fine (indemnity) of 5 billion francs.

The final settlement was delayed by a revolution in Paris. The government there was overthrown by a radical Commune that wanted to continue the war and take revenge on the governing classes. Eminent hostages including the Archbishop of Paris were shot. This rerun of the French Revolution took place as Prussian forces surrounded the capital, watching as French government forces attacked Paris and took revenge. A final humiliation for France was that the new German Empire, unifying the South German states with the North German Confederation, was proclaimed in the Palace of Versailles – the great home of the former French kings.

KEY TERM

Guerrilla war A war fought not by regular armies on battlefields but by irregular, often improvised, groups attacking enemy forces and communications.

SOURCE Y

A British war correspondent reports on French irregular troops in August 1870

How useful is Source Y in showing French military weakness?

Between Laon and Rheims I passed through Chalons and Epernay, at which places I saw, for the first time, the francs-tireurs, or free-shooters. The corps was, in the most comprehensive possible meaning of the word, irregular. The men who composed it were not only irregular in everything they did, but appeared to glory in their irregularity. They seemed to have very few officers, and the few they had were seldom, if ever, to be seen on duty with the men. The latter had evidently souls above obedience, for they did very much what they liked, and in the manner they liked. They evidently hated the regular army, and the latter returned the compliment with interest.

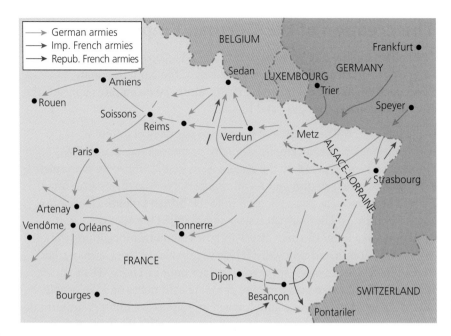

Figure 3.2 The Franco-Prussian War, 1870–71

Why was France defeated?

- The German forces, including the South German forces, were larger and efficient mobilization and transport gave them an immediate advantage. 462,000 German troops faced 270,000 French forces.
- French forces arrived at the front without the full complement of troops and equipment, as advanced guards were sent on prematurely, and had to wait for reinforcements. German forces were sent in at full strength.
- The German technical strength was in its breach-loading rifled heavy artillery. This was superior to the French muzzle-loading artillery. The French strategy of falling back on fortifications played into German hands. The French had superior rifles but the tactics of the French generals did not allow them to use this advantage to best effect.
- The French military leadership was poor and the tactics showed a lack of organization and grasp of the terrain, throwing away the advantages of French military experience and the superior French weapon – the so-called chassepot rifle.
- The decision of Napoleon III to assume leadership of his forces offered little in terms of military skill and gave the Germans the chance to capture him in September, weakening French resistance.
- After September 1870 although French resistance was desperate it lacked an overall strategy and there were divisions within France between the provisional government that took over after Napoleon III's capture and more radical groups that wanted a national resistance movement.
- The industrial growth of Germany ensured that its railways were developed enough to ensure efficient concentration of forces and also that it could produce the superior artillery that proved important at Sedan.

> **ACTIVITY**
>
> **The causes of the French defeat in 1871**
>
> Reread the section on the war and find material to put under the headings:
>
> - French weaknesses which led to defeat
> - German strengths which led to victory.
>
> Decide whether German strengths or French weaknesses were more important in explaining the outcome of the war.

The creation of the German Empire in 1871

The French Empire had been defeated and had fallen. Now the Prussian King was raised from the status of President of the North German Confederation to that of Emperor. Prussia would be an empire alongside the empires of Austria–Hungary and Russia.

Unlike those countries, it did not have large numbers of different nationalities as part of its empire. There were minorities – Danes, Poles, French speakers – but not on the scale, say, of Russia whose Russian rulers ruled vast numbers of different Asiatic peoples. Nor did the new German Empire have overseas possessions akin to the British Empire. This was an empire of princes. The German Kaiser commanded the allegiance of the royal houses of other German states and the ceremony proclaiming the empire was dominated by royalty. It was not proclaimed in Germany, but instead in occupied France at the royal palace built by Louis XIV at Versailles. The civilian governments, the state assemblies and the people were not involved. Bismarck gave himself an impressive military uniform (to which he was not entitled) for the occasion in line with the array of princely military garb. The contrast between 1871 and 1848 could not have been stronger. There was no question of William I accepting 'the crown from the gutter' as Frederick William IV had said in 1848 when offered it by commoners and parliamentarians. His crown in 1871 was accepted from the princes. German unification had indeed been achieved by blood and iron with the political leaders following events dictated by the aristocratic Prince Bismarck and accepting a new imperial constitution dictated by him.

SOURCE Z

A painting of the proclamation of William I as German Emperor January 1871

> **How useful is Source Z as evidence for the nature of the German Empire?**

The Southern states were now joined to the North German Confederation with the addition of the two conquered provinces of Alsace and Lorraine, ruled under Prussia. The federal structure of the North German Confederation and its key characteristics became the basis of the empire's constitution. The individual states (Lander) remained self-governing in most internal matters. Bavaria even kept its own army. They decided on the election of representatives to their local assemblies. The overall imperial government was appointed by the Emperor – a hereditary role given to the kings of Prussia – which controlled foreign and defence matters and could introduce legislation for the whole of Germany.

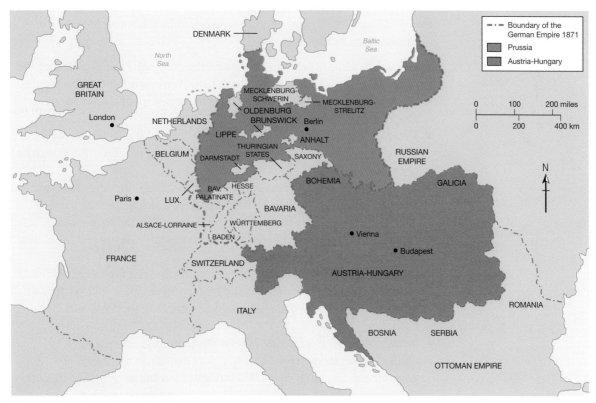

Figure 3.3 The German Empire in 1871

For the empire there was an elected lower house of parliament called the Reichstag, which met in Berlin. It could vote on imperial legislation and could control the imperial budget. However, the bulk of that was military and the only vote on that could take place every seven years, as military planning, it was argued, was long term. Adult males over 25 could vote, giving Germany one of the widest franchises in Europe.

The government was run by the Imperial Chancellor – Bismarck until 1890. Bismarck and his ministers were not elected and not responsible directly to the Reichstag, only to the Emperor.

There was also a federal assembly called the Bundesrat consisting of representatives from all the states. In both the Reichstag and the Bundesrat, Prussia as the largest state compromised two-thirds of the new empire dominated.

The domination of Prussia, Bismarck, the emperor and the central role of the army led to the view that the new empire was essentially absolutist monarchy with a facade of parliamentary rule. It was argued that this ended any hope of a liberal Germany and paved the way for the dictatorships of the twentieth century, undermining democracy and representative government. It has been argued that the new empire was a militaristic state and its power in central Europe was bound to lead to future conflict. The seeds of two world wars in the next century were sown by the whole nature of unification and by the empire of 1871.

There are elements of truth in this, given the domination of Prussia and the limited role of the imperial parliament. However, it is not the whole picture.

- Bismarck kept a constitution and did not simply adopt a Russian-style absolute monarchy.
- There were parliaments in many of the individual states that allowed for wider voting than in Prussia itself, which retained the three-tier franchise until 1918.
- Though the Liberals had accepted Bismarck's illegalities after 1862 and had been enthusiastic nationalists, they were a strong force in the new Germany. Bismarck worked with them in the 1870s to bring about economic changes such as free trade and uniform weights and measures, which were part of the liberal agenda.
- Germany remained a state governed by laws and not the whims of the state, even though those laws could be repressive and were later turned against groups whom Bismarck saw as hostile, like socialists and Catholics.
- It was not unusual for states, even when they were liberal and parliamentary, to keep foreign and defence policy in the hands of government. Bismarck controlled foreign policy but even in Britain, with a more developed parliamentary system, it was the government that decided matters of peace and war without parliamentary approval.
- Bismarck was not a member of the Reichstag and did not depend on it, but he did explain his policies to the parliament and worked to ensure that he had parliamentary support.

The downside to this is the nature of the empire itself. It emerged as a result of war and owed a lot to the manipulation of Bismarck's diplomacy. The industrial growth that allowed victory was also giving rise to a large industrial working class that would oppose the domination by the conservative elements in Germany represented by the Bismarck regime – crown, empire, civil service, landowners. Also the new empire meant that about a third of the empire were Catholics. They had a loyalty to an international Church and this set up tensions in Bismarck's Germany in the 1870s and led to a virtual war between the Protestant Prussian state and Bismarck's Catholic subjects.

In the last resort, too, Bismarck's victories had not depended on the much-despised parliamentary majority. The army had brought unification and had a special place in Germany that threatened a militarization of German society – a development that increased rapidly after Bismarck's fall in 1890 and contributed to the First World War. Finally, the empire had arisen from the defeat of France. Bismarck had been unable to persuade the Emperor to accept the type of lenient peace that he had imposed on Austria in 1866 and instead bowed to public pressure to annex Alsace and Lorraine. France never accepted this and this prevented any lasting restoration of good relations with France before the late 1940s. It was a major cause of the First World War and between 1871 and 1890 Bismarck was faced with ever-increasing complex diplomatic solutions to ensure that France was isolated from other European powers. His successors failed to maintain this, and an alliance between Russia and France in 1893 was another major cause of the First World War.

The creation of the empire gave rise to a new burst of German nationalism and pride in everything German, which Bismarck despised, and was ultimately quite a damaging and dangerous development, both for Germany itself and for Europe.

ACTIVITY

What was the most important factor in bringing about German unification?

Take each of the key reasons in the diagram below and on separate cards explain their importance. Put the cards in order of importance. Compare your order with others in the class and discuss why there are similarities and differences.

After this plan an essay: How important was Bismarck's diplomacy in bringing about German unification?

SUMMARY DIAGRAM

Why was the unification of Germany achieved by 1871?

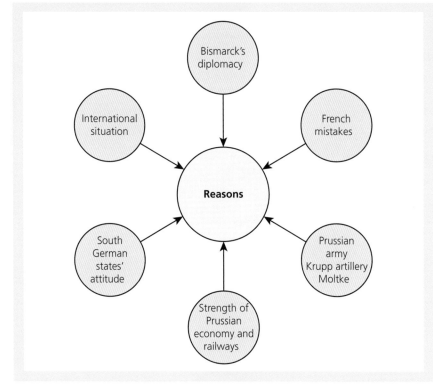

ACTIVITY

Add details and evidence to each of the factors to help explain how each factor brought about German unification.

Chapter summary

The chapter has outlined the situation in Germany after 1815 when there were nationalist hopes and a desire, especially among the students and some of the middle class, for a united and liberal Germany. These hopes ran up against the determination of Austria and its leader, Metternich, to keep Austria in overall control of a confederation of monarchies and to resist change. However, by 1848 it was no longer possible to maintain this system. The growth of the German economy and the development of a larger and more nationalistic middle class together with economic grievance among workers and peasants led to revolutions. A new German parliament assembled and the early stages of the revolutions of 1848 saw changes in many German states. However, these did not last and military forces suppressed revolutions and restored the authority of Austria and its monarchical allies. The humiliation of Olmütz showed how difficult it was going to be for even a conservative German union to be formed without Austria's permission. What developed, though, was greater nationalism and the economic power of Germany in general and Prussia in particular. However, this alone would not bring greater union. The arrival of Bismarck to power in Prussia marked a new era. He pushed through vital military reforms and by his diplomacy ensured that Austria was isolated and also that there was a reason for war. The joint war against Denmark in 1864 was a mistake on Austria's part. It strengthened Prussia's military reputation and gave Bismarck an excuse to go to war against Austria in 1866. Prussia won the war and brought about a big change in Germany with a new North German Confederation. However, with French hostility and the exclusion of South Germany, there was a dangerous situation, which was only resolved by another war. Again Prussia was successful and again war led to greater German unity with the creation of the German Empire in 1871.

Refresher questions

1 What were the signs of growing nationalism in Germany 1815–48?

2 How did Metternich try to control Germany?

3 Why was there social and economic discontent by 1848?

4 What was the Humiliation of Olmutz?

5 What were the indications of economic growth in Germany by 1871?

6 How was the North German Confederation brought about?

7 Why did Prussia and France go to war?

8 How did Bismarck ensure that no major foreign power intervened in his wars of 1866 and 1870?

9 Give any three reasons why Unification was more successful in 1871 than 1848–49.

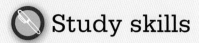 Study skills

Paper 1 guidance: Sources

Evaluating sources using contextual knowledge

In answering a source-based question on a set of sources you should aim to establish what the sources say about the issue in the question and group them. You should consider how useful the evidence is by considering provenance but you also need to test the evidence by your own knowledge of the issue.

SOURCE A

Otto von Bismarck, letter to the Prussian prime minister von Manteuffel, 1856

Because of the policy of Vienna [the Congress of Vienna, 1815], Germany is clearly too small for us both [Prussia and Austria]; as long as an honourable arrangement concerning the influence of each in Germany cannot be concluded and carried out, we will both plough the same disputed acre, and Austria will remain the only state to whom we can permanently lose or from whom we can permanently gain ... I wish only to express my conviction that, in the not too distant future, we shall have to fight for our existence against Austria and that it is not within our power to avoid that, since the course of events in Germany has no other solution.

> **How useful is this source as evidence for the view that Bismarck had a long-term plan to unify Germany?**

What contextual knowledge would help you judge this source as evidence for this particular issue?

Let's look at another source and another question.

SOURCE B

Bismarck reflects in the 1890s on the origins of the war of 1870 in Bismarck, *Reflections and Reminiscences*, 1898

I assumed that a united Germany was only a question of time, that the North German Confederation was only the first step in its solution. I did not doubt that a Franco-German war must take place before the construction of a united Germany could be realized. I was at the time only concerned with the idea of delaying the outbreak of this war until our fighting strength should be increased.

> **How far does this source support the view that Bismarck planned to unify Germany by provoking a war with France?**

Activity

Look at this analysis. Find where the answer has shown what the source is saying about the key issue and highlight. Find any comment on the provenance of the source and highlight in another colour. Find where the answer has used knowledge to assess the source as evidence and highlight in a third colour.

In your next answer highlight these elements and see if you have written about content, provenance and added any knowledge.

Though this is a source by Bismarck himself, it was written some years after the events and with the knowledge that events did indeed lead to the defeat of France and a united Germany. His memoirs may well have wished to show that he was in control of events and the unification of Germany owed everything to his master planning. The source has to be evaluated carefully.

This source indicates that Bismarck was planning a war as he says that he was delaying only until Prussia built up military strength. It suggests that Bismarck was planning unification because he says that this was 'only a matter of time'. He indicates that he saw the North German Confederation as only a first step to unification and that unification required a Franco-German War.

Other evidence suggests that he did not consider unification to be imminent even in 1869. There were problems for Prussia bringing the Catholic South German states under control and the North German Confederation and the annexations of 1866–67 had achieved major gains for Prussia. He was prepared to offer France compensation in 1867 and could not have foreseen events in Spain that led to the Spanish candidature. The risks of war with France were still considerable in 1870. However, Prussian military force had been built up, particularly heavy artillery, and there had been military planning for a war against France, for example by railway planning. Bismarck is correct in saying that a war with France would have to have taken place before South Germany would have been incorporated into a new Germany. The issue is whether the war was premeditated from 1867 or was a result of concerns about developments in South Germany and the French hostility over Luxembourg. The clear intention of Bismarck for war and further unification might be exaggerated in the source.

Try to make sure that when you answer part (b) questions you incorporate all three elements – interpretation, evaluation by provenance and evaluation by knowledge. Try to offer a distinct view of the usefulness of each source.

Now try to interpret and evaluate all the sources in the question below.

How far do Sources A to D support the view that there was every chance of success for a united Germany in 1848?

SOURCE A

Delegates from six German states issue a declaration at Heidelberg urging unity, 5 March 1848

The meeting of a national representative body elected in all the German states must not be postponed. An assembly of all men of trust from all German peoples should come together to offer cooperation for a Fatherland. With the prudent and manly cooperation of all Germans the Fatherland may hope to achieve and maintain freedom, unity and to greet the coming of a new strength and flowering of the nation.

SOURCE B

Patriotic song, popular in Berlin in 1848

Black, Red and Gold these are the colours
We Germans proudly bear on high;
Black, Red and Gold, these are the colours
For which we would gladly die.

The Black betokens death to tyrants
Who laughing nailed us to the tree;
And Red's the blood we poured as offering
For Justice and for Liberty

But Gold is freedom's blessing
That men, their duty done, may see,
So fly on highways and by-ways
The sacred German colours three.

Black, Red and Gold, these are the colours
Fill every German eye with pride.

SOURCE C

Frederick William IV of Prussia addresses the German people, from *To My People and to the German Nation*, 21 March 1848

I speak today to the Fatherland, to the German Nation. Germany is in a state of internal unrest and can be threatened by danger. It can be saved by unity of the German princes and people under one leadership. Today, I take over that leadership. My people will not desert me and Germany will follow me with confidence. I have taken the old German colours and out myself and my people under the banner of the German Nation. The assembly of the German states will deliberate about the rebirth and foundation of a new Germany, of a united but not uniform Germany, of a unity in diversity of a unity with freedom.

Bismarck gives his view of 1848 in a speech to the Budget Commission of the Prussian Landtag (Assembly), 25 September 1862

Germany does not look to Prussian liberalism, but to its power. Prussia must gather and consolidate her strength in readiness for the favourable moment which has been missed several times. Prussia's boundaries according to the Vienna Treaties [of 1815] are not favourable to a healthy political life; the great decisions of the time will not be made by means of speeches and majorities [in parliament] – that was the great mistake of 1848 and 1849 – but by iron and blood.

Comparing and contrasting two sources

It is important not just to describe each source but to explain how they agree and disagree and what might explain that by looking at the provenance of the different passages. Look again at Sources M and N on page 138 and the question which follows. Then read the two answers. Which is the better answer and why?

What accounts for the different view of the role of the Prussian monarchy in Sources M and N?

Answer 1

Source M says that there is a choice between Prussia and Austria. By this he means that Germany will be united by either Austria or Prussia. The source says that Prussia is the key power because it is 'wholly German' and that Prussia under its monarchy will merge with Germany. Source N takes a different view as the King of Prussia refuses to accept the crown and will not accept a constitution for the whole of Germany therefore he does not think that Prussia should lead Germany. Source N says that the Frankfurt Assembly 'has not the right' to offer him the Crown. One source is from a liberal in 1848 and the other source is from the Prussian king writing in 1849.

Answer 2

The two sources take a very different approach to the role of the Prussian monarchy in German unification. Source M says that the Frankfurt Assembly needs 'a powerful ruling house' to lead a new Germany and that the Prussian monarch because it is 'wholly German' is that house. However, the king of Prussia in Source N does not agree that that is the role of the Prussian monarchy. He is not prepared to accept the crown that has been tendered to him because it is offered by the assembly not the rulers and because he respects the rights of the other states above the need to have a united Germany under Prussia. Both take a view that Germany has rights which the Prussian king must respect. Source M refers to 'the rights of the German states' to decide on their future and not have a king foisted on them by the Assembly. For Source M those rights are to move forward in a 'national and reformative way' which can only happen with Prussia and its monarchy at the head. Unlike Source N though, this source argues that it is the Assembly that can define the role of the Prussian monarchy. Source N thinks that it is not the Assembly but only the other German governments. This difference can be explained by the provenance of the sources. Source M is written in the excitement of the first national parliament at Frankfurt where middle-class liberals such as Droysen dreamt of a united Germany and knew that Prussia was the only power able to deliver it. However, Source N is from the Prussian king who had very different priorities – the rights of monarchs were more important than the rights of a national assembly and he did not want a crown offered 'from the gutter'. By the time he was writing, the initial excitement and impact of the revolutions was waning and there was a reaction as the Austrian Emperor and other princes were regaining power, so it was natural for Frederick William to refuse the throne.

Show in the table which answer has:

Point by point differences	
Point by point similarities	
Explanation of differences by the use of reference to who was writing?	
Explanation by the use of knowledge of what was happening at the time?	

Paper 2 guidance: Essay questions

Avoiding descriptive answers and writing analytically

What is meant by a descriptive answer? This is when an answer has relevant supporting knowledge, but it is not directly linked to the actual question. Sometimes the argument is implicit, but even here the reader has to work out how the material is linked to the actual question. Instead of actually answering the question, it simply describes what happened.

In order to do well you must write an analytical answer and not simply tell the story. This means you must focus on the key words and phrases in the question and link your material back to them, which is why your essay plan (see pages 54–55) is crucial as it allows you to check you are doing it. You can avoid a narrative answer by referring back to the question as this should prevent you from just providing information about the topic. If you find analytical writing difficult it might be helpful to ensure that the last sentence of each paragraph links back directly to the question.

Consider the following question:

> **'The failure of French leadership was the main reason for the outcome of the Franco-Prussian war.' How far do you agree?**

In order to answer this question you would need to consider the following issues about the French leadership:
- What strategic mistakes did the French make?
- Were they too slow to bring troops to the front?
- How important was the capture of Napoleon III?

Then you would need to consider other factors such as:
- German transport organization
- the lack of allies for France
- the artillery and weapons development of Germany
- the nationalist morale of German forces.

A very strong answer will weigh up the relative importance of each factor as it is discussed, whereas a weaker answer will not reach a judgement until the conclusion, and the weakest answers will either just list the reasons or, worst of all, just describe them.

The following is part of a descriptive answer for the question above:

> The Franco-Prussian war began in 1870. The Prussians had the support of the South German states and their leader was von Moltke. The Prussians brought their troops to the French frontier and invaded rapidly. There were battles which the French resisted the advance. The French leader Bazaine decided to fall back on the fortress of Metz which was besieged. A large French force was at Sedan but this was encircled and during the battle the French Emperor was captured. The French government decided to go on with the war but the Germans besieged Paris.

This paragraph outlines some of the facts about war and is quite well informed but there is little explanation. Was Moltke a good leader and why? What was the significance of the withdrawal of Metz and the capture of the Emperor? The reader is having to do a lot of work to find the actual explanation.

The opening sentence of each paragraph

One way that you can avoid a narrative approach is to focus on the opening sentence of each paragraph. A good opening sentence will offer a view or idea about an issue relevant to the question, not describe an event or person. With a very good answer you should be able to read the opening sentence of each paragraph and see the line of argument that has been taken in the essay. It is therefore worth spending time practising this skill.

Activity

'The 1848 Revolutions stood little chance of success.' How far do you agree?

Look at the following ten opening sentences. Which of these offer an idea that directly answers the question above and which simply give facts?

1 Revolution was widespread in Germany in 1848.

2 Because there was so little agreement on the aims of unification, there was little chance that the revolutions would succeed.

3 Some revolutionaries preferred a Kleindeutsch solution.

4 Many of the grievances of the revolutionaries were economic.

5 The revolutionaries had different aims. Some wanted a new constitution, others wanted economic reform.

6 The revolutions were initially successful in some states.

7 There was little reduction in the military power of the rulers and at any time they could have suppressed the revolutions.

8 There was a great deal of enthusiasm for revolution in 1848 and hopes for change were very high.

9 There were uprisings in many cities like Berlin and Dresden in 1848.

10 The main reason for the failure of the 1848 Revolutions was the revival of Austrian power.

QUESTION PRACTICE

In order to practise the skill of directly answering the question, write opening sentences for the following essays.

 1 'How successfully did Metternich control the German states between 1815 and 1848?

2 How far was Bismarck responsible for the outbreak of the Franco-Prussian War in 1870?

EXPLAIN QUESTIONS

 1 Explain why the 1848 Revolutions failed.

2 Explain why Austria was defeated in 1866.

3 Explain why the Franco-Prussia War broke out in 1870.

4 Explain why the German Empire was declared in 1871.

It might be helpful to also write opening sentences for the short answer essay questions in the box above.

CHAPTER 4

The Russian Revolution, 1894–1921

This chapter looks at developments within Russia during a period of serious unrest that would ultimately lead to the overthrow of its ruler, Tsar Nicholas II, and the establishment of the world's first communist regime. It investigates the causes of these events and examines the reasons why there was so much instability and how the Bolsheviks, or communists, were able to emerge as the ruling power. This chapter examines these developments through the following questions:

★ What were the causes and outcomes of the 1905 Revolution up to 1914?

★ What were the causes and immediate outcomes of the February Revolution in 1917?

★ How and why did the Bolsheviks gain power in October 1917?

★ How were the Bolsheviks able to consolidate their power up to 1921?

KEY DATES

1894	Nicholas II comes to the throne	**1915**	Nicholas II takes personal command of his forces
1904	War with Japan	**1916**	Brusilov offensive
1905	Revolution	**1917**	February Revolution
	October Manifesto		July Days
1906	Fundamental Laws		October Revolution
1906–11	Stolypin prime minister	**1918**	Civil War. War Communism
1912	Lena Goldfield Massacre		Massacre of Tsar and royal family
1914	Russia enters First World War	**1921**	USSR formed

1 What were the causes and outcomes of the 1905 Revolution up to 1914?

In 1905 Russia experienced a major revolution following a build-up of social and political tensions and military failures in a war against Japan. The Tsar had to make concessions to divide the different revolutionary groups but he was able to restore his authority in 1906. Nevertheless, the Revolution led to major changes with the introduction of a national elected parliament and economic reforms.

The nature of the tsarist regime: pressures for change, social, economic and political and the reaction of Nicholas II to them

When Nicholas II became **tsar** (emperor) of the Russian Empire in 1894, he faced many problems that prevented it from being a modern state. The country was enormous, stretching across two continents – Europe and Asia – which made it very difficult to rule effectively. Most of the population lived in European Russia, where the two largest cities, Moscow, and the capital St Petersburg, were situated. The country was made up of a wide range of different peoples, nationalities and religions, which made controlling the country even more difficult.

KEY TERM

Tsar A term meaning emperor, derived from the Latin Caesar. Tsars before 1905 had total authority.

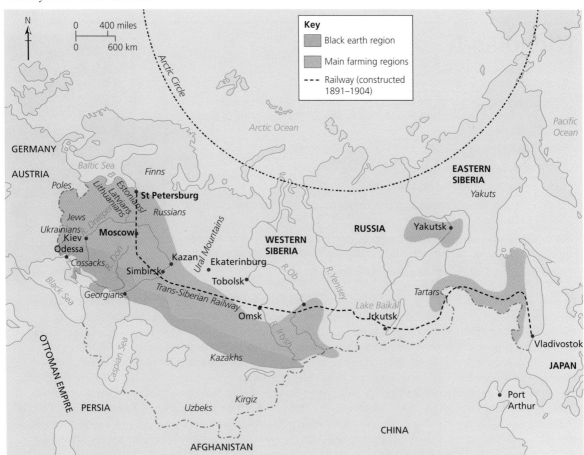

Figure 4.1 Map showing the Russian Empire

The state was ruled by one person, the tsar, who by both law and tradition was an **absolute or autocratic ruler**, appointed by God and answerable only to him. Since 1613 the tsars had come from the Romanov dynasty. They had treated the country almost as their personal estate, which suggested that the chances of major reforms or modernizations were very unlikely. Although there were official bodies such as the Imperial Council, the Cabinet of Ministers and the Senate, which gave the tsar advice, his word was final.

However, Nicholas II's personality and characteristics suggest that he was not suited for such a role. It may even be argued that it was his personality that would ultimately lead to the downfall of the dynasty in 1917. Historians have often seen him as weak-willed, lacking in confidence and a poor judge of people, and more interested in his family than in governing the country. However, he did have an enormous sense of duty and saw it as his job to keep the autocracy intact. Therefore, at the very time that Russia faced serious political, social and economic challenges, its ruler was reluctant to reform the country, prioritizing the maintenance of the dynasty and its powers.

ACTIVITY

Create a chart to show the strengths and weaknesses of Nicholas II.

Nicholas II

1868	Born into the Romanov dynasty
1894	Took over as tsar on the death of his father, Alexander III. In the same year he married the Princess Alexandra, the German granddaughter of Queen Victoria
1905	Announced the October Manifesto and new constitution
1906	Introduced the first Duma
1914	Took Russia into the First World War
1915	Ordered Russian armed forces to be placed under the personal command of the tsar
1917	Return to Petrograd halted by rebels. Senior military officials and members of the Duma advised Nicholas to stand down. Abdicated to 'save' Russia
1918	Murdered, along with his family, in Ekaterinburg

Nicholas II was the son of Tsar Alexander III and he succeeded him in 1894. He lacked his father's decisive character but shared his views about autocracy. He was influenced by his wife Alexandra of Hesse and was a devoted family man. The first part of his reign saw Russia make considerable economic progress but the Tsar's authority was shaken by defeats by Japan in 1904 and 1905. Nicholas was blamed for a massacre of demonstrators in St Petersburg in January 1905 and the Revolution of 1905 forced him to make concessions and accept a national parliament in the October Manifesto. When he had regained control he reasserted his control in the Fundamental Laws. He accepted the repression of the revolutionaries by his prime minister, Stolypin, and he himself held nationalistic and anti-Semitic views. However, he also accepted the need for reform of the land and the modernization of the armed forces. Political power, however, was not shared and the parliaments were weak. When war broke out there was a surge of patriotic feeling towards the Tsar but government incompetence and heavy losses, together with resentment about the Tsar and Tsarina's friendship with the ambitious holy man Rasputin, soon resulted in unpopularity. This was made worse by the Tsar taking personal command of his forces in 1915. By February 1917 he had lost the respect of many leading figures in government and the armed forces. A wave of demonstrations in the capital and a refusal of troops to support the Tsar led to his abdication in March 1917. He and his family were killed by revolutionaries in 1918.

Political problems facing Russia

During the rule of Nicholas II's father, **Alexander III**, opposition to tsarist rule had grown. This had been made worse because of the repressive measures his father had followed, particularly with use of **Land Captains**, rising press censorship and tighter controls over local government or **zemstva**. However, the restrictions introduced by Alexander III had not prevented more liberal ideas from entering the country. Although these ideas could not be expressed openly, they led to the growth of a range of underground and secret groups that wanted to bring about change or even revolution. The restrictions imposed by the Tsar meant that more and more were being driven towards extremist action and this had been seen in 1881 when Nicholas' grandfather was killed by a terrorist bomb. Even those who did not support such extreme measures still wanted greater representation of the people.

Social problems

There were social problems in both the towns and countryside. Although the **Emancipation of the Serfs** in 1861 had freed the peasants from the total control of the landowner, on whose land they worked, it did not solve the problems in the countryside. The peasantry made up some 80 per cent of the population, many of whom were illiterate and uneducated, and there was not a well-developed agricultural economy. Farming was backward, with many still using wooden ploughs, while standards of living were very low. The redistribution of land, which followed emancipation, had often led to many peasants seeing the amount of land they held reduced in size. They lacked the money to improve their land and the only way they could borrow was through the government, but this left them with large debts. The inefficiency in farming often led to famines, with that in 1891 leading to the deaths of some 350,000. Meanwhile the government was fearful of the '**dark masses**' whom it was believed could be held in check only by repression.

The situation in the fast-growing towns and cities was little better. As industrial development occurred so urbanization took place, but this led to a range of problems including poor housing, a lack of sanitation and water. As a result diseases spread and workers became very dissatisfied.

Economic problems

Russia was still largely agricultural. Most people lived and worked on the land. There were many famines as much of the grain that was produced was exported. However, industry was also developing. The economy had grown in the 1880s and by 1894 was averaging 8 per cent per year, but Russia was a long way behind its international rivals. Development was heavily dependent upon foreign investment, while the Tsar and his ministers controlled areas such as armaments and rail. Industry and agriculture were both backward and undeveloped, with the result that Russia could not compete economically with the major European economic powers of Britain and Germany.

Dark masses A term used to describe the mass of Russian peasantry, many of whom were illiterate. Peasant life was often characterized by violence and superstition.

Westerners Those who believed that in order to be a great nation Russia would have to adopt western values.

Slavophiles Opponents of western values. They believed they were corrupting and wanted Russia to preserve its traditional values.

Liberal democracy A system in which the people vote for national assemblies or parliaments to whom governments are responsible. Governments must keep to the laws approved by assemblies and respect the rights of citizens to free speech and freedom from punishment without trial.

Pogroms Violent attacks on Jews.

Nicholas II's response to the political, social and economic problems

As an autocrat any measures to tackle the problems that the country faced would have to come from the Tsar. However, as an autocrat he would not bring in any reforms that would undermine his position. There was also disagreement within the government over the direction the country should follow. The **Westerners** wanted Nicholas to bring in measures that were similar to those of western European states, while the **Slavophiles** argued that Russia should preserve its Slavic culture and traditions.

Although Alexander II had carried out a range of reforms to lessen opposition to the regime, his son Alexander III had been much more repressive and the period of his rule from 1881 to 1894 was known as 'The Reaction'. Nicholas II, in part because of his upbringing, continued many of the repressive policies of his father. He relied heavily on his tutor, **Konstantin Pobedonostsev**, who was his chief advisor. He was an arch-conservative who believed in the superiority of everything Russian and disliked **liberal democracy**, believing that the Russian people were ignorant and had to be controlled. Pobedonostsev was also religiously devout and determined to uphold religious orthodoxy, which often led to him encouraging **pogroms**. He also encouraged Nicholas to continue the policy of **Russification**, whereby Russian ways and values were imposed on the people.

The other important advisor was Sergei Witte and although he was a supporter of industrialization, he was conservative in his political views. However, as Minister of Finance he did oversee the **Great Spurt** which saw a growth in coal production, new technologies and railways, with the result that income from industry increased from 42 million roubles in 1893 to 161 million by 1897. Despite the economic growth, the repressive policies led to growing opposition, which became more organized and witnessed the emergence of a number of political parties, most notably the **Social Revolutionaries** and the **Social Democrats**. As Nicholas gave the impression of not being interested in either reform or modernization many began to feel alienated from their ruler.

KEY FIGURE

Konstantin Petrovich Pobedonostsev (1827–1907) was a Russian legal expert, statesman, and advisor to three tsars. He was tutor to Nicholas II and a considerable influence on his views about the importance of autocracy.

Sergei Witte

Sergei Witte (1849–1915) came from the Baltic and his family were of Dutch origin. He was an economic expert and had organized rail transport during the Turkish War 1875–78. As Minister of Finance under Alexander III he had pursued a policy of developing transport and industry. He negotiated the peace treaty with Japan in 1905 and drafted the October Manifesto, setting up a national Duma or parliament. He was prime minister 1905–06 but resigned as the Tsar moved to greater repression. He urged the Tsar not to go to war in 1914 but by then had lost all influence.

Key events of the Revolution, Bloody Sunday, wider risings and the October Manifesto

The Revolution of 1905 was not a sudden event. There were a number of areas of grievances, including the repressive nature of the regime and the political, social and economic problems that were discussed in the last section. These were added to by the disastrous Russo-Japanese War of 1904–05, which showed Nicholas' inability to manage the country. Opposition within the country had continued to grow, with increasing support for groups that were influenced by **populism** and **Marxism**, as well as student unrest, protests about poor harvests in 1902, strikes at factories and anti-war protests once the war with Japan began, and this culminated in the revolutionary events of 1905.

Causes of the 1905 Revolution

War with Japan in 1904 was hardly surprising. The two countries had quarrelled for some time over Korea and Manchuria as Russia looked to increase its influence in the Far East following the relative decline in its position in Europe. Russia also wanted to obtain an ice-free port and, according to the Interior Minister, Vyacheslav Plehve, needed 'a small, victorious war to avert a revolution' as it would distract from the domestic problems. However, the war was a shambles. The Japanese defeated the Russians at the battle of Yalu in southern Manchuria, forced Russia to surrender Port Arthur, sunk much of the Russian fleet in the battle of Tsushima Bay and then inflicted a humiliating military defeat at Mukden. As a consequence Russia lost Manchuria, Korea and Port Arthur.

Although the Russians had underestimated Japan's strength and had failed to prepare adequately for the conflict, Russia's performance led to concerns being expressed about the Tsar's ability to maintain Russia's position as a major power and the effectiveness of his rule and autocracy. Many associated military failure with the Tsar himself. The war also sparked social unrest at home and Nicholas was forced into making a number of reforms. He introduced an element of democracy by establishing the **Duma** and hoped that such actions would show the people that he was more willing to be accountable for his actions.

However, by 1905 Nicholas was faced with a combination of opposition from the peasantry, industrial workers and the growing middle class. Previous unrest had been largely caused by industrial downturns and poor harvests, but 1905 was different as it was largely caused by government policies.

Marxism The movement that was influenced by the ideas of the German writer and revolutionary Karl Marx who thought that revolution by the workers would be an inevitable consequence of industrial growth and would lead to a reborn society. After a period of dictatorship by the workers, class distinctions would fall away as would the state and there would be an ideal community led by the principle 'from each according to his ability, to each according to his needs'. Marxist states have never got beyond the dictatorship stage.

Duma The Russian word for assembly or parliament.

Bloody Sunday

The Revolution began with Bloody Sunday on 22 January 1905, although there had already been a strike at the Putilov steelworks in St Petersburg, which led to a wave of strikes across Russia. The protest on 22 January was led by a priest, **Father Gapon**. He attempted to lead a peaceful protest of workers and their families to the Tsar's Winter Palace to present a loyal petition calling on him to improve their conditions (see Source A).

KEY FIGURE

Father Georgy Gapon (1870–1906) was a zemstvo official who became a priest and tried to help workers in St Petersburg. However, although he founded a trade union organization he was also working for the secret police whose policy was to infiltrate workers' organizations. He led a march in January 1905 to petition the Tsar for better conditions but this led to deaths (Bloody Sunday). He fled to England but returned to Russia at the end of 1905 and resumed contact with the police and workers' organizations but he was killed by revolutionaries as a traitor in 1906.

SOURCE A

From a petition intended to be delivered by the Marchers to Tsar Nicholas II on Sunday 22 January 1905

We working men and inhabitants of St Petersburg, our wives and children, and our parents, helpless and aged men and women, have come to You, our ruler, in quest of justice and protection. We have no strength at all, O Sovereign. Our patience is at an end. We are approaching that terrible moment when death is better than continuance of intolerable sufferings.

Our first request was that our employers should discuss with us but this they refused to do. They regard as illegal our other demands: reduction of the working day to eight hours, the fixing of wage rates in consultation with us, and investigation of our grievances against the factory managements. We have been in slavery with the help and co-operation of Your officials. Anyone who dares to speak up in the defence of the interests of the working class and ordinary people is jailed or exiled. Is this, O Sovereign, in accordance with the laws of God, by whose grace You reign?

> **What can we learn from Source A about economic and social hardship in Russia by 1905?**

However, the march created panic among the police who opened fire and sent in the cavalry. This led to the death of some 200 protestors, with many more injured. This was seized on by tsarist opponents and used to show the brutal and uncaring nature of the regime. Nicholas was not in St Petersburg, but the events did much to damage the ideal of the tsar as the 'little father'.

SOURCE B

A painting of the Bloody Sunday massacre

> **What message does the artist of Source B wish to convey?**

> **ACTIVITY**
> Research the Bloody Sunday massacre and assess how accurate a portrayal Source B is.

The Revolution spreads

In response to the events of Bloody Sunday disorder spread. There were strikes in the major towns and cities. Government officials were attacked, Grand Duke Sergei and Plehve were assassinated by Social Revolutionaries, and unrest spread to the countryside where landlords were also targeted. Public buildings were seized and peasants squatted in landlords' houses. The workers organized themselves into trade unions, and sailors on the ship *Potemkin* mutinied. As the government struggled to contain the unrest, the non-Russian minorities seized the opportunity to assert themselves; Georgia declared its independence, the Poles demanded self-government and the Jews asked for equal rights. Meanwhile, the **Kadets** led by Paul Milyukov persuaded other liberal groups to form the Union of Unions in the attempt to organize an alliance with workers and peasants to force the government to establish a **Constituent Assembly**.

The response of Nicholas II

Nicholas turned to Witte to help restore order. Firstly, he secured peace with Japan and then became chairman of the Council of Ministers. Witte advised the Tsar to issue a new declaration of his policy, or manifesto, in August 1905. This offered concessions, most notably the promise to create an assembly of elected representatives, in an attempt to reduce tensions. But the limits to the concessions, with the Tsar stating that he reserved 'to ourselves exclusively the care of perfecting the organization of the Assembly' failed to

KEY TERMS

Potemkin A battleship named after the aristocratic favourite and lover of the eighteenth-century Empress Catherine the Great. While stationed in Odessa on the Black Sea its crew mutinied in 1905.

Kadets The party that supported a constitutional liberal democracy. Its membership was largely middle class and it never achieved mass support.

Constituent Assembly An elected body whose task is to draw up a new constitution, or a set of rules under which a country is to be run.

KEY TERM 🔑

Soviets Russian word for a council, made up of elected workers.

ACTIVITY

Which of the following statements best explains Nicholas II's response to the events of 1905?

- Nicholas II followed a policy of repression.
- Nicholas II followed a policy of reform.

Explain your choice.

How much change was there as a result of the 1905 Revolution?

restore order and more strikes followed. By October 1905 this had grown into a general strike and workers in the cities of St Petersburg and Moscow formed themselves into **soviets**, demanding better conditions. This united opposition was a serious threat and the government was forced to act to try to divide it. In October Nicholas issued a new manifesto. This went further than August and offered:

- a legislative Duma or parliament
- freedom of speech, assembly and worship
- the legalization of political parties and trade unions.

This won Nicholas the support of the liberals. Nicholas then pacified the peasants by announcing that mortgage repayments on land were to be reduced and then ended. However, the policy towards the workers was more repressive and the soviet in St Petersburg was crushed and the leaders arrested. Similar, but more brutal, action was taken in Moscow where some 1000 people were killed.

The events had shown that, provided the government retained the support of the army, it could crush opposition that had been shown to be divided and lacking in a common purpose.

The reassertion of tsarist authority; the Dumas and Stolypin's reforms

Having survived the challenge to his power, Nicholas was soon able to reassert his power. In April 1906 he announced the Fundamental Laws. These stated that 'The Sovereign Emperor possesses the initiative in all legislative matters. No law can come into force without his approval.' This was clear evidence that the Tsar was determined to maintain control even if there was a legislative assembly. He would control how the Duma worked. It appeared as if 1905 had changed nothing as Nicholas reasserted his autocratic powers. Repression continued and it is estimated that within a year some 15,000 people were killed and 70,000 arrested as opponents continued to be persecuted.

The Dumas

Although the Duma was an elected body and had appeared to be a liberal reform, the first meeting coincided with Nicholas issuing the Fundamental Laws. The electoral process also ensured that any changes would be minor as elections for the first Duma in 1906 were based on the following rules:

- Only males over the age of 25 had the right to vote.
- Women were not allowed to vote.
- Members of the armed forces could not vote.
- Electoral districts within provinces were not equally represented.
- A second chamber, appointed by the tsar, had the right to veto measures.

Although the electoral rules did mean that there were representatives from a broad range of opinions and political groups, it also ensured that it was highly critical of tsarist policy. However, the Second Chamber ensured there was little reform and in despair some members of the Duma reassembled at Vyborg, in the neighbouring province of Finland close to St Petersburg, where they drew up an appeal calling on the people of Russia to oppose their government. This led to some violence and gave the government the excuse it needed for retaliation. Not only were the Vyborg deputies arrested but **martial law** was introduced and military courts were set up to crush unrest, with some 2500 executed between 1906 and 1911. As a result, the first two Dumas were in session for only short periods and achieved very little.

The unrest also led to Stolypin changing voting rights so that those elected were more likely to come from the nobility and therefore more conservative and less critical of the Tsar. As a result, the third and fourth Dumas were more successful and a series of reforms to the army and navy, in the judicial system and an insurance scheme for workers were introduced. This has led some to suggest that it was only the government's attitude that prevented the Dumas from bringing about even more significant change (see Source C).

> ### The Four Dumas
>
> 1906   First Duma: achieved little
>
> 1907   Second Duma: achieved little
>
> 1907–12   Third Duma: carried out social reforms
>
> 1912–17   Fourth Duma: continued social reforms but was also critical of the government

SOURCE C

Comment made by Mikhail Rodzianko, chairman of the Duma, 1913

We are accustomed to think that part of the executive power of the crown is delegated to ministers and to the nominated members of the council. But what do we see? Your Majesty will agree that members of the government either do not wish to execute your will, or do not take the trouble to understand it. The population does not know where it is. Each minister has his own opinion. The cabinet is for the most part split into two parties, the state council form a third, the Duma a fourth, and your own will is unknown to the nation; this is not a government, it is anarchy.

Despite the success of the reforms, there were still unresolved issues and Nicholas' attitude towards the Dumas had shown clearly that he was unwilling to support major change.

Stolypin's reforms

Petr Stolypin, a conservative, was appointed chairman of the Council of Ministers in July 1906. His main aim was to strengthen the position of the Tsar and this was seen in his reaction to the unrest that followed the Vyborg

KEY TERM

Martial law Rule by the military.

KEY FIGURE

Petr Stolypin (1862–1911) was the son of a general. He studied agriculture and became interested in land reform. Rising in state service, he became governor of Grodno province in 1902 and by a mixture of repression and reform kept the province under control in 1905. He was rewarded by being appointed Minister of the Interior and then Prime Minister in the same year, 1906. Affected by his family being injured in a bomb attack he met terrorism with increased police repression but pursued a reforming policy to help the peasantry. Faced with feuds within government he resigned in 1911 and was subsequently assassinated.

> **How useful is Source C in explaining the problems in governing Russia?**

ACTIVITY

What was the significance of the Dumas?

Manifesto, with suppression being his priority. The number of trials and executions led to the name '**Stolypin's necktie**'. However, the unrest peaked by 1907 and Stolypin was ordered to reconsider government policy over land distribution. His aim here was to derevolutionize the peasantry, many of whom had supported the 1905 Revolution, and create a class of better and more prosperous peasants. This policy was known as 'the wager on the strong', and was aimed at creating a class of peasants who would be more likely to support the tsarist regime. Unused or poorly used land was made available and peasants who still farmed strips were given the opportunity to consolidate this land into smallholdings that were more efficient.

However, Stolypin's chances of success were limited as the peasantry were very conservative and resistant to change. Despite this, there was an expansion in the numbers joining the wealthier class of peasants, reflected in the number paying increasingly higher taxes. But it would be a slow process to transform the peasantry and the outbreak of war in 1914 brought it to a halt, making any judgement on its success difficult. Stolypin also faced the problem that many peasants were leaving the land to work in the cities, creating a labour shortage on the land which created difficulties in supplying the rapidly growing towns and cities with food.

The extent of opposition to tsarist rule

The first two Dumas had clearly shown that there was political opposition to the Tsar with both the Social Democrats and Social Revolutionaries gaining support. However, the changes to the electoral rules saw their support in the Dumas decline. The liberal members, or Kadets, were disappointed by developments, but were unwilling to openly oppose the Tsar. Radical beliefs, such as Marxism, did attract some support, as did **anarchism**. However, many of the radicals, such as Lenin, had been forced into exile and therefore the radical groups lacked enough support to offer a serious challenge to the regime. They did send back revolutionary material, which evaded censorship, but its impact was limited. As a result, it appeared, at least on the surface, as if the country was politically stable.

This does not mean that there was not disquiet. Although industry continued to grow, the conditions in the factories were often appalling. This led to many disaffected workers on the streets of the major cities in protest between 1911 and 1914. Government policy following the assassination of Stolypin in 1911 was one of repression, but this caused more disorder. The number of strikes that the Ministry of Trade and Industry described as political rose from 24 in 1911 to 2401 in 1914. Workers were faced with rising inflation and static wages, while growing class consciousness led to the potential for workers to challenge the authority of the Tsar.

Strikes and unrest became more common. There was unrest among the peasantry who were unable to keep up their payments for land they had bought. In towns poor living conditions added to the disquiet. By 1914 only

200 out of over 1000 towns had piped water and just 38 had a sewerage system. It was therefore hardly surprising that in 1910 there was an outbreak of cholera in St Petersburg, which killed over 100,000. Therefore, even if there was not political unrest as such, there was widespread dissatisfaction with the system.

Worker unrest came to a head in 1912 at the Lena Goldfields in Siberia. The miners demanded better pay and conditions, but the employers called in police to arrest the leaders of the strike. However, when the police moved in a considerable number of strikers were killed or injured, a clear indication of the willingness of the regime to enact brutal policies. This seemed to have an impact throughout the country (see Source D).

SOURCE D

A Secret Police agent describing the situation in St Petersburg, 1912

There has never been so much tension. People can be heard speaking of the government in the sharpest and most unbridled tones. Many say that the 'shooting' of the Lena workers recalls the 'shooting' of the workers at the Winter Palace of January 9 1905. Influenced by questions in the duma and the speeches which they called forth there, public tension is increasing still more. It is a long time since even the extreme left have spoken in such a way, since there have been references in the duma to 'the necessity of calling a Constituent Assembly' and 'overthrowing the present system by the united strength of the proletariat.'

How useful is Source D for assessing how stable Russia was before 1914?

Union militancy continued when a general strike brought St Petersburg to a halt in July 1914 and was probably only prevented from developing further due to the outbreak of the First World War. Industrial development had created problems that the government seemed unable to deal with, adopting ever more brutal methods of repression, which caused further disquiet and protest. Although the police and army might be able to crush unrest, they could not eliminate it and it led to the following speech by Guchkov at the Octobrist Party Conference in 1913:

SOURCE E

Guchkov speaking at the Octobrist Party Conference, 1913

The attempt by the Russian public, as represented by our party, to effect a peaceful, painless transition from the old condemned system to a new order has failed. Let those in power make no mistake about the temper of the people; let them not take outward indications of prosperity as a pretext for lulling themselves into security. Never were the Russian people so profoundly revolutionized by the actions of the government, for day by day faith in the government is steadily waning, and with it is waning faith in the possibility of a peaceful issue of the crisis.

Compose and contrast Sources D and E as evidence for the view that revolution was inevitable by 1913.

Despite this view, there are many historians who believe that the country was relatively stable on the eve of the First World War. In February 1913 the

Romanovs celebrated 300 years of rule with a nationwide tour deisgned to inspire loyalty and reverence. A few years earlier it would have been unthinkable for them to carry out such an engagement without being assassinated. The October Manifesto had not weakened Nicholas' authority and the Dumas were not a threat to his position. The Liberals or Kadets would not openly challenge him and the revolutionary parties, such as the Social Democrats and Social Revolutionaries, were incapable of mounting a serious challenge. Not only did they lack support and organization, but many of the leaders were either in internal or external exile. The economy was improving and Russia was developing into a modern industrial state. There was rising production and a growing labour force. Although that created its own problems, there was little evidence to suggest that the regime would collapse within three years. However, it must not be forgotten that the Tsar was unwilling to change and this made the system vulnerable to a severe challenge. After all, in 1914, Russia was still largely an unreformed autocratic state.

SUMMARY DIAGRAM

What were the causes and outcomes of the 1905 Revolution up to 1914?

Outcome of 1905 revolution

Unstable	Stable
Defeat to Japan Lena Goldfields strikes Opposition from Dumas	Duma reforms Growing economy Romanov celebrations Support for war 1914 Fundamental Laws

What were the causes and immediate outcomes of the February Revolution in 1917?

The long-term weaknesses of the Russian regime were made worse by the strains of war and in February 1917 unrest in the capital led to the government losing control and the abdication of the Tsar. This led to an unstable situation where power was shared between a parliamentary provisional government and a workers' and soldiers' council (soviet) and a second revolution in October.

Political, social and economic effects of the First World War, impact of military defeats

Just over a month after the assassination of the Austrian Archduke Franz Ferdinand by a Serbian terrorist group, Austria declared war on Serbia. This ultimately forced Nicholas II to mobilize the Russian army, which led to Germany and later Austria–Hungary declaring war on Russia. These events would have devastating consequences for the country and led to the downfall of the tsarist autocracy. However, at the outbreak of war it seemed to improve the position of the Tsar. There was support for the declaration of war from most of the Duma and there were popular demonstrations in support of war, with only the **Bolsheviks** opposing it.

The First World War played a crucial role in Russia's drift to revolution. The war showed that politically, economically and socially the country was not equipped to face the challenges of a modern war.

Economic impacts of the war

The Russian economy was unable to cope with the demands of **total war**. Although there were attempts to gear both agriculture and industry to the demands of war, it was simply unable to cope and this had a massive impact on the lives of ordinary Russians.

This was seen most clearly in rising inflation and prices. The cost of the war was some 3 billion roubles, whereas peacetime expenditure was 1.5 billion roubles. In order to meet the shortfall the government borrowed from overseas and at home and raised taxes and printed more money. The result was rampant inflation. By 1917 prices had risen 400 per cent since the start of the war, while average wages had only doubled.

There were also food shortages despite the average output of cereals being higher than it had been before the war. The problems were caused by a rising population, food requisitioning by the army, a decline in the availability of fertilizers and transport problems which meant that food could not be distributed. In particular the cities suffered badly. St Petersburg, or Petrograd as it was now named, was, by 1917, receiving less than a quarter of the amount of bread that had been available in 1914.

Much of the food shortages were the result of transport problems. The military had priority in using the transport system. They took control of both the railways and roads so that moving food supplies to civilian areas became increasingly difficult. Despite the growth in the railway system in the years before the war it simply was not enough and it became chaotic as the military attempted to move troops and armaments. As the system broke down trucks could not be moved and food often rotted in trucks. In the northern port of Archangel the pile-up of goods was so great that the weight of goods led to trucks sinking into the ground. In Moscow, which required 2200 wagons of grain per day, only 700 were reaching the city by February 1917.

Social problems

The disruption to food supplies made living and working conditions very difficult (see Source F). In desperate situations many of the workers turned to alcohol, particularly vodka, but Nicholas introduced prohibition of alcohol consumption at the start of the war. However, revenue from alcohol taxes brought in a third of government funds, which the government could not afford to lose. Prohibition also deprived workers of their one source of relaxation. By 1916 it was evident that the measure was not working as workers turned to other illicit methods to make drink, but by the time of the repeal the damage had been done.

SOURCE F

A report by the secret police (the Okhrana), October 1916

Even if we estimate the rise in earnings at 100 per cent, the prices of products have risen on the average, 300 per cent. The impossibility of even buying many food products and necessities, the time wasted standing idle in queues to receive goods, the increasing incidence of disease due to malnutrition and unsanitary living conditions (cold and dampness because of lack of coal and wood), and so forth, have made the workers as a whole, prepared for the wildest excesses of a 'hunger riot'.

In the future if grain continues to be hidden, the very fact of its disappearance will be sufficient to provoke in the capitals and in the other most populated centres of the empire the greatest disorders, attended by pogroms and endless street rioting.

How useful is Source F for supporting the view that the war brought about revolution in 1917?

Political impact

The Duma voted in August 1914 for its own suspension for the duration of the war. This was because a wave of patriotic feeling and support for the Tsar led to a belief that the Duma might only hinder the war effort. However, Russia's poor military performance led to it demanding its own recall less than a year later. Nicholas finally agreed to this in July 1915. However, his ministers failed to work with non-governmental bodies, such as the Union of Zemstvos and the Union of Municipal Councils, which joined to form the **Zemgor**. The success of this body was important as it suggested that there other ways to govern other than the tsar.

The Tsar also refused to listen to the Duma and refused its demands to dismiss his cabinet and replace it with a 'ministry of national confidence'. This was the last chance that Nicholas would have of maintaining the support of moderate parties as many Duma members now established the **'progressive bloc'**. This grouping tried to persuade him to make concessions, but the Tsar was unwilling to listen and it turned previous supporters into opponents. Meanwhile, all the Tsar did was to change his ministers, but they were not up to the task and so government slipped further into chaos.

Military events

The best chance for Russia to win the war was probably a quick victory, but there were early defeats at Tannenberg and Masurian Lakes. These defeats lowered the morale of the Russian troops, who were let down by poor commanders and strategy. By 1915 there was a supposed shell shortage, but this was more of an excuse for failings, and in the same year the **Great Retreat** was underway. The Russians had lost twice as many men as the enemy during these early campaigns and hopes of victory declined, leading to a loss of morale at home. This was not helped by shortages whereby Russian soldiers were forced to take shoes and weapons from dead colleagues to be able to continue to fight. These defeats led Nicholas to take personal control of the army by the end of 1915 with all the problems associated with such a decision.

Nicholas II as a war leader; implications of personal leadership of the war effort

The defeats during 1915 and the lack of strong leadership that the war needed led to Nicholas II taking direct command of the Russian forces in August 1915. Although he can be commended for trying to rally the nation and lift morale, it was a disastrous decision. Nicholas had been trained as a soldier, but he was not a natural commander and he had to rely on his generals. He did not know enough about the actual fighting and did not bring any new ideas of strategy. It appeared as if his decision to leave the capital and join his troops on the front line fighting the enemy, as a commander, was due more to his desire to escape Petrograd than because he had anything useful to bring to the front. His appointments were poor, based more on social standing than military expertise. However, the situation was not helped as senior officers were reluctant to tell him the truth of what was happening. But the biggest problem for Nicholas was that now he was commander all the defeats were blamed on him.

Despite these problems 1916 did appear to offer some respite. There was a more successful campaign led by General Brusilov, but this did not bring victory and had to be brought to an end. A million men were lost in the year. The failure of the Brusilov offensive and the development of a **war of attrition** showed that the Tsar was incapable of bringing the war to a successful conclusion.

The longer the war went on the more apparent were Russian military weaknesses (see Source G). It was not just the Tsar's failings as a commander that had an impact on the government of the country, but his decision to leave it in the hands of his wife, **Alexandra**, and **Rasputin**, who had become a personal advisor to the Tsarina. The decision to leave Alexandra in charge caused suspicion among the Russian people because she was German and because she took advice from Rasputin, who was despised by other of the Tsar's advisors. Rasputin was disliked by the Russian nobility, in part because of his peasant background, but also because of his growing influence over the Tsarina because of his apparent ability to lessen the **haemophilia** from which the Tsar and Tsarina's son suffered. He was also seen as a sexual predator, which made him appealing to many women at court, but angered their husbands. It was therefore difficult for even the most ardent supporters of the Tsar to defend a system whereby, at Russia's darkest hour, the country was ruled by 'that German woman' and a 'mad monk'.

KEY TERM

War of attrition A war where both sides try to wear down the enemy by killing more men and exhausting their resources rather than winning decisive victories.

KEY FIGURES

Tsarina Alexandra (1872–1918) was a German princess – Alix of Hesse and granddaughter of Queen Victoria of Britain. She met Nicholas in 1884 and they were married in 1894 when she became Empress. Shy, nervous and reclusive, she was unpopular in Russia and was ready to give Nicholas extreme advice. She was devoted to her family and to Rasputin, which made her popularity sink lower. She was killed with her husband and children by the Bolsheviks in 1918.

Grigori Rasputin (1869–1916) was a Siberian peasant who established himself as a self-professed holy man. These wandering mystics were a common feature in Russia and widely revered. He met the Tsar in 1905 and captivated the royal family. He was thought to be able to cure the haemophilia (a disease that prevents the blood clotting) of the Tsar's son and was influential before and during the war in advising the Tsarina, whose lover he was believed to be. Intensely unpopular, he was assassinated in December 1916 possibly with the connivance of the British.

How useful is Source G for explaining why the Tsar lost support in the course of the war?

How useful is Source H in assessing how far the problems of Russia by 1916 were the fault of the government?

SOURCE G

A report on the Russian army, January 1917

When this mass is at last demobilized and poured out over the country, it will wash away old landmarks and destroy dykes which have kept back the flood. All will join in one general demand: that the government should answer for bringing the country to the state it is in. To what extent the Government is really responsible will not concern them. Everyone agrees there will be a revolution. On this occasion the Army will be on the side of the people.

Among the better class of officers I note a great change of late. It daily grows greater and franker, daily more freely expressed. That is their attitude towards the Emperor. From time immemorial they have abused the Government. In the last year, I have noticed a new and sinister trend of feeling towards the Emperor. One by one they have fallen away from him, louder and louder they declare the existing state of affairs to be impossible. They condemn the Emperor as being weak and vacillating, ruled by the Empress and keeping in office not only utterly incompetent, but with pro-German tendencies.

On 30 December 1916 Rasputin was murdered by a group of aristocrats. He was poisoned, shot at close range, battered and was still alive when he was thrown into the icy river Neva where he finally died of drowning. By this stage, most supporters of the Tsar had deserted him. In November 1916 the leader of the Kadet party outlined the divisions within Russia (Source H).

SOURCE H

Paul Milyukov, leader of the Kadet party, speech to the Fourth Duma, November 1916

This present government has sunk beneath the level on which it stood during normal times in Russian life. And now the gulf between us and that government has grown wider and become impassable. Today we are aware that with this government we cannot legislate, and we cannot, with this government, lead Russia to victory. We are telling this government, as the declaration of the Progressive Bloc stated: We shall fight you, we shall fight you with all legitimate means until you go.

There had been challenges to Nicholas II before, most notably in 1905 (see pages 174–178) but the Duma had also demanded the sacking or removal of incompetent ministers and generals. However, by the start of 1917 things were very different. This time the range of opposition to the Tsar was much greater. There were rumours of serious unrest breaking out in the capital Petrograd and this was confirmed by the Duma president in early February, when he told the Tsar that serious protests were imminent. This seemed to confirm the reports of the Secret Police – the Okhrana – who had reported in January 1917 that the industrial workers were on the verge of revolution (Source I).

SOURCE I

Report from the Okhrana, January 1917

The mass of industrial workers are quite ready to let themselves go to the wildest excesses of a hunger riot. The working masses, led in their actions and sympathies by the more conscious and already revolutionary-minded elements, are violently hostile to the authorities and protest with all means and devices against a continuation of the war. Thus left-wing revolutionary circles are convinced that a revolution will begin very soon.

Compose and contrast Sources H and I as evidence for the causes of revolution in February 1917.

But it was not just the workers who had deserted the Tsar, even his traditional supporters had. At the front there were army mutinies and stories of the hardships the soldiers were suffering reached home. Many soldiers deserted, fearful that their families would die if they did not return home and it was they who provided a focal point of dissatisfaction in many of the cities where unrest developed. The scale of the dissatisfaction became apparent when soldiers were ordered to restore order in the cities and the Cossacks, that traditional arm of autocracy, refused to fire on protestors.

The Revolution of February and the abdication of Nicholas II

The Russian dating system, which follows the older Julian rather than the Gregorian calendar, puts forward the view that the Revolution lasted from 18 February to 4 March 1917.

Events of the February Revolution	
18 February	Strike begins at the Putilov steel works in Petrograd
19 February	Rumours that bread rationing is to be introduced
23 February	International Women's Day. This leads to marchers and workers from the Putilov plant joining to protest for female equality and improved conditions
25 February	General strike. Troops fire on workers
27 February	The Petrograd Soviet is formed. Some members of the Duma establish a Provisional Committee
28 February	Nicholas II is prevented from returning to Petrograd
1 March	Soviet Order Number 1 passed. This gives the Petrograd Soviet control over the military
2 March	The Provisional Committee declares itself the Provisional Government. Nicholas signs abdication decree
3 March	Provisional Government declares a revolution has taken place
4 March	Abdication of Nicholas announced

Given the situation in the major cities it should not be a surprise that unrest started at the Putilov steel works. This was the largest factory in Petrograd. Over the next few days the numbers on the streets increased dramatically.

This was initially encouraged by rumours that there would be further cuts in the bread supply. Although this was not true, the tensions within the city led to it being believed. International Women's Day brought more people out onto the streets. Many of the women were demanding equality, but they joined with other protestors who were demanding an end to the war, an improvement in food supplies and in their living and working conditions.

Within two days the protests had grown and a city-wide strike had started. Workers occupied factories and the authorities were unable to disperse them due to the sympathy among many of the police. This led to troops firing on protestors, while the president of the Duma, Rodzianko, urged the Tsar to change his methods of ruling. The events were still largely chaotic and many of the protests appeared to be about food shortages and problems created by the war, rather than politically driven and calling for the removal of the Tsar.

The Tsar was still at the front, some 400 miles (650 km) away, while the Tsarina remained in Petrograd. It was Alexandra who provided her husband with details of the developments within the capital. He ordered the commander of the Petrograd garrison to restore order, but was told that some members of the police and militia had joined the demonstrators and that the garrison was disobeying orders. The breakdown in law and order within the city was such that martial law could not be declared. However, the most important development was the desertion of the garrison.

The Provisional Committee and the Petrograd Soviet

It was this that prompted Rodzianko to inform the Tsar that the situation could be saved and the Tsar's position preserved only if major concessions were made. Nicholas' response was to dissolve the Duma. However, a group of twelve defied the order and established the Provisional Committee. This was a significant moment as it marked the first unconstitutional defiance of the Tsar and was soon followed by a call from Alexander Kerensky, a member of the Duma, for the Tsar to stand down.

A photograph of Kerensky at his desk in his office in the Winter Palace, 1917

Alexander Kerensky

Alexander Kerensky (1881–1970) was the son of a teacher. He studied law and history at university and became associated with radical opposition groups, defending revolutionaries of 1905 in trials. He was prominent in the Duma as a socialist and spoke against the government. After the February Revolution he was a member of both the provisional government and the committee of the Soviet. He was Minister for War and in July 1917 became the Prime Minister. Wavering between supporting the radical revolutionaries and a military coup he lost support and was overthrown by the Bolsheviks in October. He lived in exile until his death in the USA in 1970.

At the same time, another important event took place. This was the formation of the 'Petrograd Soviet of Soldiers', Sailors' and Workers' Deputies'. This, and the Provisional Committee, which although self-appointed now became the unofficial government of Russia, gave a clear indication that they viewed the Tsar as unfit to govern. It marked what would later be called the start of Dual Authority, whereby the two powers would rule the country. This situation lasted until October. The Soviet soon made its position very clear and announced its intention to summon a Constituent Assembly that would be elected on the basis of **universal suffrage**.

The abdication of the Tsar

As the situation deteriorated most ministers abandoned the government and left Petrograd. This led to Rodzianko informing the Tsar that only his abdication could save the crown and resulted in Nicholas' decision to return to his capital. He believed that by returning it would help to calm the situation, but his train was intercepted and forced to divert to Pskov. The members of old Duma and the high command of the army informed him how bad the situation was and advised him to abdicate. He accepted their advice and renounced the throne and also on behalf of his son. The abdication document he signed named his brother, the Grand Duke Michael, as the new tsar. However, Michael refused to accept it, using the excuse that it had not been offered to him by the Constituent Assembly.

His refusal left the Provisional Committee, now called the Provisional Government, responsible for ruling Russia. The rule of the Romanovs was over and Nicholas' formal abdication was announced.

The abdication of Nicholas had been brought about by events in the capital, with very few instances of unrest elsewhere. The Bolsheviks, the most revolutionary of the political parties, played little direct part in the regime's downfall, with many of their leaders still in exile. What is also noticeable is that there were no groups willing to defend the autocracy.

The overthrow of the autocracy was not completely bloodless, but probably no more than 2000 people were killed or wounded. But whether the events that took place in the capital should be seen as overthrowing the monarchy is another question. An examination of the timeline at the start of this section suggests that developments were haphazard and there was no real plan. Perhaps the most important reason for the eventual downfall was that those in power lacked a plan to save the monarchy. It was the desertion of high-ranking officers and the refusal of members of the Duma to disband that brought it down. Once Nicholas lost the support of the army and police, it was virtually impossible for him to remain in power. It was this loss of support that was very different from 1905 and, along with the refusal of Michael to take up the reins of power, that ended tsardom in Russia.

KEY TERM

Universal suffrage
A system of election in which all adults have the right to vote.

ACTIVITY

Discussion point:

Why was Nicholas II able to survive the 1905 revolution but not the February 1917 revolution?

The formation and purpose of the Provisional Government

Although the Tsar had gone, it did not mean that the new government did not face serious problems. In fact it faced not only the problems that the Tsar had faced:

- continuation of the war
- land redistribution
- economic dislocation.

Added to these issues was the problem that the provisional government lacked real authority as it was not an elected body and had come into being because of the refusal of some members of the old Duma to disband. It also faced challenges from the Petrograd Soviet, which would further limit its authority.

However, it was the task of the Provisional Government, initially led by **Prince Lvov**, to pick up the government of the Tsar. It was provisional, or temporary, as it was to hold power until elections could be held for a Constituent Assembly, which was to be elected on the basis of universal suffrage and a secret ballot.

Although some have argued that because the Provisional Government was not democratically elected and consisted of members of the old Duma it was weak, but as its main task was to establish a Constituent Assembly this was not a major issue. A far greater challenge was presented by the existence of the Petrograd Soviet, which although it did not set out to be an alternative government was soon opposing virtually everything that the Provisional Government attempted to do. This was particularly the case over the big question of the war. The Provisional Government was keen to continue Russia's involvement and push for a decisive victory, while the Soviet wanted 'peace without annexations or indemnities'. This division would be crucial and play a major role in the failure of the government.

The issuing by the Petrograd Soviet of Order Number 1 also created problems for the Provisional Government as it meant that their orders were not binding unless they were approved by the Soviet. The Order also placed control of the armed forces in the hands of the Soviet, which further restricted the power of Provisional Government (Source J).

KEY FIGURE

Prince Lvov (1861–1925) was a member of an eminent noble family who became a liberal and joined the Kadets after 1905. He was prominent in the opposition in the Duma after 1915 and was the first prime minister of the Provisional Government after the fall of the Tsar. Lacking support he resigned in July. Imprisoned by the Bolsheviks in 1918 he was lucky to survive and lived in exile until his death in France in 1925.

> **How useful is Source J as evidence for the view that the Dual Authority of 1917 fatally weakened the Provisional Government?**

SOURCE J

The Petrograd Soviet of Workers' and Soldiers' Deputies Order Number 1, 14 March 1917

The Soviet of Workers' and Soldiers' Deputies has decided:

- *In all companies, battalions, squadrons and separate branches of the military service of all kinds and on warships, committees should be chosen immediately.*
- *The order of the State duma shall be carried out only when they do not contradict the orders and decisions of the Soviet of Workers' and Soldiers' Deputies.*

- *All kinds of arms, such as rifles and machine guns, must be under the control of the company and battalion committees and must in no case be handed over to officers even at their demand.*

- *The addressing of officers with titles such as 'Your Excellency', 'Your Honour', etc., is abolished and these are replaced by 'Mr General', 'Mr Colonel' and so on.*

These orders meant that compromise with the Soviet was now essential and until April, when the Bolshevik leader, Lenin, returned this appeared to work. However, Leon Trotsky saw it rather differently from the moderate socialists and suggested that Soviet was the dominating force (see Source K).

SOURCE K

Leon Trotsky, *A History of the Russian Revolution*, 1932

From the moment of its formation the Soviet, in the person of its Executive Committee, begins to function as a sovereign. It elects a temporary food commission and places it in charge of the mutineers and of the garrison in general. The tasks and functions of the Soviet grow unceasingly under pressure from the masses. The revolution finds here its indubitable centre. The workers, the soldiers, and soon also the peasants, will from now on turn only to the Soviet. In their eyes the Soviet becomes the focus of all hopes and all authority, an incarnation of the revolution itself.

> **How useful is Source K as evidence of the importance of the Soviet in the period after the abdication of the Tsar?**

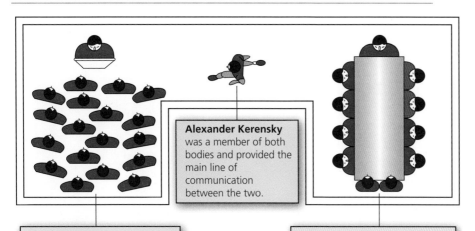

Petrograd Soviet

Made up of:
- Workers' and soldiers' representatives
- Socialist intellectuals, mainly Mensheviks and Socialist Revolutionaries

Chairman of the executive committee:
Chkheidze

Role:
To protect the interests of the working classes and soldiers

NB Socialist intellectuals formed the leadership of the Soviet

The Petrograd Soviet and Provisional Government held meetings in different wings of the Tauride Palace

Alexander Kerensky was a member of both bodies and provided the main line of communication between the two.

Provisional Government

Made up of:
Leading figures from the Kadets and other liberal parties

Leader:
Prince Lvov

Role:
To run the country until a Constituent Assembly had been elected

NB The Provisional Government had been chosen by a committee of the Duma; it had not been elected by the people

Figure 4.2 The membership and role of the Petrograd Soviet and the Provisional Government

Vladimir Ulyanov (Lenin)

1870	Born as Vladimir Ilyich Ulyanov, to a minor aristocratic family of Jewish ancestry
1897	Exiled to Siberia, took the alias Lenin
1900	Joined the Social Democratic Party
1903	Led the Bolshevik breakaway movement in the SDs
1906–17	In exile abroad
1917	Returned to Petrograd to lead the Bolsheviks in the October Revolution
1917–22	Led the Bolsheviks in consolidating their hold on Russia
1921	Introduced the New Economic Policy
1924	Died

Vladimir Ulyanov (1870–1924), better known to history as Lenin, turned against the tsarist regime following the execution of his brother in 1887. In his writing he adapted Marxist theory to fit Russian conditions. He argued the Bolshevik party would direct a revolution from above regardless of the scale of popular support. He returned to Russia after the abdication of Nicholas II, writing his April Theses and after seeing the party virtually destroyed in the July Days organized the overthrow of the Provisional Government in October. He was largely responsible for the creation of the new state, overcoming opposition from both foreign powers and within Russia. He was forced to backtrack on his socialist principles and introduce the New Economic Policy. He suffered from ill health following a series of strokes and died after being incapacitated for two years.

Lev Bronstein (Trotsky)

1879	Born into a Ukrainian Jewish family
1905	Became Chairman of St Petersburg soviet
1907–17	Lived in various European countries and in the USA
1917	Principal organizer of the October coup
1918	Negotiated the Treaty of Brest-Litovsk
1918–20	Created the Red Army
1924–27	Outmanoeuvred in the power struggle with Stalin
1940	Assassinated in Mexico

Trotsky (1879–1940) was originally a Menshevik and it was in this role that he was appointed Chairman of the St Petersburg Soviet in 1905. He was exiled between 1907 and 1917 but used that time to develop his theory of 'permanent revolution' or continuous international class warfare. He returned to Petrograd after the February Revolution and joined the Bolsheviks, becoming Chairman of the Petrograd Soviet, using the position to help organize the October Revolution. He became Commissar for Foreign Affairs and was chief negotiator in the peace talks with Germany. He was responsible for the organization of the Red Army in the Civil War. However, having been a Menshevik he was never fully accepted by some Bolsheviks and lost out to Stalin in the struggle for power following Lenin's death. He was exiled in 1929 and in 1940 was assassinated by an agent of Stalin.

The Provisional Government issued a set of eight principles by which it would rule. These were liberal in nature and further weakened it as it allowed for opposition groups, such as the Bolsheviks, to develop. The Provisional Government also faced the challenge of very high levels of inflation and low wages, which it found virtually impossible to resolve. The land redistribution issue was also difficult and the best answer it could offer was to suggest that only an elected assembly could resolve it and therefore the matter would have to wait, which did little to please the peasantry and encouraged further seizures of land. This also encouraged soldiers to desert as they did not want to miss out on land seizure, further weakening the armed forces.

Despite the challenges it faced the Provisional Government did have some early successes:

- Political prisoners were released from jail.
- There were improvements in working conditions as trade unions were recognized and an eight-hour day was brought in.
- Full civil rights were granted.
- Religious freedom was allowed.

It did appear as if Russia was moving towards a more liberal and modern state with the adoption of these progressive measures.

However, the return of Lenin to Russia in April 1917 and his call for 'all power to the Soviets' drove a wedge between the two powers and ended the initial co-operation. An attempt was made in May 1917 to heal the divisions with the formation of a coalition government, with Lvov inviting six members of the Soviet to join it. However, this did not satisfy the more radical members of the Soviet and problems continued. National elections to a Constituent Assembly were postponed and the other issues of the war and land were ignored. This led to a loss of support for the Provisional Government and increasingly radical demands from the Soviet, so that by June they were demanding an even greater say in national government.

Long-term causes	Short-term causes	Immediate outcomes
Growth of opposition parties Economic problems Unwillingness of Tsar to reform Repressive policies Growing worker unrest and strikes	Impact of war Nicholas going to the front Loss of Tsar's traditional supporters Military defeats Strikes in factories Actions of the Duma Actions of the police, army and garrison in Petrograd Developments in Petrograd	Abdication of the Tsar Establishment of the Provisional Government Struggle between Provisional Government and Petrograd Soviet Lack of authority

SUMMARY DIAGRAM

Why was there a Revolution in February 1917 and what were the immediate outcomes?

ACTIVITY

Briefly explain how each of the causes mentioned in the summary diagram brought about revolution.

How and why did the Bolsheviks gain power in October 1917?

In February 1917 when the tsarist autocracy fell very few people would have thought that by the end of October 1917 the Bolsheviks would have been able to seize power. They lacked mass support, most of their leaders were in exile and most expected that a Constituent Assembly would establish a new form of government for Russia. However, a series of mistakes, as well as the leadership of Lenin and the skill of Trotsky, meant that by October the Bolsheviks were in a position to stage a successful **coup**.

Crises of the Provisional Government

The Provisional Government made a series of mistakes in the period from March to October 1917. Changes they made allowed political groups such as the Bolsheviks to develop. Firstly, Stalin and **Kamenev** returned to Petrograd from exile in Siberia in March and then Lenin returned from exile in Switzerland in April. It was Lenin's return that was particularly significant. He made it very clear to members of the party that he was opposed to the Provisional Government and the day after his return he set out his ideas in his April Theses.

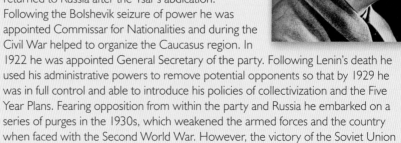

Josef Stalin

Stalin (1879–1953) was born Iosif Vissarionovich Dzhugashvili in Georgia. He was expelled from a seminary in Tbilisi in 1899 because of his political views. By 1905 he was representing the Bolshevik party at conferences in Georgia and South Russia. He became a member of the Party's Central Committee and helped to found the party newspaper. Exiled, he returned to Russia after the Tsar's abdication. Following the Bolshevik seizure of power he was appointed Commissar for Nationalities and during the Civil War helped to organize the Caucasus region. In 1922 he was appointed General Secretary of the party. Following Lenin's death he used his administrative powers to remove potential opponents so that by 1929 he was in full control and able to introduce his policies of collectivization and the Five Year Plans. Fearing opposition from within the party and Russia he embarked on a series of purges in the 1930s, which weakened the armed forces and the country when faced with the Second World War. However, the victory of the Soviet Union in 1945 strengthened his position. He died in 1953.

In the April Theses Lenin:

- condemned the Provisional Government for being **bourgeois** and called for its overthrow
- called for co-operation with other political parties to be ended
- called for the Soviets to seize power and create a workers' government.

 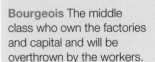
This message led to two very important propaganda slogans to emerge:

- 'All power to the Soviets'
- 'Peace, Land and Bread'

These were very important as they reinforced Lenin's call for the Soviets to take political power and for Russia to withdraw from the war and deal with food shortages and the land issue. Such calls would win large-scale support among the workers and peasants. These calls were in complete contrast to the policies of the Provisional Government which had continued with the war, which was having a large negative impact on both the workers and peasants, and had failed to tackle either the problem of food shortages or the land issue.

In an attempt to try to win support for the Provisional Government Lvov ordered a new offensive in the war. This was organized by the Minister of War, Alexander Kerensky, and proved to be a disaster. There were heavy losses and mass desertions, which led to further protests against the war. The protests culminated in July when sailors at the naval base of Kronstadt mutinied.

These events led to what have been called the July Days when the Bolsheviks believed that the Soviets should take power. However, they were not supported by other political groups, and the government was able to summon enough loyal troops to put down the protests. The successful crushing of the unrest was credited to Kerensky who, despite the failings of the offensive, was appointed Prime Minister. He now launched an offensive against those who were behind the July Days, particularly the Bolsheviks. Leading members of the party were either exiled or arrested while their newspaper, *Pravda*, was closed down. It appeared as if Bolshevik hopes of taking power were over.

However, there were two developments that prevented the complete crushing of the Bolsheviks. The first was the Bolshevik attitude to the land question. The Bolsheviks had initially believed that it was only the industrial masses who were revolutionary, but the continued seizure of land by the peasantry convinced them that the peasants might also be won over. Therefore they adopted a campaign of land to the peasants, which soon won them support given the failure of the Provisional Government to tackle the question. The second was the issue of General Kornilov (see Source L on page 200).

Victor Chernov, Founder of the SR Party, *The Great Russian Revolution,* **1936**

At that time it would not have been difficult to suppress the Bolshevist organization completely. Nevertheless, the Soviet did not go so far. It did not even expel the Bolsheviks. Why? Because to take such strong steps against the Left while continuing to compromise with the Right, when General Kornilov was beginning his political demonstrations, meant breaking forever with democracy and openly joining the counter-revolution. To disarm the Bolsheviks and their sympathisers completely was possible only for a government which could win the sympathy of the toiling masses by far-reaching social reforms, by a firm policy in the question of war and peace and by creating radically new conditions for nationalities in Russia. But the government was paralysed by its alliance with the bourgeois nationalists. It had to counterbalance its concessions to them by equal tolerance of Left-wing extremism. In other words it had to be weak on both fronts.

> **How useful is Source L in explaining why the Bolsheviks were not suppressed by the authorities?**

> **ACTIVITY**
> Outline and explain the changing fortunes of the Bolshevik party in 1917.

Kornilov brought his troops to Petrograd with the intention of closing down the Soviet and then hoped to replace the Provisional Government with a military-style dictatorship, which might even restore tsardom. He made a patriotic appeal to the people of Russia for support, claiming that he was saving the country (Source M).

SOURCE M

Kornilov's declaration to the people of Russia, 26 August 1917

People of Russia! Our great motherland is dying. The moment of death is near. I, General Kornilov, declare that the Provisional Government, under pressure from the Bolshevik majority in the Soviet, acts in full accord with the German General Staff, and concurrently with the imminent landings of the enemy forces on the coast of Riga, destroys the army and convulses the country from within.

I, General Kornilov, declare to each and all that I personally desire nothing but to save Great Russia. I swear to lead the people through victory over the enemy to the Constituent Assembly, where it will decide its own destiny and choose its new political system.

> **Read Source M. Using your own knowledge, how far are Kornilov's criticisms of the government justified?**

His plan collapsed, in part because railway workers refused to transport his troops, but also because the Bolsheviks prepared quickly to resist him. Kerensky called on all loyal citizens to defend the city and released Bolsheviks from prison, while others came out of hiding and took the weapons being offered by the Provisional Government to defend the city. Their response turned the Bolsheviks into heroes as they were willing to defend the Revolution and Petrograd. This gained them more support, but it also showed how weak the Provisional Government was as they had been forced into arming the Bolsheviks to prevent a potential counter-revolution. There was a considerable shift in the position of the Bolsheviks from the low point of the July Days and this was reflected in their gaining majorities in

both the Petrograd and Moscow Soviets by the end of September. This
change was largely the result of the failings of the Provisional Government,
but it did not mean that they had secured mass support.

Lenin's leadership of the Bolsheviks

Although Lenin had spent long periods in exile, most notably from 1906 to
1917 he was a major influence on the Bolshevik party and would play a
crucial role in their seizure of power. Even from his exile his writings had
given the Bolsheviks a sense of direction and his oratory skills had been
seen when he returned in April 1917 and issued the April Theses. However,
his greatest importance was in the events of the autumn of 1917. He had
been constantly appealing to the party to prepare for the overthrow of the
Provisional Government. His call became more intense as the government
failed to solve the problem of the war or the land question and appeared to
be more reactionary in their outlook. Lenin argued that the Bolsheviks must
seize the moment and on 12 September wrote 'History will not forgive us if
we do not assume power.'

Lenin was concerned that if the Bolsheviks did not act they would lose their
chance. In particular, he was concerned by two events that were due to take
place:
- The meeting of the All Russian Congress of Soviets in late October
- The elections to the Constituent Assembly.

Lenin was convinced that it was essential for the Bolsheviks to seize power
before either of these events took place (see Source N below).

SOURCE N

A letter by Lenin to the Central Committee, 24 October 1917

*The situation is critical in the extreme. In fact it is now absolutely clear that to delay the
uprising would be fatal. With all my might I urge comrades to realize that everything
now hangs by a thread. We are confronted by problems which are not to be solved by
conferences but only by the masses and by the struggle of the armed people. We must
at all costs, this very evening, this very night, arrest the government, having first
disarmed the officers. We must not wait! We may lose everything!*

*Under no circumstances should power be left in the hands of Kerensky and his group,
not under any circumstances. The matter must be decided without fail this very
evening, or this very night. History will not forgive we revolutionaries for delaying
when we could be victorious today (and we certainly will be victorious today), while we
risk losing much tomorrow, in fact, risk losing everything.*

*It would be an infinite crime on the part of the revolutionaries if we let the chance slip,
knowing that the salvation of the revolution, the chance of peace, salvation from famine,
and the transfer of the land to the peasants depend upon them. The government is
tottering. It must be given the death blow at all costs.*

> **How useful is Source
> N for assessing the
> view that Lenin was
> the key to Bolshevik
> success in October
> 1917?**

He believed that if they overthrew the Provisional Government before the Congress of Soviets met then they could claim authority as it would have been carried out in the name of the Soviets and handed them power. Just as importantly, Lenin was concerned about the outcome of the elections to the Constituent Assembly and was uncertain how the Bolsheviks would perform and therefore they needed to be in power before the results as this would give them the authority to go against the results if they did badly.

In order to try to bolster the Provisional Government Kerensky announced plans for a pre-parliament, which was a body to advise the government. Lenin condemned this and, following his orders, Bolsheviks in the Soviet criticized it and then walked out. As a result, the pre-parliament was undermined, and this gave Lenin the confidence to pressurize his party to overthrow the Provisional Government. However, he faced considerable opposition from within the Bolshevik Central Committee. In order to overcome this opposition, Lenin secretly returned to Petrograd on 7 October and spent a lot of time trying to convince opponents that this was the correct course of action. On 10 October the Central Committee agreed to an armed rising, but did not agree on a date. It was the actions of the Provisional Government that forced the Bolsheviks to act.

Rumours that the Bolsheviks were about to act had been spreading around Petrograd for some weeks. However, it was an article written by two members of the Bolshevik Central Committee, **Grigory Zinoviev** and Lev Kamenev, that appeared to provide the Provisional Government with the proof they needed. Zinoviev and Kamenev argued that it would be a mistake to attempt to seize power (Source O), showing the divisions there were within the Bolshevik party.

ACTIVITY

Construct a spider diagram to show the reasons for the failure of the Provisional Government. Explain each factor, which do you think was the most important? Explain your choice.

KEY FIGURE

Grigory Zinoviev (1883–1936) was a close colleague of Lenin following the formation of the Bolshevik party. He was executed during Stalin's purges.

Compare and contrast Source O with Source N on page 201 as evidence for Bolshevik views about the timing of the revolution.

SOURCE O

Article by L. Kamenev and G. Zinoviev, 11 October 1917

We are most profoundly convinced that to declare at once an armed uprising would mean to stake not only the fate of our party, but also the fate of the Russian and international revolution. There is no doubt that there are such historical situations that an oppressed class has to acknowledge that it is better to join battle and lose than to surrender without a fight. Is the Russian working class in such a position now? No, and a thousand times no.

This convinced Kerensky that a date had been set and rather than wait he ordered a pre-emptive strike. On 23 October the Bolshevik newspapers were closed down and attempts were made to arrest the leading Bolsheviks. This left Lenin with no choice; he ordered the rising to begin.

The role of Trotsky and the Military Revolutionary Committee (MRC)

Trotsky's role in events went back to 1905 when he was appointed Chairman of the Petrograd, or as it was called then St Petersburg, Soviet. Although he was subsequently exiled, he resumed his role as Chairman in September 1917. In this role he persuaded the Petrograd Soviet to establish the Military Revolutionary Committee (MRC). However, more important was his appointment as one of three co-ordinators of the MRC, which had been established on 9 October to organize the defence of the city against a possible German attack or a Kornilov-style coup. It was Trotsky who actually organized the rising. He realized that by having control of the MRC the Bolsheviks would control Petrograd. By having control over the MRC it meant that he controlled the only effective military force in the city. Not only that, but any actions it took would be viewed as lawful because it acted on the authority of the Soviet.

These developments meant that Trotsky was in a position to draft plans for the overthrow of the Provisional Government. Therefore, when Lenin gave the orders for the Revolution to start, Trotsky was in a position to implement the plans. It would be Trotsky who would direct the **Red Guards** and organize the seizure of the key strategic points in Petrograd, namely the telegraph offices, bridges, the main railway station and the power stations.

The key events of the October Revolution

The Bolsheviks had been planning for the revolution for some time, but it was Kerensky's decision to close down their newspapers and attempt to arrest their leaders that triggered the revolution. The Bolshevik Revolution started on 24 October and it took just three days for Petrograd to fall to them, during which time there was very little fighting.

Key events of the October Revolution

7 October	Lenin returns from exile after the July Days
9 October	Petrograd Soviet establishes the Military Revolutionary Committee
10 October	Bolsheviks start to plan the Revolution
11 October	Kamenev and Zinoviev oppose the idea of a revolution
23 October	Kerensky closes down Bolshevik newspapers and attempts to arrest Bolshevik leaders
24 October	First Session of the Congress of Soviets
24–26 October	Bolsheviks seize Petrograd
25–26 October	Members of the Provisional Government arrested, Kerensky flees, Bolsheviks seize the Winter Palace
27 October	Lenin informs the Congress of Soviets that the Bolsheviks have taken power

The seizure of power was relatively straightforward for the Bolsheviks. They faced virtually no military opposition as the Provisional Government simply lacked a military force. The Petrograd garrison did not come to its aid and desertions had weakened it further. Even the seizure of the Winter Palace faced little opposition and the Bolsheviks did not have to storm the gates, as is often shown on films, as there was no one there defending it (Source P).

SOURCE P

A report from the British newspaper the *Manchester Guardian*, 10 November 1917

Towards five o'clock on Wednesday the Soviet, which has become master of the whole city, began to isolate the Winter Palace, where practically the whole of the Government remained. Detachments occupied all routes giving access to the Palace. Barricades were erected haphazard, made of logs taken from neighbouring wood depots, and planks from works under construction. Traffic was gradually stopped, and in the area isolated only troops, armoured cars and two anti-aircraft guns placed near the police headquarters on the Nevsky Prospekt remained. Trams were stopped on this part of the route, but a short distance beyond they are running as usual, and the ordinary service will be maintained. The disturbances which the actions of the Committee [MRC] have occasioned are therefore purely local and temporary. Ordinary life is going on with almost a tinge of indifference.

How useful is Source P as evidence for the nature of the Bolshevik takeover?

Once they had entered the building, those who were supposed to be defending it simply gave up and lay down their arms. The sounding of the guns by the cruiser *Aurora* convinced those members of the government who remained that their position was hopeless and those who could escaped.

The Bolshevik seizure of power had been easy, in part because there was a power vacuum and power simply fell into their hands.

ACTIVITY

Compare and contrast Source P and Source Q in their view of the Bolshevik seizure of power in October 1917.

SOURCE Q

A painting made in the 1930s by Sokolov-Skalya showing the storming of the Winter Palace

Why were the Bolsheviks successful in seizing power?

- They were viewed as heroes because they had defeated Kornilov.
- They refused to work with other parties and were therefore not associated with unpopular policies, such as the continuation of the war.
- They rejected the creation of the Constituent Assembly.
- Owing to the mistakes of the Provisional Government, particularly allowing the leading Bolsheviks to return from exile.
- Bolshevik use of propaganda; slogans such as 'Peace, Land and Bread' were very popular.
- The role of Kerensky. He failed to crush the Bolsheviks after the July Days and then armed them to defeat Kornilov.
- The skills of Lenin and Trotsky.

The All-Russian Congress of Soviets, which had begun their meeting, were soon told by the Bolshevik Chairman, Lev Kamenev, that they were now the supreme authority and that the Petrograd Soviet had seized power in their name and formed a new government. This shocked the Congress and this sense of bewilderment was only added to when Kamenev read out a list of the new government that they had supposedly appointed. The new government was made up of all Bolsheviks and Left SRs, but at the head of the **Sovnarkom** was Lenin. The SRs and Mensheviks walked out, arguing that this was just a Bolshevik coup. However, Trotsky's response to them was forthright (Source Q), arguing that seizure of power was a popular uprising, while other parties had abandoned the ideals of the revolution.

ACTIVITY

Rank the factors listed for the success of the Bolsheviks in seizing power. Explain your order.

KEY TERM

Sovnarkom Council of People's Commissars, or a governing committee for the new Russian state, set up by Lenin in October 1917.

SOURCE Q

Trotsky, speech to the Congress of Soviets, January 1918

The insurrection of the masses stands in no need of justification. What is taking place is not a conspiracy but an insurrection. We moulded the revolutionary will of the Petrograd workers and soldiers. The masses gathered under our banner, and our insurrection was victorious. But what do they, the other socialists, offer us? To give up our victory, to compromise, and to negotiate – with whom? With whom shall we negotiate? With those miserable cliques which have left the Congress or with those who still remain? But we saw how strong those cliques were? There is no one left in Russia to follow them. And millions of workers and peasants are asked to negotiate with them on equal terms. No, an agreement will not do now. To those who have left us and to those proposing negotiations we must say: You are a mere handful, miserable, bankrupt; your role is finished, and you may go where you belong – to the garbage heap of history.

How useful is Source Q for assessing the view that the Bolshevik Revolution was a popular revolution rather than a coup?

Although the Bolsheviks had taken power in Petrograd, they faced a harder struggle elsewhere, even in Moscow. In Kiev there was much fighting between the Ukraine regiments and the Bolsheviks, with the former gaining the upper hand and declaring its autonomy. The major naval port of Odessa, on the Black Sea, declared for a coalition socialist government, while in the Cossack region they continued to maintain their independence. Bolshevik control over the rest of Russia would have to be fought for and this would eventually lead to a civil war that would last until 1921.

Was the Bolshevik Revolution a popular takeover?

The Communist party argued that Lenin, supported by the Russian people, brought the Bolshevik party to power and then went on to create a workers' state. This view fulfilled the writings of **Karl Marx** who, writing in the nineteenth century, had argued that economic forces determined history and that economic changes would eventually give power to the workers, or proletariat, who would defeat the **capitalists** or bourgeoisie.

The extent of Bolshevik support is very difficult to gauge, but it does appear as if support for the Bolsheviks was growing; membership appears to have risen from 10,000 in February 1917 to 250,000 by October the same year. Their performance in the Moscow municipal elections also supports this view as the table below shows.

	July	October
Social Revolutionaries	375,000 (58%)	54,000 (14%)
Mensheviks	76,000 (12%)	16,000 (4%)
Bolsheviks	75,000 (11%)	198,000 (51%)
Kadets	109,000 (17%)	101,000 (26%)

However, the extent to which the October Revolution was a mass movement of the workers is hotly debated. Even Trotsky argued that the Revolution needed Lenin's drive to make it happen when it did. Instead Trotsky suggested that Lenin had created a tightly knit and well-disciplined cadre that was able to seize power in the name of the workers.

Much of the dispute about the nature of the Revolution has centred round how popular the Bolsheviks were or whether Lenin simply led a minority party to power. But even in this interpretation the role of Lenin was still important, even if the Revolution was not inevitable even though Marxist historians believe that it was. Instead, these interpretations have put forward the view that events followed the course they did because of decisions that were made by those taking part, particularly Lenin and Trotsky, but also Kerensky.

Trotsky also argued though that the Revolution was still a genuine workers' revolution and that its achievements were betrayed later by Stalin in particular. There may be some truth in Trotsky's claim that the Revolution was popular as politics in Russia had become more radical in 1917 and there were worker and soldier demonstrations against the Provisional Government. Some historians have also argued that even before the war Russia was heading towards revolution. Previous sections of this chapter have shown that a gulf was developing between the tsarist autocracy, the growing middle class and the workers such that a revolution was likely and that all the Bolsheviks had to do was to exploit this to gain power. It is unlikely that there will be agreement as to why the revolution occurred and the extent to which it was unavoidable, or whether it was decisions made after the abdication of the Tsar that brought it about. However, one thing is clear; having seized power, or perhaps even just picked it up, the Bolsheviks would face a struggle to consolidate their hold over Russia.

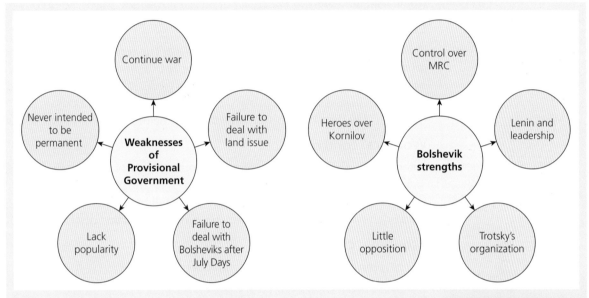

SUMMARY DIAGRAM

How and why did the Bolsheviks gain power in October 1917?

 # How were the Bolsheviks able to consolidate their power up to 1921?

Although the Bolsheviks had taken power in the October Revolution, their authority did not extend much beyond Petrograd and Moscow. It would therefore be very difficult for them to introduce the revolutionary policies that some of the supporters wanted and expected. They also faced a number of problems, most notably the question of the First World War. It was this, the issue of land and the elections to the Constituent Assembly that first had to be addressed.

Bolshevik reforms and the establishment of a dictatorship

In order to deal with the problems created by the war the Bolsheviks issued a number of decrees.

Peace

The first Decree, on Peace, issued in October 1917 called for nations to enter into talks for 'a democratic peace without annexations'. This laid the foundations for an armistice, which was signed on 2 December 1917 and would lead ultimately to the Treaty of Brest-Litovsk (see pages 210–211).

Land reform

In November 1917 the Decree on Land was issued. This accepted the seizure of private land by the peasants and gave authority to a process that had already started. However, it did state that the division and redistribution was to be carried out by the village soviets. In many ways it was similar to the proposals that the SRs had been putting forward and therefore helped in winning over some.

Workers' control

The same month also saw the Decree on Workers' Control. As with the Decree on Land, this largely authorized what had been taking place. It accepted the takeover of factories by workers, but due to the fall in output it also ordered the workers' committees to maintain 'the strictest order and discipline'.

Economic changes

The government, despite lacking control of the whole country, also began to establish state control of the economy and in December 1917 established **Gosplan**, which nationalized the banks and railways, cancelled foreign debts and began to develop the transport network. There was also a Decree on Nationalization issued in June 1918 which brought nearly all the major industrial enterprises under central government control.

Political control

The other problem that the Bolsheviks faced was the elections to the Constituent Assembly. They hoped that they would win a majority as this would further legitimize their power, but as the table below shows, this did not happen.

Table 4.1 Results of the election to the Constituent Assembly

Party	Votes	Seats
Socialist Revolutionaries	17,490,000	370
Bolsheviks	9,844,000	175
National minority groups	8,257,000	99
Left SRs (pro-Bolshevik)	2,861,000	40
Kadets	1,986,000	17
Mensheviks	1,248,000	16
Total	**41,686,000**	

These results were a clear indication that there was considerable opposition to Bolshevik rule. Aware that they would not be able to consolidate power through future elections, Lenin decided to use military force to end the Assembly and it was closed down after just one day. Lenin justified his actions by arguing that the elections had been rigged and that the Assembly had been elected using the old system, producing a result similar to that under the Tsar. It must also be remembered that the position of the Bolsheviks was weak and that many did not believe that they would be able to hold on to power and, therefore, faced with threats both at home and abroad they were not willing to share power. Lenin himself was not a democrat. He believed that the only way to rule was by crushing the opposition; however, he defended his actions by arguing that it was necessary to destroy the bourgeoisie in order to give power to the people (Source R).

SOURCE R

Lenin, speech, January 1918

Those who point out that we are now 'dissolving' the Constituent Assembly although at one time we defended it are not displaying a grain of sense, but are merely uttering pompous and meaningless phrases. At one time, we considered the Constituent Assembly to be better than tsarism and the republic of Kerensky with their famous organs of power; but as the Soviets emerged, they, being revolutionary organizations of the whole people, naturally became incomparably superior to any parliament in the world, a fact that I emphasized as far back as last April. By completely smashing the bourgeois and landed property and by facilitating the final upheaval which is sweeping away all traces of the bourgeois system, the Soviets impelled us on to the path that has led the people to organize their own lives.

Our cry was, All power to the Soviets; it is for this we are fighting. The people wanted the Constituent Assembly summoned and we summoned it. But they sensed immediately what this famous Constituent Assembly really was. And now we have carried out the will of the people, which is – All power to the Soviets.

> **Using your own knowledge how far are the claims in Source R justified?**

The closure of the Constituent Assembly was agreed by the Third All-Russian Congress of Soviets in January 1918, which also announced the establishment of the Russian Soviet Federative Socialist Republic.

However, the dissolution of the Assembly did create unease and this was added to by Lenin's desire to take Russia out of the war and reach a peace with Germany. This led to many, particularly among the SRs, arguing that Lenin had not only betrayed the Revolution but was a German agent. Even among his own supporters there was unease, there was criticism of his methods and some believed that he was destroying democracy. Lenin, however, argued that the country was faced with challenges on all fronts and therefore harsh measures were needed, and he stressed the concept of democratic centralism, whereby party members obey the leadership.

The impact of the Treaty of Brest-Litovsk

The rule of both Nicholas II and the Provisional Government had fallen largely because they had failed to bring the war to a satisfactory conclusion, and Lenin was determined that the same fate would not befall the Bolsheviks. However, even within the party there were disagreements as to how this was to be achieved, with Lenin arguing for an immediate peace and Trotsky for a delay.

Lenin was aware that the war had exhausted Russia and it was impossible to bring the war to a successful conclusion and therefore there was little point in continuing. He was also receiving considerable sums of money from the German government, which had allowed him to return from exile in 1917, and therefore the best way to ensure this financial support continued was to make peace. Although Trotsky did not want to continue the war and agreed with Lenin's view that Russia had no chance of emerging victorious, he did adopt a slightly different view. He hoped that German forces would collapse in the west and that there would be a revolution in Germany and therefore wanted to drag out negotiations in the hope that such developments would occur.

Trotsky's approach angered the Germans who failed to understand that the Bolsheviks were not concerned by national defeat. They were international revolutionaries, who had little interest in Russia as a nation; their first concern was to spread the revolution, but Lenin was also aware of the practical situation with the Germans willing to advance on Petrograd. However, Sokolnikov, who signed the Treaty on 3 March 1918, did argue that the peace was a *diktat* enforced on a defenceless country.

The treaty gave up large amounts of Russian territory (see Figure 4.3) and Russia had to pay reparations for the damage it had caused of 3 billion roubles.

Divisions within the Bolshevik party over the Treaty

The treaty created opposition within the party as many wanted a revolutionary war against what they saw as imperialist Germany. Lenin, however, argued that peace was the only realistic option and that Russia simply could not continue the struggle and needed time to recover. He did, though, argue that Russia would, at a later date, be strong enough to take back the land. Lenin thought that there would be continuing rivalry between capitalist powers which would weaken them and allow Russia to take back lost lands. Despite this, there was a fierce debate in the Central Committee and the treaty was approved by only one vote. It is important to understand why Lenin was willing to give up such large amounts of Russian land. It was not simply that Russia was too weak to continue to fight, but that both he and Trotsky believed that a worldwide workers' revolution would begin, which was of far greater significance than the peace terms.

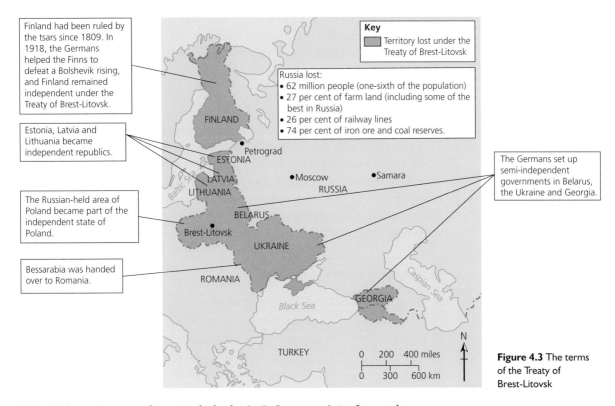

Finland had been ruled by the tsars since 1809. In 1918, the Germans helped the Finns to defeat a Bolshevik rising, and Finland remained independent under the Treaty of Brest-Litovsk.

Estonia, Latvia and Lithuania became independent republics.

The Russian-held area of Poland became part of the independent state of Poland.

Bessarabia was handed over to Romania.

Key
- Territory lost under the Treaty of Brest-Litovsk

Russia lost:
- 62 million people (one-sixth of the population)
- 27 per cent of farm land (including some of the best in Russia)
- 26 per cent of railway lines
- 74 per cent of iron ore and coal reserves.

The Germans set up semi-independent governments in Belarus, the Ukraine and Georgia.

Figure 4.3 The terms of the Treaty of Brest-Litovsk

Not all the party agreed, particularly the **Left Communists**. It was the developments on the Western Front in August 1918 that allowed Lenin to triumph. The German collapse in the west and the total withdrawal of German forces from Russia meant that the treaty was meaningless. More importantly, it strengthened Lenin's hold over the party and allowed him to expel the Left SRs from government and ban them as an organization.

Reasons for the Bolshevik victory in the Civil War

The origins of the Civil War, which would last for four years, can be traced back to the October Revolution. Some groups saw this as a chance to launch a counter-revolution against the Bolsheviks, while others saw it as an opportunity to gain independence. The dissolution of the Constituent Assembly, Bolshevik attempts for absolute power and the weakness of the Bolsheviks only added to the likelihood of war. However, some have argued that Lenin himself wanted a war as it would provide him with the opportunity to destroy his opponents.

The events of the war

The events of the war are very complex, in part because it was fought between three groups. It was not just the Bolsheviks – the Reds – fighting their opponents, the Whites. There were also a considerable number of national minorities, such as Ukrainians and Georgians, and peasant forces known as the Greens who fought to establish their independence from Russia.

KEY TERM

Left Communists A group of Bolsheviks led by Nikolai Bukharin who in 1918 opposed Lenin's more practical measures. Rather than make peace with Germany, they hoped to wage revolutionary war through Europe.

The actual date of the start of the war is debatable. Some have argued that it began when Kerensky launched an offensive in October to try to retake the capital, but these clashes were minor. It was not until the spring of 1918 that the war really started.

The Bolshevik Red Army controlled most of central western Russia and the main cities and industrial centres. Their opponents, the Whites, were attacking from different directions and could not concentrate their forces. They got some help from foreign powers, Britain, France, the US and Japan. Polish forces also fought against the Red Army. French assistance was important in preventing the Red forces taking Warsaw in 1920 but generally foreign intervention only tended to make the Reds more popular. Both sides fought with considerable brutality, but the Whites could not gain enough support or assemble sufficient numbers of forces on one front to win.

ACTIVITY

Research the contribution of each of the foreign powers (overseas forces) to the White cause in the Civil War.

KEY TERM

Czech Legion Largely composed of Czechs who had been fighting for the allied cause on the Eastern front in the First World War. Their attempts to leave Vladivostok were stopped and so they rose up against the Bolsheviks.

KEY FIGURES

Admiral Alexander Kolchak (1873–1920) was the former commander of the Russian Black Sea Fleet.

General Anton Denikin (1872–1947) was an ex-tsarist general who supported Kornilov in 1919.

General Nicolai Yudenich (1862–1933) was an ex-tsarist general who fought in the Russo-Japanese War.

Baron Pyotr Wrangel (1878–1928) had served in the army during the Russo-Japanese War and First World War. He had been decorated for bravery.

The main events of the war

January 1918	Red Army is established
March 1918	Treaty of Brest-Litovsk. British troops arrive
Spring 1918	Opposition from the Cossacks is defeated
April 1918	Kornilov's army is defeated and Lenin announces the war is about to end. Foreign intervention to support Bolshevik opponents
May 1918	**Czech Legion** revolts and becomes a focus for those fighting the Reds. Conscription into the Red Army is introduced
June 1918	The Tsar and his family murdered
August 1918	Trotsky starts to execute deserters, USA sends troops to aid the Whites and establish anti-Bolshevik government
September 1918	Opposition government is established at Ufa
November 1918	**Admiral Kolchak** becomes Supreme Ruler of White Armies
December 1918	French army lands at Odessa
February 1919	**Denikin** assumes command of White forces in south-east
March 1919	Kolchak's forces cross the Urals but driven back by Red Army
April 1919	French evacuate Odessa
June 1919	Denikin and southern army take Kharkov
July 1919	Denikin takes Tsaritsyn
September 1919	Allies evacuate Archangel
October 1919	Red Army starts to score victories, defeats General Denikin at Orel and General **Yudenich** at Petrograd
January 1920	Admiral Kolchak resigns
February 1920	Kolchak captured and executed by Bolsheviks
April 1920	Polish forces attack Russia and reach Kiev. Reds counter-attack, but are then pushed back. Denikin is succeeded by **Wrangel**
October 1920	Russo-Polish armistice
November 1921	White troops under Wrangel driven from southern Russia

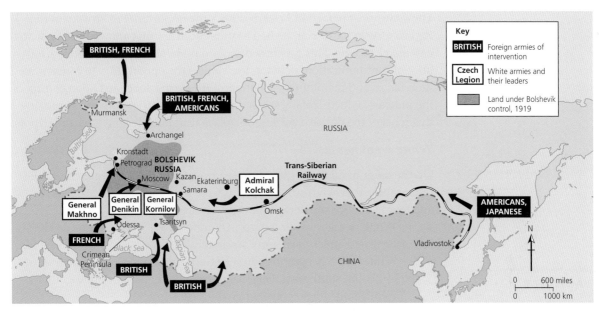

Figure 4.4 The Civil War, 1918–21

Why did the Reds win?

There were a number of reasons why the Reds won and this can be split into two parts: Red strengths and White weaknesses.

Red strengths

- They retained control of the key cities of Moscow and Petrograd.
- They had control over a concentrated area of land in the west of Russia, which they were able to supply, helped by maintaining control over much of the rail network.
- The Reds had most of their support in the industrial areas, which gave them supplies and munitions, things the Whites lacked.
- The Reds were able to claim that they were fighting for Russia and the nation against the Whites who were in league with foreigners.
- The Red Army was well organized and led by Trotsky, who was War Commissar. He turned the old Red Army of workers and peasants into a well-disciplined force. By 1920 he had some 3 million men under arms.
- Trotsky used former experienced tsarist officers to counter White experience. Similarly, he created cavalry units to counter the Cossacks.
- Trotsky realized the importance of the rail network and used it to move troops quickly and in large numbers for defence and attack.
- The morale of the Red Army was sustained by Trotsky and Lenin. They used propaganda trains to spread the Bolshevik message.
- The imposition of brutal measures by **Cheka** allowed strict wartime measures, such as War Communism (see page 215) and the militarization of labour, to be enforced.
- The **Red Terror** helped to maintain discipline.

KEY TERMS

Cheka The Bolshevik political militarized police force.

Red Terror The deliberate policy of gaining control by brutality and the killing of suspected and actual opponents.

The summary on page 213 clearly shows the importance of Trotsky in the Red victory. In particular, he had a simple strategy that allowed the Reds to emerge victorious. This was based around maintaining Bolshevik internal lines of communication, denying the Whites the opportunity to concentrate their forces and maintain their supplies. All of this depended upon control of the railways, which Trotsky saw as crucial, and it is therefore not surprising that most of the decisive battles took place near railway junctions and depots.

White weaknesses

On the other hand the Whites suffered from a number of weaknesses. Most importantly, they were not united and were fighting for a range of causes and fought as separate detachments.

- The Whites were unwilling to form a united front and this allowed the Bolsheviks to attack each army separately.
- The Whites were geographically scattered with armies in the north-west, the south and south-east. This meant that they could not put together a sufficiently large force to challenge the Red Army.
- The Whites were heavily reliant on supplies and support from abroad and therefore the Bolsheviks could portray them as anti-Russian.
- The Reds were able to portray the Whites as supporters of the Tsar.
- The leadership of the Whites was not as good as the Reds.
- The White army numbered only 500,000.

The Civil War allowed the Bolsheviks to further increase their control and eliminate their enemies. Terror through the Cheka and the Red Army played a crucial role, with the Cheka destroying political opposition (see Source S).

ACTIVITY

Prepare for a debate. One side should argue that it was Red strengths that best explains their success in the Civil War and the other should argue that it was due to White weaknesses. Which view do you find most convincing? Why?

SOURCE S

How far does Source S support the view that Terror was the key reason for Red victory in the Civil War?

A speech by Felix Dzerzhinsky, Head of the Cheka, December 1917

This is no time for speech making. Our Revolution is in serious danger. We are ready to do all to defend the attainments of our Revolution. Do not think that I am on the look-out for forms of revolutionary justice. WE have no need for justice now. Now we have need of a battle to the death! I propose, I demand the use of the revolutionary sword, which will put an end to all counter-revolutionaries. We must act not tomorrow, but today at once. Do not demand evidence to prove that the prisoner has opposed the Soviet government; your first duty is to ask him to which class he belongs, what are his origins. These questions should decide the fate of the prisoner.

Answerable only to Lenin, the Cheka operated as a law unto itself and was given virtually unlimited powers, which were used brutally. This was particularly evident following an attempt on Lenin's life in August 1918 and was used to justify a reign of terror, the Red Terror, which saw the Tsar and his family killed at Ekaterinburg. They were shot without trial. At the same time the Cheka attacked wealthier peasants, the kulaks. Forced labour camps were also established to detain 'enemies of the Revolution' or potential enemies. There was also a series of show trials of the leading members of the banned political parties. At the same time, the Red Army imposed their authority over the population as a whole.

War Communism

In 1918 Lenin also introduced very restrictive economic measures, known as War Communism. The key features of this were:

- nationalization of major industries
- the partial mobilization of labour
- the forced taking or requisitioning of grain and agricultural products.

Every part of people's lives was subjected to winning the Civil War. However, the measures of war communism had a devastating impact on both agricultural and industrial production. Peasants refused to hand over grain and refused to produce more food until the government was willing to pay a reasonable price for it. This led to the Cheka sending out requisition units to seize food. However, the result was that even less food was available. By 1921 this policy, along with a drought, led to a major famine as less than half the grain produced in 1913 was harvested. The situation was very similar in industry. Nationalization had not led to an increase in production and the Civil War made matters worse as military needs took priority. Manpower was reduced as men were conscripted to fight and **hyperinflation** only added to the problems.

Despite these difficulties, the Bolsheviks were able to impose their control and terror appeared to work. Lenin was able to destroy his opponents, perhaps supporting the view that he wanted a civil war for just such a purpose. However, opposition grew. In Tambov province a peasant army was formed and they attacked the requisition squads and were able to take over large areas of the surrounding countryside. The peasant army grew to some 20,000 and the Red Army was able to take back control of the area only with the greatest difficulty. The Red Army then took revenge on the locals and their resistance was ended by the summer of 1921.

KEY TERM 🔑

Hyperinflation The very rapid rise in prices.

ACTIVITY

What evidence is there to support the claim that Lenin wanted a civil war to destroy opposition to the Bolsheviks?

Kronstadt and the introduction of the New Economic Policy (NEP)

Although Lenin upheld War Communism for as long as possible, it did become evident to him, with the famine, that changes were needed. The anti-Bolshevik rising in Tambov was followed by growing opposition in the party to War Communism and strikes in Petrograd in early 1921.

The Kronstadt Rising

However, the most serious challenge occurred in February 1921 when large numbers of Petrograd workers crossed to the naval base of Kronstadt. The workers joined with mutinying sailors and workers from the dockyard to demand greater freedom. This was particularly worrying as the protestors had been the supporters of the October Revolution. The protestors demanded:

- new and free elections to the soviet
- elections to be held using secret ballot
- freedom of assembly
- rights for trade unions
- the ending of the Communists as the only socialist party
- freedom for the press
- freedom to bring in food from the countryside.

As their demands increased, Trotsky ordered General Tukhachevsky to recapture Kronstadt. Between 50,000 and 60,000 troops were sent across the ice, but their success was at the cost of the deaths of some 10,000 Red Army soldiers. The leaders of the rising were condemned as Whites and shot, while those who escaped were hunted down by the Cheka.

Lenin argued that the brutality of the Red Army was justifiable as the rising had been the work of bourgeois enemies of the Revolution. Despite this clear propaganda statement, Lenin realized that he had to take action and ensure that there was not another challenge to the party and therefore it was time to bring an end to the harshness of War Communism.

The New Economic Policy

Lenin's decision to introduce the NEP was largely intended to tackle the problem of famine and reduce opposition to the Bolsheviks. The measure was purely economic and there was no intention that Lenin was willing to reduce his political control, if anything that would be tightened.

NEP was intended to persuade farmers to grow more food. Requisitioning was ended and peasants were allowed to sell surpluses at local markets. The decree making it official policy included a range of measures. Small-scale enterprises were denationalized so that small-scale workshops could flourish. However, the state retained control over heavy industry, what Lenin described as 'the commanding heights'. Internal trade was encouraged as restrictions on the sale of private goods and services were lifted and a new rouble was introduced to try to restore confidence in the currency and end inflation. Foreign trade and investment was also to be encouraged.

Although there were objections to these measures within the party, the disastrous economic situation and famine ensured that the measure was approved unanimously even though it was a clear retreat from the principle of the state control of the economy. In order to conciliate opponents, Lenin made it clear that it was a temporary measure.

Even though it was a success economically with industrial output increasing rapidly, opponents objected to the emergence of private traders or **nepmen** who they viewed as enemies of the Revolution. It appeared as if the divisions

KEY TERM 🔑

Nepmen The name used to describe those who gained from the New Economic Policy as a result of the free trade and the ability to sell their products.

over the policy might split the party and therefore at the Tenth Party Congress in 1921 Lenin introduced a measure 'On Party Unity'; this measure banned factionalism to prevent criticism of government decisions. Lenin also banned all other socialist parties, thus completing the suppression of opposition that had started in 1918. It was now very difficult for any members of the party or others to challenge policy as they would be seen as challenging the party.

By the end of 1921 Lenin had been able to increase his control. The party was more centralized and less democratic. All the key government posts were held by senior Bolsheviks, and the administration was dominated by the top members of the party. However, given the weak position they were in after the October Revolution their survival was a remarkable achievement. However, at what cost had it been achieved? Had they upheld the ideals of the Revolution? These are issues to think about now that you have completed your study of this period in Russian history.

SOURCE T

NEP poster. The text reads: 'Out of NEP Russia there will be a socialist Russia (Lenin)'

> **What does the poster in Source T suggest about the role of Lenin in the NEP?**

SUMMARY DIAGRAM

How were the Bolsheviks able to consolidate their power up to 1921?

ACTIVITY

Find evidence to support each of the points made in the summary diagram.

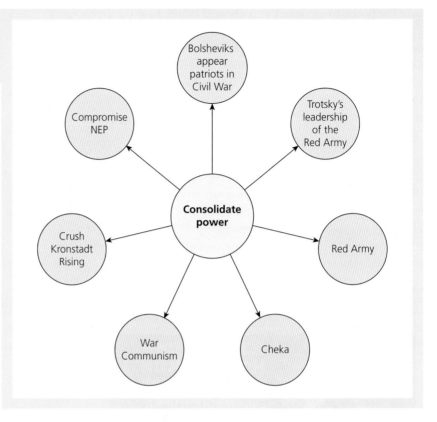

Chapter summary

The centuries of tsarist system was coming under pressure at the start of this period as a result of the impact of economic change and the desire for political change. The countryside was restless because of population growth and land hunger. There were growing radical and revolutionary groups, though these were not extensive. Tsar Alexander III had relied on repression of discontent, control of the countryside and a policy of peace. His successor Nicholas II unwisely went to war in 1904 and the poor performance of Russian forces, losses and inflation created the conditions in which longer-term discontents could erupt into revolution. This was the most serious challenge to tsarism in modern times

and the Tsar was forced to offer concessions in October 1905. These divided the revolutionaries and the middle-class liberals and the revolutionaries split, allowing the Tsar to regain control. He restated the principle of autocracy in 1906 and his minister Stolypin ruthlessly repressed the opposition while gaining peasant support by land reforms. The creation of an elected parliament gave the semblance that Russia had changed politically. However, the regime could do little to stop growing discontent and only the outbreak of war in 1914 prevented further disturbances as the nation was gripped by patriotic feelings. However, the initial defeats in 1914 and the retreat of 1915 brought criticism of the Tsar and his government. A patriotic bloc in the Duma was formed and criticized the Tsar's inefficient ministers. The influence of the disreputable holy man Rasputin made matters worse. Despite a military resurgence in 1916 the war did not look winnable and there were increasing shortages, rising prices and casualties. Discontent erupted in February 1917 and the Tsar lost control of the capital and could no longer rely on the loyalty of his army. He abdicated and for the first time Russia became a republic. However, the continuation of the war and the failure to bring in rapid measures to solve social and economic problems and set up a new constitution allowed radical forces to take their chance. The new Provisional Government was fatally weakened by a dual authority of a parliamentary government and a council or Soviet of workers and soldiers. Though a seizure of power failed in July, the disruption caused by a failed military coup gave Lenin and the Bolsheviks a window of opportunity in October 1917 despite limited support in the country as a whole and not being the biggest revolutionary group.

Lenin and Trotsky masterminded the takeover of Petrograd and other cities and then fought a successful war to defend the socialist state they created. Their opponents were too divided to be effective and the ruthless efficiency of Lenin and his commissars resulted in victory by 1920 and the establishment of the world's first communist state and a new Union of Soviet Socialist Republics.

Refresher questions

1 What powers did Tsar Nicholas II have?

2 Why was it so difficult to reform Russia?

3 What led to the growth of opposition parties in Russia in the period before the First World War?

4 Why did Russia do so badly in the Russo-Japanese War?

5 What was the impact of the 1905 Revolution on Russia?

6 What evidence was there of growing tensions in Russia in the period from 1906 to 1914?

7 What did the Dumas achieve?

8 How did the First World War damage the Russian economy?

9 How well did the Russian army cope with the demands of the First World War?

10 What led to the emergence of Dual Authority?

11 What problems did the Provisional Government face?

12 Why did the Bolsheviks survive the July Days?

13 What roles did Lenin and Trotsky play in the events of October 1917?

14 How did Lenin establish Bolshevik control of Russia?

15 What did the Kronstadt Rising show about the problems facing the Bolsheviks?

16 What were Lenin's main achievements?

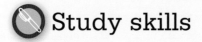 Study skills

Paper 1 guidance: Sources

Visual sources

You may be asked to use a visual source like a cartoon or a poster. It is important to be able to see its meaning in relation to the issue in the question and to test its validity by considering its purpose and origin and also to use contextual knowledge.

Take this example:

From a Russian satirical magazine, 1916

How would you assess this source as evidence that the Revolution of February 1917 was caused by the mistakes of the Tsar?

Think about the cartoon itself:

It shows that it was believed that Rasputin dominated a group of high-ranking Russians including the Tsar and the Tsarina. Nicholas is shown in a position in which he is lower than Rasputin and holding his leg in an undignified way.

Alexandra is holding a picture of the German Emperor, suggesting her disloyalty.

This suggests that Rasputin had a large influence at court. Rasputin is shown as a somewhat sinister figure.

Looking at the following evaluation:

> The source is a critical magazine and may be exaggerating for effect. There is little evidence of the Tsarina admiring Wilhelm II. However, the source does reflect much popular opinion. When the Tsar went to the Front in 1915 it was widely thought that Rasputin was dominant over the Empress who was left in charge. Rasputin was unpopular enough for a group of high-ranking Russians including Prince Yusupov to connive in his murder. The Tsar was criticized for the misjudgement of having this disreputable holy man in his court.
>
> It is evidence that the Tsar was thought to have poor judgement. This misjudgement was also evident in his appointment of incompetent ministers and leaving the capital.

 ## Activity

Look at the cartoon and assess how far it supports the view that the Tsar's concessions after the Revolution of 1905 were not enough to bring stability. The cartoon comes from a French magazine of 1905.

Seeing stars of liberty.—Philadelphia Inquirer.

1 What is the message of the cartoon?

2 What can you say about the provenance of the cartoon?

3 What details from your own knowledge can you apply to the cartoon?

Paper 2 guidance: Essay questions

Writing a conclusion

What is the purpose of a conclusion? A conclusion should come to a judgement that is based on what you have already written and should be briefly supported. It should not introduce new ideas – if they were important they should have been discussed in the main body of the essay. You must also take care to avoid offering a contrary argument to the one you have pursued throughout the rest of the essay as that will suggest to the examiner that you have not thought through your ideas and are unclear as to what you think.

It might be that you are largely restating the view you offered in the vital opening paragraph, or in stronger answers there might be a subtle variation to the judgement – you confirm your original view but suggest, with an example, that there were occasions when this was not always correct.

If the question has named a factor then you should give a judgement about that factor's relative importance, either explaining why it is or is not the most important, and the role it played in the events you have discussed. If the question asks you to assess a range of factors, the conclusion should explain which you think is the most important and should support the claim. At first sight a claim might appear to be judgement, but without supporting material it is no more than an assertion and will not gain credit.

Consider the following essay question:

> 'The loyalty of the army was the main reason for the Tsar's survival in 1905.' How for do you agree?

In order to answer this question you may consider:
- the use of military force to put down revolution
- the concessions made in the October Menifesto
- the divided aims of the revolutionaries
- the lack of peasant support.

Now consider this sample conclusion:

The Revolution of 1905 failed in the last resort not so much because of the use of force by a loyal army, though this was an important factor and the effects of army disloyalty can be seen in February 1917 when it was more of a key factor. However, the ability to divide the revolutionaries by the introduction of concessions was more important. The Revolution was not a single movement but a number of different discontents linked by the reaction to the failures of the war and the horror of Bloody Sunday. No single plan united the revolutionaries, some of whom wanted national independence, some a constitution, some a full-scale Marxist revolution and some concessions to the peasantry or a re-division

This is an excellent final paragraph because:

- it focuses immediately on the issue in the question
- it provides a clear judgement on that issue
- that judgement is supported with good argument and evidence
- it briefly summarizes what the author believes was the main reason.

of land. The workers' groups were too small and divided to take a lead as they were to do in October 1917. The middle-class liberals were concerned about the break-up of Russia by revolts of nationalities and the radical actions of workers. Once the Tsar made the concessions of the October Manifesto on the advice of Witte, and the war with Japan ended, important grievances were met. Thus more radical elements could be dealt with by military force.

QUESTION PRACTICE

In light of these comments and the sample conclusion, write conclusions to the following questions:

1 'War Communism was the main reason why the Reds won the Civil War.' How far do you agree?

2 How successful were the reforms of the Tsar's governments 1905–14?

3 How important were the failures of the Provisional Government in bringing about the Bolshevik Revolution in October 1917?

You have now covered all the main skills you need to write a good essay. It is worth looking back at these skills before you write each essay you are set. This will help you to build up and reinforce the skills you need for the examination and ensure that you are familiar with the skills needed to do well.

EXPLAIN QUESTIONS

1 Explain why the Tsar survived the 1905 Revolution.

2 Explain why the February Revolution ended tsarist rule.

3 Explain why Lenin held on to power 1917–21.

4 Explain why the Whites lost the Civil War.

 Activity

Answer one of the questions in the box above and highlight where you have explained and where you have described.

Further reading

Chapter 1 France, 1774–1814

D. Andress, *The French Revolution and the People* (Hambledon, 2004)

T. Blanning, *The Pursuit of Glory* (Penguin, 2007)

M. Broers, *Napoleon, Soldier of Destiny* (Faber, 2015)

M. Crook, *Revolutionary France* (OUP, 2002)

W. Doyle, *Origins of the French Revolution* (OUP, 1980)

G. Ellis, *Napoleon Profiles in Power* (Longman, 1997)

S. Englund, *Napoleon, A Political Life* (Harvard, 2005)

E. Hazan, *A People's History of the French Revolution* (Verso, 2014)

A. Horne, *The Age of Napoleon* (Modern Library, 2006)

C. Jones, *The Great Nation, France from Louis XV to Napoleon* (Columbia UP, 2002)

P.M. Jones, *The French Revolution, 1787–1804* (Longman, 2003)

M. Lyons, *Napoleon and the Legacy of the French Revolution* (Palgrave, 1994)

P. McPhee, *Liberty or Death* (Yale, 2016)

D. Rees and D. Townson, *Access to History, France in Revolution* (Hodder, 2016)

J.M. Robert, *The French Revolution* (OUP, 1997)

A. Roberts, *Napoleon the Great* (Allen Lane, 2014)

J. Tulard, *Napoleon, the Myth of the Saviour* (Weidenfeld and Nicolson, 1984)

S. Waller, *France in Revolution* (Heinemann, 2002)

M. Wells, *The French Revolution and the Rule of Napoleon* (Hodder, 2018)

Chapter 2 The Industrial Revolution in Britain, 1750–1850

J.V. Beckett, *The Agricultural Revolution* (Blackwell, 1990)

J. Belchem, *Industrialisation and the Working Class: The English Experience* (Scholar Press, 1990)

M. Berg, *The Age of Manufactures: 1700–1820* (Routledge, 1994)

P. Deane, *The First Industrial Revolution* (CUP, 1979)

J. Dinwiddy, *From Luddism to the Great Reform Act* (Blackwell, 1986)

E. Evans, *The Forging of the Modern State* (Routledge, 2001)

M.W. Flinn, *Origins of the Industrial Revolution* (Longman, 1966)

R. Floud and D. McCloskey, *The Economic History of Britain Since 1700, Vols I and II* (CUP, 1994)

E. Hobsbawm, *Industry and Empire* (Pelican, 1984)

P. Hudson, *The Industrial Revolution* (Arnold, 1993)

P. Mathias, *The First Industrial Nation* (Methuen, 1987)

A.E. Musson, *The Growth of British Industry* (MUP, 1978)

M. Overton, *Agricultural Revolution in England* (CUP, 1996)

E. Royle, *Modern Britain, A Social History 1750–2011* (Bloomsbury, 2012)

E.P. Thompson, *The Making of the Working Class* (Penguin, 1980)

Chapter 3 Liberalism and Nationalism in Germany, 1815–71

D. Blackbourn, *The Fontana History of Germany 1780–1918: The Long Nineteenth Century* (Blackwell, 1997)

J. Breuilly, *The Formation of the First German Nation-state* (Palgrave, 1996)

C. Clarke, *The Iron Kingdom: The Rise and Downfall of Prussia 1600–1947* (Allen Lane, 2006)

G. Craig, *Germany 1866–1945* (OUP, 1980)

E. Crankshaw, *Bismarck* (Macmillan, 1981)

E. Feuchtwanger, *Bismarck* (Routledge, 2002)

M. Fulbrook, *A Concise History of Germany* (CUP, 2004)

M. Kitchen, *A History of Modern Germany, 1800 to the Present* (Wiley-Blackwell, 2011)

H. Schulze, *The Course of German Nationalism* (CUP, 1991)

H. Schulze, *Germany, A New History* (Harvard UP, 2001)

J. Steinberg, *Bismarck, A Life* (OUP, 2011)

A. Stiles, *Access to History, The Unification of Germany 1815–90* (Hodder, 1986)

A.J.P. Taylor, *Bismarck, The Man and the Statesman* (Hamish Hamilton, 1958)

M. Wells, *Bismarck* (Collins, 2004)

M. Wells, *Unification and Consolidation of Germany and Italy, 1815–90* (CUP, 2013)

D.G. Williamson, *Bismarck and Germany, 1862 to 1890* (Longman, 2011)

Chapter 4 The Russian Revolution, 1894–1921

E.H. Carr, *The Russian Revolution from Lenin to Stalin 1917–1929* (Palgrave, 2004)

D. Christian, *Imperial and Soviet Russia* (Macmillan, 1997)

R. W. Davies, *From Tsarism to the New Economic Policy Cornell* (UP, 1991)

O. Figes, *A People's Tragedy* (Pimlico, 1997)

G. Hosking, *Russia and the Russians* (Allen Lane, 2001)

D. Lieven, *Nicholas II: Emperor of All the Russias* (Pimlico, 1993)

R. Pipes, *Russia Under the Bolshevik Regime 1919–24* (Collins Harvill, 1994)

R. Pipes, *Russia Under the Old Regime* (Penguin, 1995)

R. Pipes, *The Russian Revolution 1899–1919* (Collins Harvill, 1990)

R. Service, *Lenin: A Biography* (Macmillan, 2004)

R. Service, *The Penguin History of Modern Russia: From Tsarism to the Twenty-first Century* (Penguin, 2009)

S.A. Smith, *Russia in Revolution 1890–1928* (OUP, 2017)

S.A. Smith, *The Russian Revolution: A Very Short Introduction* (OUP, 2002)

A. Wood, *The Origins of the Russian Revolution* (Routledge, 2003)

Glossary

Absolute monarchy This is rule by a monarch who is free to pursue any policy and has no responsibility to any elected assembly or to their people. Absolute monarchs often claimed they had been chosen by God and were responsible only to God.

Absolute/autocratic ruler The total rule of one man with complete control over his subjects.

Anarchism A belief that all government is oppressive and should be abolished.

Barrowmen Men who hauled wagons of coal.

Bill of Rights A legislative guarantee to citizens of a country that their liberties will be respected and that they will not be subject to arbitrary rule.

Blacklegs Workers who break a strike and continue to work during trade disputes.

Bolsheviks One faction of the Social Democratic Party; the term means the majority.

Bourgeois The middle class who own the factories and capital and will be overthrown by the workers.

Bread riots A common feature of French life was riots by poor and often hungry people to seize corn or take bread from bakers.

Capitalism The system by which private owners and companies increase their wealth by trade and invest for profit.

Capitalist The owners of the factories or capital who exploited the workers, but would be overthrown by them in the revolution that was to come.

Cheka The Bolshevik political militarized police force.

Cholera An infectious disease contracted from infected water causing vomiting and diarrhoea and possibly leading to death.

Chouans The name given to those who fought against the Revolution in Western France, especially in Brittany and Maine from 1793. They were a mainly peasant force.

Civil Constitution of the Clergy The name given to the new official position of the church in the Revolution which placed it under state control.

Common land Village land where everyone who was not a landowner could graze animals and use it as a source of wood and food.

Congress of Vienna This is the name given to the meeting to discuss the peace terms with France after the fall of Napoleon in 1814 and the reorganisation of post-war Europe. It was interrupted by the return of Napoleon in 1815. The Congress resulted in the Treaty of Vienna.

Constituent Assembly An elected body whose task is to draw up a new constitution, or a set of rules under which a country is to be run.

Constitution A set of rules by which a country is run.

Constitutional monarchy A state where the hereditary ruler shares power to a greater or lesser extent with an elected assembly.

Consul for Life In 1802 Napoleon Bonaparte declared himself the ruler of France, or Consul for Life. The term consul derives from the Republic of Ancient Rome.

Corn Laws The Corn Laws were a series of tariffs and duties brought in after the Napoleonic Wars in 1815 to protect British agriculture. They prevented the import of corn until British corn reached a certain price, which opponents argued kept the price of British corn high and impacted the workers who had to pay more for bread. However, they did help guarantee that British farmers continued to grow corn. The laws were repealed in 1846.

Corvée This was an obligation to work on the public roads or the king's highways. It was unpopular and as the nobles and clergy were exempt it caused a lot of resentment.

Coup Literally a blow; in French refers to a forceful takeover of power.

Crimean War (1854–56) This was a war between Britain, France and the Ottoman Empire on one side and Russia on the other. France and Britain were eager to prevent Russian expansion into the Ottoman Empire. The war was fought in the Crimean peninsula. Austria did not support Russia despite the help it had received in 1849. A series of costly battles led to a British and French victory which excluded Russian warships from the Black Sea and destroyed the Russian naval base at Sebastopol.

Czech Legion Largely composed of Czechs who had been fighting for the allied cause on the Eastern front in the First World War. Their attempts to leave Vladivostok were stopped and so they rose up against the Bolsheviks.

Dark masses A term used to describe the mass of Russian peasantry, many of whom were illiterate. Peasant life was often characterized by violence and superstition.

Day of Tiles On 7 June 1788 popular protest against the French government in Grenoble involved throwing down roof tiles into the streets.

Diets The name given to the assemblies of parliaments of the German states.

Direct taxes Taxes levied on personal income or property.

Domestic system The making of goods within the home whereby clothiers would purchase the raw materials, bring them to workers in their cottages and collect the finished product.

Duma The Russian word for assembly or parliament.

East India Company A powerful trading company that controlled much of Britain's trade with India.

Emancipation of the Serfs Before 1861 there were millions of people who were the property of landowners and who could be bought, sold and even gambled away. By the mid-nineteenth century this was increasingly seen as a sign of backwardness which was preventing Russia's social and economic development. Thus in 1861 the serfs were freed (emancipated) from being the personal property of nobles, Church, crown and landowners.

Enclosure The enclosing of land by hedges or fences in order to divide up large open fields.

Enlightenment This is the name given to the growth of scholarly and intellectual writing on many aspects of philosophy, science, the arts, economics, government, religion and politics in the eighteenth century. These writings were often critical of and questioned established religion, monarchical rule and social inequality, and were seen as a major cause of revolution.

Feudal dues Payments made to lords by peasants based on traditional privileges not contractual obligations.

Franchise The right to vote in elections.

Friendly societies Associations of workers set up to provide insurance, pensions and savings or co-operative banking.

Furnace men, **puddlers** and **rollers** These were all jobs done in the iron industry: furnace men were responsible for the blast furnaces, puddlers were responsible for stirring molten iron with iron oxide to produce wrought iron, and rollers rolled the iron into sheets.

Gosplan The government body responsible for national economic planning.

Great Retreat The name given for the withdrawal of Russian forces in 1915 to a new front line well into Russian territory.

Great Spurt A name given to a period of rapid industrial growth encouraged by the finance minister Witte by direct government support of trade and industry, railway construction and a stable currency which encouraged foreign investment.

Gross Domestic Product The annual total value of goods produced and services provided in Britain.

Guerrilla war A war fought not by regular armies on battlefields but by irregular, often improvised, groups attacking enemy forces and communications.

Habeas Corpus This is the process by which a person who was arrested was required to be brought before a court or they had to be set free.

Haemophilia A genetic condition in which the blood does not clot. It can lead to severe bruising, internal bleeding and has the potential to be life-threatening.

Holy Roman Empire This is the name given to the lands of central Europe that owed allegiance to an overall emperor. There was little in the way of central government in this medieval union of princes and cities, which had its origins in the coronation of Charlemagne in 800, and in practice the lands were independent. Since the fifteenth century the emperor had been the rulers of Austria, the Habsburg royal family. It was formally dissolved by Napoleon Bonaparte in 1806.

Hyperinflation The very rapid rise in prices.

Indemnity Bill The word indemnity means that Bismarck was freed from all responsibility or blame for having ignored the constitution. In effect, the Liberals were saying that military and political success justified illegality – a dangerous precedent to set.

Inflation Rising prices.

IOU A way of writing 'I owe you' – a promise to repay a loan.

Irish famine Potatoes were the staple food of most of the Irish peasant population. However, a potato blight in 1845 which destroyed the crop led to mass starvation and emigration.

Junker The term for a Prussian landed aristocrat, often seen by the use of the word 'von' (of). Bismarck's full title was 'von Bismarck-Schonhausen'.

Kadets The party that supported a constitutional liberal democracy. Its membership was largely middle class and it never achieved mass support.

Land Captains Leading landowners appointed to control the peasants.

Landed class A term used to describe landowners who owned sufficient land so that they could live entirely from rental income.

Left Communists A group of Bolsheviks led by Nikolai Bukharin who in 1918 opposed Lenin's more practical measures. Rather than make peace with Germany, they hoped to wage revolutionary war through Europe.

Legislative Assembly The parliament of France October 1791 to September 1792.

Liberal Early nineteenth-century liberals believed that there should be elected assemblies to which governments should be accountable; and that states should not be allowed to ignore the rights of their citizens. These rights included freedom of expression and opinion, freedom to trade, freedom from arrest without charge and punishment without a lawful trial.

Liberal democracy A system in which the people vote for national assemblies or parliaments to whom governments are responsible. Governments must keep to the laws approved by assemblies and respect the rights of citizens to free speech and freedom from punishment without trial.

Marling A mixture of clay and lime that was applied as a fertilizer.

Martial law Rule by the military.

Marxism The movement that was influenced by the ideas of the German writer and revolutionary Karl Marx who thought that revolution by the workers would be an inevitable consequence of industrial growth and would lead to a reborn society. After a period of dictatorship by the workers, class distinctions would fall away as would the state and there would be an ideal community led by the principle 'from each according to his ability, to each according to his needs'. Marxist states have never got beyond the dictatorship stage.

Mercantilism The belief that colonies existed for the economic benefit of the mother country.

Napoleonic Wars (1803–15) Napoleon fought a series of wars against the European powers of Britain, Austria, Russia and Prussia, as well as in Spain and Portugal. Throughout the period the British were the only power who, at some point, did not make peace with France. The wars came to an end following Napoleon's defeat at Waterloo in 1815, but he had already been weakened by a long struggle in Spain and Portugal and war against Russia.

National Guard An armed force of citizens formed to keep order in July 1789.

Neo-Jacobins The main impetus of radical revolution had been slowed by the fall of Robespierre and the suppression of the more extreme groups. However, the ideas of the Jacobins had not died and there was a radical opposition to the Directors that saw the regime as betraying the core principles of the Revolution. These groups were not a united party and have been known as the neo- (or near) Jacobins. They were later suppressed severely after a failed attempt on Napoleon's life.

Nepmen The name used to describe those who gained from the New Economic Policy as a result of the free trade and the ability to sell their products.

Open field system The division of large open fields into strips where each villager was allocated a number of strips across the fields.

Outdoor relief The giving by local authorities of poor relief in the form of money, food, clothing or goods to those who needed it without them having to enter an institution.

Parlements and parliaments The parlements were not elected. They were courts of law consisting of small numbers of aristocratic judges that acted as final courts of appeal and also registered royal edicts (orders) to give them the status of laws. If they refused to register a royal edict then the king could pass it anyway. This is very different from a parliament, such as that of Britain in the eighteenth century, which consisted of a lower house of elected representatives who could vote on the government's budget and whose consent was needed to make law.

Picketing Action by those who are on strike: standing outside the place of work to stop others from entering and working.

Pit ponies Ponies that worked underground in the mines hauling coal.

Pitt's Combination Act 1799 The Act prohibited trade unions and collective bargaining. It was passed partly in response to fears following the French Revolution, but also because the government was concerned that workers would strike during the war against France.

Pogroms Violent attacks on Jews.

Poor Law Guardians Poor Law Guardians were responsible for the administration of poor relief in their areas, which were made up of a group of parishes.

Populism The name given to those who wanted greater power to go to the ordinary people in Russia. The movement was active in the 1870s.

Potemkin A battleship named after the aristocratic favourite and lover of the eighteenth-century Empress Catherine the Great. While stationed in Odessa on the Black Sea its crew mutinied in 1905.

Progressive bloc A loose union of moderate and liberal members of the Duma.

Proletariat Karl Marx, the theorist of Communism, gave this term to the industrial working class that had emerged from the industrial revolution and the growth of large-scale factories.

Protestants Followers of the religious reforms begun in the sixteenth century. There were wars between Catholics and Protestants in the sixteenth century. Protestants were granted toleration in 1598 but this was ended in 1685 when the Protestants, or Huguenots as they were called, were persecuted.

Realpolitik Politics that considers not ideals or aspirations but takes a hard look at national interests.

Red cap of liberty This was a soft conical hat based on the headgear of ancient eastern European people such as the Phyrigians. It came to symbolise Revolutionary liberty and was often worn by the sans-culottes.

Red Guards A force of about 10,000 men largely recruited from those who worked in the factories.

Red Terror The deliberate policy of gaining control by brutality and the killing of suspected and actual opponents.

Revolutionary calendar In order to break from the past, the Revolution in October 1793 renamed the months and started numbering the years from the start of the Revolution. The months were named after their characteristics – so November, for example, became Brumaire – the foggy month. Year 1 was 1793–94.

Rotten borough A borough that although it had very few voters was still able to return an MP, often due to corruption or bribery or where a family controlled who was elected.

Russification There were many languages and cultures in the Empire and Russification was a deliberate policy to impose Russian language and way of life on a wide variety of non-Russian people. 'Russia' referred only to the western part of a very large empire made up of many different racial groups.

Sans-culottes Richer men wore breeches and stockings on their legs but the poorer men wore trousers – so they were literally 'without breeches'. The sans-culottes were politically active and often not the very poorest of the people of Paris but small shopkeepers and artisans who resented the rich and were influenced by the radical ideas of clubs like the Jacobins. They took a key role in many of the political disturbances of the Revolution in Paris.

Second Coalition The First Coalition or alliance of different European states against France had broken down in 1797. Britain was ready to finance another group of nations and in 1798 Britain, Austria, Russia, Portugal, Naples, some German states and the Ottoman Empire (Turkey) signed alliances to co-operate in a coalition against France. The coalition was weakened by Bonaparte's victory over Austria in 1800.

Slavophiles Opponents of western values. They believed they were corrupting and wanted Russia to preserve its traditional values.

Social Democrats Followers of Karl Marx who believed that the Russian workers would spearhead a revolution. They were less numerous and influential as a group than the SRs because Russian workers made up a relatively small part of the population.

Social Revolutionaries (SRs) The name given to revolutionaries who gained support from the peasants by their policies of a proposed redistribution of land and ending the power of landlords. Some were terrorists and assassinated officials, minsters and even royalty.

Socialism This is the political belief that the state should own the major means of production and should be run for the benefit of those who produce, not those who own land and factories or businesses or make themselves rich through investing money (capital). Their profits are seen as a result of exploiting workers.

Sorbs or Wends By the mid-nineteenth century there were about 165,000 of these Slavonic people with their own language, customs and culture living in the area between modern-day Germany and Poland.

Soviets Russian word for a council, made up of elected workers.

Sovnarkom Council of People's Commissars, or a governing committee for the new Russian state, set up by Lenin in October 1917.

Stolypin's necktie The name given to the hangman's noose following 2500 executions between 1906 and 1911.

Subsistence farming Poorer farmers with limited or infertile land could survive only by growing enough for themselves and their families to eat in order to stay alive rather than producing crops for sale.

Three-tier system Each district was divided into three classes of voters according to the amount of tax paid. Generally the richest (Class 1) were around 5 per cent, the next richest (Class 2) were 13 per cent while the majority (82 per cent) were Class 3. Elections were held in the open and only men aged over 21 could vote. Each class in each electoral area chose a third of electors who in turn voted for the deputies of the parliament. So the richest 18 per cent voted for two-thirds of the electors while the bulk of the population opted for one-third. This undemocratic system persisted in Prussian elections until 1918.

Total war War that involves using all the resources of a country and includes not just armies but the entire population.

Trades Union Congress The federation of trade unions in England and Wales which represents most trade unions. It was formally established in the 1860s.

Transportation The removal of those who had been convicted of an offence to a penal colony, usually Australia.

Tsar A term meaning emperor, derived from the Latin Caesar. Tsars before 1905 had total authority.

Typhoid An infectious bacterial fever leading to spots and stomach pains.

Tyranny Oppressive rule

Universal male suffrage The right of all adult men to vote.

Universal suffrage A system of election in which all adults have the right to vote.

War of American Independence Fighting broke out between British forces and the British colonists in North America in 1775 and in 1776 the Americans declared independence. Britain tried to suppress this rebellion but was unsuccessful and in 1778 France joined the war on the colonists' side. Though Britain lost, French gains in the peace of 1783 were not great and costs were high. Also, the war gave rise to greater interest in liberty and opposition to arbitrary rule in France.

War of attrition A war where both sides try to wear down the enemy by killing more men and exhausting their resources rather than winning decisive victories.

War of the Austrian Succession 1740–48 and the **Seven Years War 1756–63** France had fought two prolonged wars in the eighteenth century. In both France had opposed Britain. Both had resulted in greater British than French success and both had been costly, increasing the French debt by over 2 billion livres.

Westerners Those who believed that in order to be a great nation Russia would have to adopt western values.

Wheeled corf A wheeled wagon or basket used for bringing coal out of the mines.

White Terror This was politically inspired violence used by the enemies of the Revolution (the so-called 'Whites') against its supporters.

Workhouse Parishes were required to set up places where poor people would have to work to earn money. In 1782 parishes had been allowed to join together to build and maintain workhouses and the 1834 Act made sure that by 1868 all parishes were in unions that had a workhouse.

Zemgor (from the Russian for zemstvo and 'town'– gorod) A union of representatives of local government members, businessmen and influential townsmen set up to support the war effort in 1915. Its first chairman was Prince Lvov, later the first leader of the provisional government of 1917 after the Tsar's abdication.

Zemstvo (plural zemstva) Councils created by Nicholas II's grandfather Alexander II to run local areas and to administer matters such as road maintenance, law and order and education.

Zollverein This means customs (zoll) union or association (verein). A customs union is an area in which members trade without paying tariffs or payments when goods are moved from one area to another. A German customs union was established in 1834 to manage tariffs and economic policies between a number of German states.

Index

A

absolutism
  Austria 139
  France 4, 6, 7, 10, 17
  Russia 176
agriculture
  Britain
    agricultural
      revolution 57–60, 94
    Corn Laws 77, 78
    and popular unrest 96–7
  Germany 130, 131, 132
  Russia 177
  steam power 63
  subsistence farming 4, 57
Alexander III, Tsar 177, 178
Alexander II, Tsar 177, 178
Alexandra, Tsarina 176, 189, 192
American independence, War
  of 4, 5, 11, 15
aristocracy
  France 3, 4, 5, 6, 43, 45
  German 143
Arndt, Ernst 127
Austria
  and the Frankfurt
    Assembly 137–8
  and French Revolutionary
    wars 24–5, 30, 33, 34–5,
    119
  and the German
    Confederation 121, 128,
    129, 130, 133, 148
  and German unification 136,
    138–40, 142, 144, 148,
    154–5, 162
    Schleswig-Holstein
      issue 149–50
  war with Prussia 146,
    148, 150–4
  and the Holy Roman
    Empire 118, 119
  and Italy 138, 156
  Metternich and
    Germany 120–2, 123, 133,
    135, 138
  and the Napoleonic Wars 30,
    119–20
  War of the Austrian
    Succession 4

B

Babeuf, François Noel
  (Gracchus) 31
banks 40, 45, 61, 142
Barras, Paul, Vicomte de 30, 32, 36
Bismarck, Otto von 118, 143–54
  and the Austro-Prussian
    War 150–4
  diplomacy with France 155–7,
    165
  and the German Empire 162–5
  and German unification 154–65
  and the Indemnity Bill 154
  planner or improviser 148–9
  and the Prussian
    parliament 144–5, 146–8,
    153–4
  Schleswig-Holstein issue
    149–50
  see also Prussia
Bolsheviks 187, 197
  Civil War 205, 211–16
  consolidation of power 207–18
  Constituent Assembly
    elections 201, 202, 207,
    208–9, 211
  Left Communists 211
  Lenin's leadership 201–2
  October Revolution (1917) 186,
    203–7, 211, 216, 217
  Red Army 212, 213, 214,
    215, 216
  the Red Terror 213, 214–15
  reforms and dictatorship 208–9
  rise to power 198–209
Boulton, Matthew 62
Brest-Litovsk, Treaty of 210–11, 212
Bridgewater Canal 66, 70
Brissot, Jacques-Pierre 18, 19, 24
Britain
  and French Revolutionary
    wars 25, 29, 34, 104
  Great Reform Act (1832) 78,
    97, 99, 107, 125
  industrialization 56–116
    causes of 57–66
    government reforms
      89–93, 107–8
    living conditions 80–3
    and popular protest
      94–104, 107
    population growth 80
    and social class 86–9
    see also factory system
  and the Napoleonic Wars 30,
    45–6, 77, 94–5
  political reform 97–100
British Empire 76–7
Brunel, Isambard Kingdom 71

C

Calonne, Charles de 8–9
canals 66, 69–70
capitalism 60–2

Carlsbad Decrees (1819) 121

Carnot, Lazare 26

censorship
  Germany 122, 123, 124–5
  Napoleonic France 46

Chadwick, Edwin 81, 89, 90

Chartism 97, 99–100, 108

child labour 84–6, 90–1, 94, 130

Chouans 19

coal 75
  iron industry 73, 74, 141
  transport of 64–5, 66, 75

Cobden, Richard 77, 78

Coke, Thomas 60

Cordeliers 17, 18, 20

Corn Laws 77, 78, 106, 107

Cort, Henry 74

cotton industry 63–4, 66,
  68–9, 141
  child labour 84, 85

Crimean War 151

D

Danton, Georges-Jacques 17,
  18, 19

Darby, Abraham 73, 74

Declaration of the Rights of
  Man and of the Citizen 14, 15

Denikin, General Anton 212

Denmark 149–50, 159

Desmoulins, Camille 17, 18, 19

Diderot, Denis 7

the Directory 1, 20, 21, 27–38
  coup of November 1799 32,
    36–8
  financial reforms 32
  and the Revolutionary
    wars 31, 32, 33–5

Doherty, John 102

Ducos, Pierre 32, 36

E

education, Napoleonic
  France 39–40, 44

Enghien, Duc d' 41

Enlightenment 2, 6–8, 11, 15,
  16, 41

factory system 67–9, 83–4, 141
  child workers 84–6, 90–1
  reforms 91–3
  working conditions 83–6

F

Feuillants 17, 18

First World War 165
  and Russia 185, 186–91,
    194–5, 199, 207

food riots 4, 6, 15, 23, 96

food shortages
  Britain 104–5
  Russia 187–8, 194, 199, 215

Fouché, Joseph 46

France
  Ancien Regime 3–11
  Consulate 30, 37–8
    domestic reform 39–41
  economic problems 6, 21–3, 29
  Estates General 2, 5, 6, 8, 10,
    11–13, 17, 20
  and Germany
    the Bund 122, 123, 128
    the German Empire 162,
      165
    Prussia 151, 155–61
  parlements 4, 9–10
  Third Estate 3, 6, 10, 11, 13
    Tennis Court Oath 12
  see also Louis XVI, King of
    France; Napoleon Bonaparte;
    Napoleonic Wars;
    Revolutionary Wars (France)

Frankfurt Assembly 133, 136–8,
  140

Frederick William IV, king of
  Prussia 133, 134, 135, 137, 138,
  140, 144

French Revolution 1, 11–16, 134
  causes and immediate
    outcomes 2–16
  Constituent Assembly 15, 16, 20
  Constitution (1791) 20, 21, 28
  counter-revolutionary
    groups 17, 28–9, 29
  émigrés 19, 22, 24, 25
  and Germany 119, 121
  March of the Women 15
  and Napoleon 41, 46
  National Assembly 13, 14, 15,
    16, 20
  October Days 15
  the Revolutionary calender 29
  revolutionary groups 17–20
  sans-coulottes 22, 23, 25,
    28, 29
  storming of the Bastille 13–14
  the Terror 17, 19, 20, 21, 22–3,
    25–6, 28, 46
  see also the Directory;
    Revolutionary wars (France)

G

Gapon, Father Gregory 180

Germany
  culture and the arts 123,
    127–8
  economic growth 123, 124,
    125, 130, 141–2
  French émigrés in 24
  German Confederation (the
    Bund) 120–9, 152
    and the 1848
      Revolutions 130,
      133–5
    Frankfurt
      Parliament 133,
      136–8, 140
    Schleswig-Holstein
      issue 149–50

social and economic
    problems 130–2
the Zollverein 129–30,
    141, 142–3, 157
German Empire 141, 162–5
Holy Roman Empire 118, 119
industrial development 130–1,
    141–2
Metternich system 118,
    120–3, 124–5, 126, 127, 130,
    138
and the Napoleonic Wars 30,
    119–20
nationalism 121, 124, 125,
    126–9, 130, 134, 142, 155
and Bismarck 143, 145,
    164, 165
North German
    Confederation 153–4, 160,
    162, 163
parliaments 144–5, 146–8,
    153–4, 163–4, 165
rural population 129, 131,
    132, 141
and Russia 121, 157, 162,
    210, 211
unification 136, 138–40, 140,
    142, 148–9, 154–65
see also Prussia
Girondins 18, 19, 20, 22, 24, 25

H

handloom weavers 63, 64, 66,
    88, 96, 100, 131
Holy Roman Empire 118, 119
Hungary 138, 139, 140

I

Irish famine 107
iron industry 66, 73–4, 75, 77,
    96, 141
    wages 88
Italy 138, 155, 156

Napoleon's campaign in 33,
    34–5

J

Jacobins 17, 18, 21, 22–3, 28, 32
    neo-Jacobins 29, 32
Japan 176, 179

K

Kamenev, Lev 198, 202, 205
Kerensky, Alexander 192, 199,
    200, 202, 203, 206, 212
Kolchak, Admiral Alexander 212
Kornilov, General 199–200, 205,
    212
Kronstadt Rising 199, 215–16

L

Lenin, Vladimir 184, 195, 196, 197
    April Theses 198–9
    and the Civil War 211, 216
    leadership of the
        Bolsheviks 201–2
    NEP (New Economic Policy)
        216–17
    and the October
        Revolution 203, 205, 206
    One Party Unity policy 217
    peace treaty with
        Germany 209, 210–11
    and War Communism 215–16
    see also Bolsheviks
liberalism
    Germany 120, 121, 124–6,
        130, 140, 153–4, 164
    Russia 177, 178, 182
Liverpool, Lord 105–6
Louis XIV, king of France 6, 7, 152
Louis XVI, king of France 2, 3,
    24, 41, 49
    constitutional monarchy 17,
        18, 19, 20–1, 22, 23

overthrow and execution 19,
    25, 134
policies and reform
    attempts 4–5, 8–11
and the Revolution 11–15, 19, 20
Luddites 95–6, 105
Ludwig I, king of Bavaria 134
Luther, Martin 127
Lützow, Adolf von 127
Luxembourg Crisis 156–7
Lvov, Prince 194, 197, 199

M

Marie Antoinette, queen 2, 4, 8,
    24, 26
Marie-Louise of Parma 43
Marshall, William 57, 60
Marxism 179, 184
Marx, Karl 131, 133, 142, 179,
    206
mechanization 62–4, 94–6, 101
Méricourt, Théroigne 20
Metternich, Prince Clemens
    von 118, 120–3, 124–5, 126,
    127, 130, 134, 135, 138
middle class
    Britain 71, 87, 89, 107
    France 4, 5, 6, 10–11, 45
    Germany 124–6, 127, 130,
        132, 137, 140, 153
    Russia 179
Moltke, Helmuth von 146, 151,
    159–60
Montesquieu, Baron de 7

N

Napoleon Bonaparte 1, 20,
    33–48, 49, 76
    background and career 30
    as Consul for Life 30, 37, 39, 41
    coup of 1799 32, 36–8

domestic reforms 38–48
    as Emperor 41–6
    as First Consul 39–41
    Egyptian campaign 27, 30, 32, 33–4, 35
    inauguration of the Empire 41–3
    Italian campaign 33, 34–5
    marriages 32, 43
    and Metternich 118
    military reputation 33–5, 43
    overthrow of the Directory 27, 29, 30, 32, 36–8
    political ambitions 35–6
Napoleonic Wars 30, 45–6, 77
    and Britain 94–5, 96, 100, 101
    and Germany 118, 119–20, 123, 126, 127
Napoleon III, French Emperor 151, 155–6, 157, 159, 160, 161
Necker, Jacques 8, 10, 11, 13
Nicholas II, Tsar 175–6, 178, 214
    abdication 191, 193, 207
    and the First World War 187–8, 189–91
    Fundamental Laws 176, 182
    opposition to tsarist rule 184–6
    and the Revolution of 1905 179, 180, 181–2
nobility see aristocracy
Nogaret, Dominique-Vincet Ramel de 32

O

Olmütz, Declaration of 140, 143, 144
Ottoman Empire 151
Owen, Robert 102

P

Peel, Sir Robert 78, 107
Peterloo 97–8, 106

Philosophes 6
Pillnitz, Declaration of (1791) 24
Pitt, William the Younger 77, 104, 105
Pobedonostsev, Konstantin 178
police in Napoleonic France 46–7
population growth
    Britain 57–8, 80, 82, 85
    France 4
    Germany 124, 130–1
Prairial, Revolt of 23
Prussia 117, 123, 143–54
    Bismarck as Minister President of 143–54
        army reforms 144, 146–8, 151
    constitution 139
    Franco-Prussian War 159–61
    and the Frankfurt Assembly 137, 138
    French Revolutionary Wars 24–5
    and the German Confederation (the Bund) 123, 128, 129, 130, 134
    and the German Empire 164
    and German unification 140, 142, 148–9, 154–65
    Hohenzollern Candidature and war with France 157–9
    Luxembourg Crisis 156–7
    March Days 133
    Napoleonic Wars 30, 119–20
    and the North German Confederation 153–4
    Schleswig-Holstein issue 149–50, 150–1, 153
    Sorbs/Wends 128
    war with Austria 146, 148, 150–4
    see also Bismarck, Otto von; Germany

R

Radowitz, Joseph von 140
railways 63, 70–3, 76, 129, 213, 214
Rasputin, Grigori 176, 189–90
religion
    Catholic emancipation in Britain 98–9
    France 3, 7, 9, 21, 44, 45
        the Concordat 40
        Cult of the Supreme Being 19–20, 28
    Germany 119, 126, 136, 157, 165
    Russia 178
Revolutionary wars (France) 21, 22, 23, 24–6, 29, 30, 32
    and Britain 25, 29, 34, 104
    and the Directory 31, 32, 33–5, 36
    and Germany 119, 127
    Napoleon's campaigns 27, 30, 32, 33–5
    see also Napoleonic Wars
Revolutions (1848-49) 122, 123, 130–43, 144
Ricardo, David 76, 77
river transport 64, 65
roads 64, 65, 124
Robespierre, Maximilien 17, 18, 19, 21, 24, 46
    Cult of the Supreme Being 19–20, 28
    fall of 23, 29, 30, 45
Roon, Albrecht von 144
Rousseau, Jean-Jacques 7, 8
Russia
    and Austria 139, 140, 148, 151
    Dumas (parliaments) 179, 182, 182–3, 184, 192, 194, 195
        progressive bloc 188

February Revolution (1917) 186–97
and the First World War 185, 186–91
and Germany 121, 157, 162, 201, 211
industrial development 177, 178, 186
industrial workers 179, 182
    Bolshevik reforms 208
    and the February Revolution 190–1, 192
    strikes and unrest 184–5
Kadets (liberals) 181, 184, 186, 190, 194, 195
Lena Goldfields strikes 185, 186
and the Napoleonic Wars 30, 119–20
October Manifesto 176, 186
peasantry 177, 179, 182, 184
    land reforms 197, 199, 208
Petrograd Soviet 193, 194–5
Provisional Government 186, 192–3, 194–7, 198
    crises and overthrow of 198–205
Revolution of 1905 174–5, 176, 179–82, 184, 186
Social Democrats 178, 179, 186
Social Revolutionaries (SRs) 178, 179, 181, 186
Tsarist regime 175–8
war with Japan 176, 179
see also Bolsheviks; Nicholas II, Tsar

S

Schleswig-Holstein 149–50, 150–1, 153
Schurz, Karl 135
Seven Years War 4
Shaftesbury, Earl of 91, 92
Sieyès, Emmanuel-Joseph 32, 36, 37
Smith, Adam 65, 76, 77
socialism 102, 131, 132
Spain 125, 158
Stalin, Josef 198, 206
steam power 62–3, 64, 66, 75
    and the factory system 67–8
    in Germany 124, 141
    iron industry 74
    railways 63, 70–3
    steamships 63, 73
Stephenson, George 71
Stolypin, Petr 176, 183–4
Swing Riots 97, 103, 107

T

tax farmers 5, 6
Tennis Court Oath 12
textile industry 63–4, 66, 77, 96, 141
    factory system 67–9, 84
Thermidorians 28, 29
Tolpuddle labourers 103, 107
trade unions 94, 101–4
transport developments
    Britain 61, 64–6, 69–73
    Germany 124

Trotsky, Leon 195, 196, 203, 205, 206, 210
    and the Civil War 212, 213, 214, 216

V

Valmy, Battle of (1792) 25
Vendemiarie, royalist uprising of (1795) 31
Vienna, Congress of (1815) 118, 120, 145

W

wages 68, 82, 83, 87–8
    women and children 84, 85
War Communism (Russia) 215–16
water power 62, 67, 74
Watt, James 62
William I, king of Prussia 144, 145, 146, 148, 158, 159
    as German Emperor 162, 165
Witte, Sergei 178, 179, 181
women 20, 84, 86, 130
workhouses 107
working class
    Britain 81–6, 87–8
    Germany 130–1, 142
Wrangel, Baron Pyotr 212

Y

Young, Arthur 58, 59, 60, 80

Z

Zinoviev, Grigory 202

The Publishers would like to thank the following for permission to reproduce copyright material.

Photo credits

p.2 © Shutterstock/Everett – Art; **p.9** © Josse Christophel/Alamy Stock Photo; **p.12** © Niday Picture Library/Alamy Stock Photo; **p.18** From The New York Public Library, https://digitalcollections.nypl.org/items/510d47da-2950-a3d9-e040-e00a18064a99; **p.30** image courtesy National Gallery of Art, Washington, Samuel H. Kress Collection 1961.9.15; **p.31** © Bettmann Archive/Getty Images; **p.42** © Painters/Alamy Stock Photo; p.64 https://wellcomecollection.org/works/nzvb3s6b. Wellcome Collection. https://creativecommons.org/licenses/by/4.0/; **p.81** © Pictorial Press Ltd/Alamy Stock Photo; **p.83** © INTERFOTO/Alamy Stock Photo; **p.98** © Classic Image/Alamy Stock Photo; **p.118** https://www.metmuseum.org/art/collection/search/436887, https://creativecommons.org/publicdomain/zero/1.0/; **p.123** © Alfredo Dagli Orti/REX/Shutterstock; **p.128** https://commons.wikimedia.org/wiki/File:Caspar_David_Friedrich_-_Wanderer_above_the_sea_of_fog.jpg; **p.135** © bpk/Geheimes Staatsarchiv, SPK/Thomann; **p.136** © Pictorial Press Ltd/Alamy Stock Photo; **p.146** © INTERFOTO/Alamy Stock Photo; **p.147** © Granger Historical Picture Archive/Alamy Stock Photo; **p.152** © Bettmann Archive/Getty Images; **p.155** Public Domain. https://commons.wikimedia.org/wiki/File:Napoleon_III._of_France.jpg; **p.162** © Pictorial Press Ltd/Alamy Stock Photo; **p.176** © Everett Collection Historical/Alamy Stock Photo; **p.178** Library of Congress Prints & Photographs Division, Washington/LC-USZ62-128298; **p.181** © The Granger Collection/Alamy Stock Photo; **p.192** © Fine Art Images/Heritage Images/Getty Images; **p.196** *t* © Thinkstock/ Photos.com/Getty Images; **p.196** *b* Illustrated London News; **p.198** Library of Congress Prints and Photographs Division Washington, LC-USW33-019081-C; **p.204** © A. Burkatovski/Fine Art Images/SuperStock; **p.217** © Heritage Image Partnership Ltd/Alamy Stock Photo; **p.220** © Pictorial Press Ltd/Alamy Stock Photo; **p.221** Provided courtesy HarpWeek.